THE AUDITORY SETTING

Music and the Moving Image

Series Editors
Kevin Donnelly, University of Wales Aberystwyth
Beth Carroll, University of Southampton

Titles in the series include:

Film's Musical Moments
by Ian Conrich & Estella Tincknell (eds)

Music and the Moving Image: A Reader
by Kevin Donnelly (ed.)

Music, Sound and Multimedia
by Jamie Sexton (ed.)

Music Video and the Politics of Representation
by Diane Railton & Paul Watson
Contemporary Musical Film
by Kevin J. Donnelly and Beth Carroll (eds)

British Music Video: Art, Commerce and Social Critique 1966–2016
by Emily Caston

The Auditory Setting: Environmental Sounds in Film and Media Arts
by Budhaditya Chattopadhyay

www.edinburghuniversitypress.com/series/MAMI

THE AUDITORY SETTING

Environmental Sounds in Film and Media Arts

Budhaditya Chattopadhyay

EDINBURGH
University Press

Edinburgh University Press is one of the leading university presses in the UK.
We publish academic books and journals in our selected subject areas across the
humanities and social sciences, combining cutting-edge scholarship with high editorial
and production values to produce academic works of lasting importance. For more
information visit our website: edinburghuniversitypress.com

© Budhaditya Chattopadhyay, 2021, 2022

Edinburgh University Press Ltd
The Tun – Holyrood Road
12(2f) Jackson's Entry
Edinburgh EH8 8PJ

First published in hardback by Edinburgh University Press 2021

Typeset in 10/12.5 Adobe Sabon by
Servis Filmsetting Ltd, Stockport, Cheshire, and
printed and bound by CPI Group (UK) Ltd,
Croydon, CR0 4YY

A CIP record for this book is available from the British Library

ISBN 978 1 4744 7438 2 (hardback)
ISBN 978 1 4744 7439 9 (paperback)
ISBN 978 1 4744 7440 5 (webready PDF)
ISBN 978 1 4744 7441 2 (epub)

The right of Budhaditya Chattopadhyay to be identified as the author of this work
has been asserted in accordance with the Copyright, Designs and Patents Act 1988,
and the Copyright and Related Rights Regulations 2003 (SI No. 2498).

CONTENTS

List of Figures — viii
Acknowledgements — ix

PART 1: INTRODUCTION

1 The First Sound and the Curiosity — 3
  1.1 Foregrounding environmental sound — 3
  1.2 Mise-en-sonore — 6
  1.3 Ambient sound in films — 7
  1.4 Ambient sound in other audiovisual media arts — 10

2 The Auditory Context and Signification — 14
  2.1 Film sound research — 14
  2.2 The audiovisual relationship — 17
  2.3 Sound studies — 18
  2.4 Film and media arts — 19
  2.5 The phenomenology of ambient sound — 20
  2.6 Digital aesthetics — 23

3 Key Concepts and Definitions — 26
  3.1 Diegetic sound — 26
  3.2 Mimesis — 28
  3.3 Presence — 29
  3.4 Rendering — 31
  3.5 Soundscape and the soundmark — 32

CONTENTS

4	Approach and Method	35
	4.1 Historical overview	35
	4.2 Ethnographic research	36
	4.3 Personal inputs	38
	4.4 Artistic research	38
	4.5 Self-reflective analysis	39
	4.6 Structure of the book	40

PART 2: SONIC TRAJECTORIES

5	Monaural Soundtracks and Recording (Sonic) Reality	45
	5.1 Mechanical and optical recordings, sound film and direct sound	45
	5.2 The monaural aesthetics	49
	5.3 Magnetic recording	51
	5.4 Audiographic realism	53
	5.5 Dubbing	55

6	Stereo Sound and the Expanded Space	59
	6.1 Studio-centric sound	59
	6.2 Hyper-real sound effects	60
	6.3 Stereophonic space	62
	6.4 Sounding media arts	64

7	Digital Surround Sound and the Mimetic Site	67
	7.1 The state of the digital	67
	7.2 Sync sound	72
	7.3 Sound design and deconstruction of the soundtrack	73
	7.4 Surround sound	76
	7.5 Digital technology, field recording and multi-channel sound artworks	80

PART 3: ON LOCATION AND OTHER STORIES

8	Land, Field, Meadow	87
9	Forest, Jungle	92
10	Village, Rural Environment	97
11	Indoors	102
12	Riverbank, Beach, Island	112
13	Street, Public Squares, Urban Neighbourhood	119
14	Public Transport	131

15	Airport	135
16	Underwater, Outer Space	139

PART 4: CRITICAL LISTENING

17	Mapping the Aesthetic Choices in Sound Production	147
	17.1 Listening through film and media arts	147
	17.2 Locating models in sound production	150
	17.3 Sonic mediation and expanding the notion of rendering	152
18	Auditory Presence and Better Practice	155
	18.1 Comparative analysis: film sound/sound in media arts	155
	18.2 Constraints of the sonic environment in film	157
	18.3 Challenging best practice in film sound production	158
	18.4 Tracing an emergent spatiality	160
	18.5 Rethinking the concept of auditory presence in film and media arts	163
19	The God of Small Sounds	169
	19.1 Anthropocenic listening	169
	19.2 Environmental sounds lost	170
20	Emerging Trends and Future Directions	175
	20.1 Post-digital sound and future listening	175
	20.2 Post-immersion	178
	20.3 Remoteness	183

Bibliography	187
List of Works/Media Cited	198
Index	202

Listening and viewing examples to support the text can be accessed via the QR code on the back cover or at https://budhaditya.org/projects/auditory-setting/

FIGURES

5.1	Direct recording outside of Melies Studio	44
6.1	Inside a sound studio	58
7.1	Digital sound recording on location	68

ACKNOWLEDGEMENTS

This book is a culmination of many years' intensive thinking, research and sensitive listening to films and audiovisual media, and, most importantly, engagement with locations during extensive travel across the globe. The personal enquiry that germinated into this book started in 2002 when I was fresh out of engineering school and contemplating joining film school. At that time, I was a cinephile and a film buff – indeed, I still am – but my earlier innocence has been partly replaced by a critical attitude. My interest and curiosity for sound in film and media arts are distilled in this book. First, I would like to acknowledge the inspiration I have drawn from fellow sound artists and practitioners.

This book is inspired by the extensive research conducted for my doctoral project at Leiden University, Netherlands, which I completed in 2017. I warmly thank Prof. dr Marcel Cobussen and Prof. Frans de Ruiter of the Academy of Creative and Performing Arts for their valuable comments and suggestions towards developing the final version of the dissertation. I am particularly grateful to Marcel Cobussen for kindly agreeing to become my supervisor during the final and crucial stages of the PhD, providing me with valuable guidance. This book has also been enriched by the following three years of extensive writing and further research, partly produced during my Mellon Postdoctoral Fellowship at the Center for Arts and Humanities, American University of Beirut, Lebanon, 2018–2019. I would like to thank the Center for Arts and Humanities for hosting me and facilitating an inspiring writing environment in AUB's wondrous campus with all those friendly cats. I also thank the Faculty of Humanities at the University of Copenhagen,

Denmark, for supporting and financing earlier parts of this research from 2011 to 2015.

I would like to thank several people who have remained supportive throughout the development of this project. Thanks to Professor Brandon LaBelle at the University of Bergen, Norway, who invited me to join the seminar series Dirty Ear Forum – his continuing support has been immensely helpful. Thanks also to Morten Michelsen of the Department of Arts and Cultural Studies, University of Copenhagen, who invited me to hold a panel at the ESSA2014 Sound Studies conference, where I had the chance to discuss this project with fellow film sound scholars such as Martine Huvenne, who read parts of the manuscript and gave helpful advice and comments. I would like to thank Prof. Debasish Ghoshal at SRFTI, who listened patiently to my idea. I thank Sharon Stewart, who helped me edit the final version of the dissertation. I sincerely thank Associate Professor Ulrik Schmidt, who invited me to work as a guest researcher at Roskilde University, Denmark, to further develop the project. Interaction with students, who took part in the courses I taught at the University of Copenhagen and the American University of Beirut, has considerably enriched my research. My heartfelt thanks go to Prof. Andrew Lewis at the School of Music in Bangor University, North Wales, UK, for providing hospitality during my residency to develop the sound artwork *Elegy for Bangalore* while working at Studio 4. I would also like to thank the Charles Wallace India Trust, London, for funding my travel and stay in Bangor. Thanks to Deutschlandradio, Berlin, for broadcasting the work and to Gruenrekorder for publishing the work on CD. I would like to thank the Prince Claus Fund, Netherlands, for providing financial support for the fieldwork conducted in India to develop the project *Decomposing Landscape*. I thank ICST, Zurich University of the Arts, Switzerland, for providing the resources, funds and technical facilities for the development of the piece during a residency at their Computer Music Studio equipped with an Ambisonics system. My heartfelt thanks go to composer Johannes Schütt for providing technical guidance and all the other support offered during this residency. I thank the Institute of Electronic Music and Acoustics at the University of Music and Performing Arts, Graz, Austria for having me in the IEM residency 2015–2016, supporting the project *Exile and Other Syndromes*.

Thanks to Professor Cathy Lane and Professor Angus Carlyle of Creative Research into Sound Arts Practice (CRiSAP), University of the Arts London, for inviting me to be part of the book *In the Field: The Art of Field Recording* (2013) where I talk at length about my work. I would also like to thank the invited guests and participants to the two-day seminar, Affective Atmospheres: Site-specific Sound, Neighborhood Music and the Social Formation (2018), that I organized at the American University of Beirut and to the International Ambiances Network for supporting the event. Thanks to Ernst Karel, on whose invitation I presented the developing book at the Center for Experimental Ethnography, University of Pennsylvania, USA, receiving stimulating comments. Thanks to Professor Anna Morcom, at the UCLA Herb Alpert School of Music, California, USA, for reading a section of the book in progress and providing helpful comments. Thanks so much to Sarah Waring for reading through the book's entire manuscript with helpful comments and editorial suggestions. Thanks to Copper Leg Residency, Estonia, for hosting me while finishing the manuscript in the COVID-19 lockdown.

Finally, I would like to thank my late father Satya Sadhan Chattopadhyay for setting my cinematic taste higher. I also thank my mother Shipra Chattopadhyay for her personal sacrifices and quiet support. On this occasion, I heartily express my gratitude to close friends, associates and well-wishers, especially Arild Fetveit, Heiko Aufdermauer, Matteo Marangoni, Lasse-Marc Riek, Ashish Avikunthak, Sukanta Majumdar, Tirtha Sankha Majumder, Tobias Lintl, Adi Hollander, Subrata Sarkar, Sreya Chatterjee, Tanya Toft, Nicola Di Croce, National Film Archive of India Pune, and the SilentFilm Media Collective Berlin – without their support this project would not have seen the light of day.

PART I

INTRODUCTION

You can't show everything; if you do, it's no longer art. Art lies in suggestion. The great difficulty for filmmakers is precisely not to show things. (Robert Bresson 1983[1])

PART I

INTRODUCTION

1 THE FIRST SOUND AND THE CURIOSITY

1.1 Foregrounding Environmental Sound

My first cinematic experience was at the age of seven when my father took me to experience Sergei Eisenstein's unfinished magnum opus ¡*Que viva México!* (1932). The film was screened with his other works at an international festival in our small town. This visually stunning yet silent film (albeit accompanied by an asynchronous musical score and voiceover in Grigoriy Aleksandrov's 1979 version) opened my eyes and ears to an intriguing and appealing mediated world for the first time – a world I remain curious about. I imagined sounds recorded in the evocative and dreamy landscapes of post-revolution Mexico. My fervent anticipation of environmental sounds for each of the majestically shot sequences, depicting mythical landscapes crowned with cactus plants and ancient pyramids, met with the obtrusive musical score, which bothered me. Environmental sounds were missing, though I knew they existed somewhere due to my own experience of sounds from the countryside, fields and grasslands around our small town. Even though the moving images were powerful enough to engage me, I was frustrated and annoyed that these sounds were not included in the cinematic experience. These thoughts gathered in my mind as I left the movie theatre with imagined sonic menageries resonating in my head. Outside, I was sensitive to the sounds around me. This experience instilled in me a deep affinity with film and the filmic experience, as well as arousing my curiosity about the construction of its sonic world, leading to the development of a critical attitude towards sound, the sonic environments and media production.

I started going to the cinema frequently and enrolled myself at the SRFTI, India's prestigious national film school, as a film sound student. While fascinated by the tone, texture and layered composition of sounds from nature and environmental or 'ambient'[2] sounds of places I encountered, I also listened critically to the sonic universe of film each time I went in the cinema. Through my experiences of various cinematic genres, I confronted the absence of 'ambience' or sounds from the film's 'actual sites'. In my first scholarly paper (Chattopadhyay 2007),[3] I focused on how ambience could contribute to a sense of place if given enough scope in filmmaking. I argued that the imposed limitations practised in standard film sound production create lapses in the existence and recognition of site-specific sonic information for each film's 'soundscape'. By this time, in 2007, I was already making field recordings and composing with ambient sound in response to the screen-centric and visually dominated field of film production. My shift to artistic practice as opposed to becoming a film industry sound technician can be seen as a critical inclination and personal choice. The above-mentioned paper was the beginning of my work's critical articulation within a growing interest for sound studies and academia in general, not only to voice my concerns on these issues but also to situate my artistic practice within this conundrum and the genealogy of sound practice in general. At a certain stage, these considerations were instrumental in initiating and unfolding this book project.

My sound art practice was simultaneously driven by environmental concerns. Through field recordings in sites torn by industrialisation, I was exposed to the environmental decay in many parts of a rapidly developing and re-emerging India. I questioned how many of these transitory sites and environmentally troubled landscapes were frequented and depicted in film and media productions, and how sensitive they were towards sonic environments disappearing at the hands of the profit-hungry consuming natural resources, including fields, grasslands and various other natural sites. I was aware that the intricate layers of environmental sounds from these sites would be lost through technological exploitation and mediation, turning the landscape into a site of spectacle, consumption and entertainment. The cultural appropriation of nature and the environment and its audiovisual resources into man-made environs in architecture, buildings as well as film, media and cultural production, became a focus in my work. I was moved by the fact that natural ambience was being engulfed by mediated ambience, fulfilling human needs to the detriment of ecological organisms.

At this time, worldwide communities began waking up from their slumber to slowly face the realities of climate change. In November 1992 around 1,700 leading thinkers from around the globe, including a number of Nobel laureates, issued an ardent appeal:

> Human beings and the natural world are on a collision course. Human activities inflict harsh and often irreversible damage on the environment and on critical resources. If not checked, many of our current practices put at serious risk the future that we wish for human society and the plant and animal kingdoms, and may so alter the living world that it will be unable to sustain life in the manner that we know. Fundamental changes are urgent if we are to avoid the collision our present course will bring about.[4]

Twenty-five years later an updated letter was published in the journal *BioScience*. 'World Scientists' Warning to Humanity: A Second Notice' had 15,372 signatories from world-renowned scientists and thinkers. The letter underscores the gravity of the situation, noting how environments have continued to be exploited at great risk:

> Humanity was pushing Earth's ecosystems beyond their capacities to support the web of life. These are alarming trends. We need the services provided by nature for our own survival including a 'loss of nearly 300 million acres' of forestland and the environment.[5]

If broadened, the environment in this urgent and cautionary discourse can be understood as both the remote and immediate physical surroundings that humans inhabit, transform, misuse and manipulate for their own consumption. This is the habitual environment – not only natural but also built environments such as rural, urban, suburban, indoor and outdoor sites – that humans live in every day. These environments stem from myriad physical places. They are often perceived as the setting that provides specific atmosphere or ambience when describing, depicting, narrating, producing and reproducing increasingly mediatised worlds for film, literature, music and art. Such mediated settings also essentially include the aural domain. The sonic environment, as explained by musician and ecologist Bernie Krause (1987, 2012), has deteriorated rapidly in the last hundred years through accelerated human intervention in environments that are inhabited for industrialisation and urbanisation. Such interventions have also been made for entertainment and tourism. Environments consumed, (re)produced and mediated through technology are under pressure. An investigation of processes that are used to mediate environments for their aesthetic consumption – in other words, human agency in expending the environment – is required to gain an understanding of the complex relationship between humans and the environment, which humans are not outside of, yet are purposefully exploiting. Therefore, one of the fundamental entries in this discourse is the study of the (re)production and mediation of environmental sounds from particular places or sites for making sonic environments in film, media arts and other audiovisual media and technology-based arts that are consumed for both entertainment and aesthetic engagement. Through this knowledge, aspects of the impact humans have had on environments can be measured in relation to current environmental and ecological crises, and the prevailing Anthropocene.

1.2 Mise-en-sonore

In narrative works, the setting can be understood as the environment in which a story or event takes place. Setting includes specific information about an environmental situation as a description of place and time. It presents a backdrop for narrative action. Careful engagement with this setting can result in the meaningful portrayal of a site and its environs. The setting made within a mediated world such as film or media artwork requires information about place, the spatial situation and time arranged as aural and visual elements to evoke intricate sights, sounds and other sensations of location and 'situatedness'. I term the sonic environment crafted within a film and media production as 'auditory setting' or *mise-en-sonore*,[6] which is constructed by using a specific sound component known as 'ambience' or 'ambient sound'.[7] Ambience is a standard term used by sound practitioners to denote the site-specific sounds that provide characteristic atmosphere and spatial information in audiovisual productions. How ambience or ambient sound is used as a site-specific element to compose the auditory setting that renders a spatial sensation during the production of films, media art and sound artworks is examined throughout the book. Focus is placed on processes that (re)construct a site's presence using ambient sounds recorded from that site. In film it is often a fictional site. In field recording-based media artworks it is the site for making a recording with the purpose of developing a site-aware artistic production.

The mediated worlds within any work of sound production emerge through the narrative and descriptive accounts of a place or site[8] through the recording and spatial organisation of sounds. Audiences engage with the site by recognising its presence within this constructed world. The produced experience of presence varies in degree and intensity depending on the sound practitioners'[9] and sound artists' attention to the site's sonic details. The mediated world appears convincing if the site's resonance reverberates in the ears of its audience and triggers their sonic sensibilities long after it has been experienced. It is no surprise then that the fundamental element of establishing a site's presence through sound is of foremost importance when it comes to convincingly conveying the narrative and descriptive account of a particular site.

This leads to a crucial question: How is the sonic environment of a specific site (re)produced in film and media artwork? Certainly, specific methods and creative strategies are involved in constructing or evoking the relatively convincing presence of a site within the mediated environment by means of various forms and formats of sound recording and the spatial organisation of recorded sounds. However, to what extent can presence be achieved in sound practice? Or does the site remain elusive within the sonic experience?

The aim of this book is to question classical assumptions about sound in film and media arts (e.g., image-based relationships) and shift the focus towards the site and its sonic environment, whose presence is often carefully constructed in a film or media artwork's diegetic world[10] as a vital narrative strategy. The emphasis on site in this study enables an informed investigation of an essentially anthropogenic process of the sonic environment's mediation and (re)production. Sonic environments are inhabited, experienced, exploited and transformed every day, their corporeality augmented by human agency in mediated forms. The human agency of sonic environments is crucial to unwrap in order to understand cultural expectations from the media; greater awareness is required of narration, depiction, communication and artistic production approaches and affordances harnessed through media technologies.

This investigation will be drawn through the study of various generic and ordinary sites that have been recorded and (re)produced in film and media productions. Analyses address the similarities and differences between ambient sound recordings made to reconstruct the site within the film production's interior world and field recordings used in certain site-driven sound and media artworks. Relevant new knowledge is proposed about the extent to which sonic environments are mediated. From a practical standpoint, such knowledge challenges the idea of best practice[11] in sound production. It suggests a reconfiguration of the typically consumerist and industry-driven models of film and audiovisual media productions through a critical examination of sound art and other creative sound practices in the media arts.

1.3 Ambient Sound in Films

Since a substantial amount of sound production scholarship centres on film sound analysis, a clearer contextual picture can be drawn by considering the role of ambient sound in film. The following is based on the assumption that film sound practitioners choose to use certain layers of ambient sound among a multitude of other recorded sound components. These resources are incorporated into a strategy of narration that aims to produce a spatial realisation of the site's presence in the diegetic world. The absence or relative inclusion of ambient sound in a film's auditory setting determines the qualitative degrees and intensities of the site's presence.

Film sound scholars reference the spatial, enveloping properties of ambient sound. Take David Sonnenschein, for example, who suggests that ambient sound can 'create a space within which the audience can be enveloped'

(Sonnenschein 2001: 47). Film scholar Béla Balázs proclaims that it is sound's business to reveal the acoustic environment, the landscape that we experience every day as the 'intimate whispering of the nature' (Balázs 1985: 116). Theories of spatial cognition also suggest that natural, site-specific, environmental sounds can reinforce spatial aspects of perception 'focusing primarily on perception of sound-source direction' (Waller and Nadel 2013: 83). These varied perspectives indicate how ambient sounds provide depth and a spatial dimension to a particular filmic sequence by establishing an environment conducive to eliciting cognitive association between audience and site, reinforcing 'the impression of reality' (Percheron 1980: 17). In film, the organisation and design of ambient sound completes a perception of reality in terms of aural perspective and localisation,[12] enabling audience members to relate to the specifics of a site's sonic environment. Film sound scholar William Whittington's work (2007) focuses on science-fiction films, in which he unpacks the idea of ambiences (or 'ambient noises' in his definition) and their role in the developing craft of sound design to not only provide a 'sonic long shot' (2007: 137) but also to reveal dramatic elements. Aesthetics scholar Martin Seel sees ambient sound as the architect of the 'interconnection of filmic space with the space that is presented in the film' (Seel 2018: 9). Contemporary film scholars like Elsie Walker (2015) note 'the contextualizing space' by multi-track ambient sounds drawing on Michel Chion's coinage 'superfield' denoting to 'the space created in multitrack films by ambient natural sounds' (1994: 150). These perspectives may be consolidated in a thorough, practice-based and reflective analysis of ambient sound's specific position in cinema by a more sensitive listening.

Scholar of film sound production Tomlinson Holman states that 'ambience most typically consists of more or less continuous sound, often with a low-frequency emphasis we associate with background noise of spaces' (Holman 1997: 177). The advent of digital recording makes it possible to record these deep layers of low-frequency sounds (Kerins 2011). Earlier recording media – namely analogue optical recording and analogue magnetic recording – had a limited dynamic range and was less capable of capturing the full spectrum of ambient sounds, thus weakly affecting the way fictional sites could be portrayed in narration.

Trajectories of sound production within any national film industry such as Indian cinema or Hollywood reveal shifts in location recording practices and the mediation of myriad sonically produced environments. In both industries, certain phases have determined sound production practices. For example, the dubbing era (1960s–1990s in Indian cinema) and studio era (1930s–1950s in Hollywood) centred less on the site and emphasised typical narrative tropes such as song and dance sequences or musical scores. Since the digital era (2000s–) in both Indian cinema and Hollywood, more realistic and concrete representations of sites can be observed. Although technological advancements have predominantly determined this shift (Altman 1992; Kassabian 2013a; Kerins 2006, 2011; Lastra 2000), certain aesthetic choices have also developed as a result of sound production's historical evolution. This history needs to be introduced in order to understand the different yet concurrent ambient sound recording and designing practices, methods and approaches, and their shifting roles, in transforming the 'pro-filmic space' (Lastra 2000) into 'film space'.[13]

Based on these developments, the nature of ambient sound usage will be studied in various corresponding and intercepting phases of recording and sound production in global cinema including but not limited to Indian cinema. For methodological clarity, the history of global cinema sound production will be divided into three broad periods: (1) direct or synchronised sound (optical recording on film or electro-mechanical recording on disc), monaural soundtracks (1930s–1950s); (2) analogue recording (magnetic), dubbing, stereophonic mixing (1960s–1990s); and (3) digital recording and surround sound design (2000s–). Critical listening, informed reflections and analyses of certain sound excerpts representative of Indian, European and American films from these three sound production phases qualify the evidential component of this study from a top-down approach. The quality, texture, depth and other typical onsite characteristics of ambient sound recordings, as well as the aesthetic choices of sound organisation in the spatial settings of various post-production stages, have substantially changed alongside technological shifts that correspond with and intercept predominant sound production periods. Therefore, the contemporary use of digital tools and techniques will also be conscientiously studied in relation to previous production phases.

As film sound scholars have suggested, in the field of global cinema, American cinema has consistently utilised clean layers of ambient sound in order to 'help to develop the atmosphere and to range the image on screen into space and time' (Ribrant 1999: 19). Technological developments in the digital era have resulted in the systematic use of ambient sounds and surround design (Holman 2002; Kerins 2011) – which has facilitated 'a thicker, more realistic, sound score [...] and help[s] the audience in their spatial orientation' (Ribrant 1999: 20). However, in comparison to its American and European counterparts, Indian cinema is notorious for producing sonic experiences incorporating an overwhelming use of song and dance sequences where location-specific ambient sounds are generally given little attention or even are ignored (Gopalan 2002; Rajadhyaksha 2007). There are indeed many examples from popular Indian films in which ambient sounds are kept at bay, mostly in the interest of a loud and colourful setting, providing a detached and imaginary cinematic landscape of auditory spectacle in which the site is predominantly absent, offering a transient moment of escape for the spectator. This study will show how this general perception might be erroneous when historical trajectories are taken into consideration. The advent of digital technology has been especially successful in enabling rich layers of ambient sound components to be incorporated into the production schemes of sound organisation, which has somewhat homogenised sound production and sonic experiences across the globe. A thorough study of the historical trajectories of sound production leading to the contemporary digital domain, specifically focusing on the use of ambient sound, will help contextualise critical listening, enquiry and analyses. The comparative discussion of film examples from the wider field of global cinema, including the less-discussed Indian and Asian films alongside more-discussed American and European films will enrich the field. Indian cinema, the largest producer of films in the global film industry, is as equally a part of world cinema as European and American cinemas, though it faces a lack of critical engagement. The inclusive and wide-ranging case studies from Indian and other Asian cinema alongside their American and European counterparts can generate new knowledge and add dimensions to the field of sound studies, film sound and media art history.

1.4 Ambient Sound in Other Audiovisual Media Arts

This historical trajectory is also significant and relevant while discussing and situating sound art developed from field recordings within a contemporary context. It will be argued that functional aspects of ambient sound in sound art are often dissolved for the purpose of embracing artistic imagination and transformation. The word ambient within a sound art context relates to a rather obscure understanding of environment or atmosphere (Böhme 1993), leading to terms such as 'environmental sound art'.[14] No wonder sound artist and theorist Seth Kim-Cohen criticises the art world's recent fascination with ambient aesthetics in his book *Against Ambience* (2013). Here ambience is simplistically understood as the soothing atmospheres that prevail in contemporary sound art exhibition contexts. He identifies a non-critical attraction for immersive experiences that tend to 'wash over the senses' (Kim-Cohen 2013). He argues that a strong emphasis on ambience enhances an alleged perceptual immediacy at the expense of conceptual rigour. Kim-Cohen's analysis thus heavily critiques what he calls the 'ambient aesthetics' of contemporary sound art as 'a move toward unmediated experience without concepts' (2013).[15] However, his views do not reveal the deeper ramifications and implications of ambience in sound studies.

Ambient music pioneer Brian Eno defined ambience in the liner notes of *Music for Airports* (1978) 'as an atmosphere, or a surrounding influence: a tint' (Eno 1978). Indeed, this sense of subdued colouring permeates the field of ambient music. However, Eno's definition makes an easy association between ambient music and ambience. In contrast, this study will argue that ambient music's ready correlation with ambient sound or ambience is debatable. As Joanna Demers has shown, ambient music 'uses a slew of methods to make it sound as if it lacks a foreground and thus easily melts into its surroundings' (Demers 2010: 117), and therefore, as David Toop suggests (1995), hints at an imaginary environment rather than imposing one derived from lived experience. This study will show that ambience emerges from specific sites and that their site-specificity cannot be easily erased through artistic transformation.

Ulrik Schmidt (2012, 2013) proposed the term 'sonic environmentality' to denote an aggregation of the ways in which ambient sound can affect us. The concept of sonic environmentality further opens discourse by distinguishing between three major forms or dimensions: the ambient, the ecological and the atmospheric. This threefold dissection of ambience helps create a more comprehensive understanding of the term. This book intervenes in current discourse by considering ambient sound as a material layer in the hands of sound practitioners and artists. Specifically, it investigates the ways in which they sculpt the conditions of relative presence (or absence) and embodiment (or deliberate abstraction) through mediated processes of recording and spatial organisation that attempt to (re)produce a site's specific atmosphere and sonic environment.

Notes

1. Cardullo (2009).
2. Though both connote the same meaning, in this book, I will be using 'ambient sound' more often than 'environmental sound'. The reason is to be faithful to the practitioners' terminology, while considering 'environmental sound' to be overloaded with an ecological discourse, which I would like to let gradually unfold in the book.
3. Chattopadhyay (2007).
4. To access the article, see: https://www.ucsusa.org/about/1992-world-scientists.html
5. See: https://science.gu.se/digitalAssets/1671/1671867_world-scientists-warning-to-humanity_-a-second-notice_english.pdf
6. Mise-en-sonore is a neologism that will be explained fully while unpacking the term 'auditory setting'. The term draws on the idea of mise-en-scène, meaning the arrangement of objects within a pro-filmic space and its visual framing, but rather focuses on the arrangement of sounds within a pro-filmic space and its recording. Altman, with McGraw Jones and Sonia Tatroe coined the term 'mise-en-bande' (2000: 341), meaning the interaction of various sound components in the soundtrack. While 'mise-en-bande' is concerned with the audio-audio relationship between various elements of the soundtrack, e.g. voice, sound effects and music, my proposed coinage mise-en-sonore focuses on the sound's complex relationship with site and space in cinema, and denotes the sonorous film space constructed through the recording of the space and designing these recorded sounds for narration.
7. The terms broadly denote background sounds that are present in a scene or location: wind, water, birds, room tone, office rumbles, traffic, forest murmurs, waves from seashores, neighbourhood mutterings, etc. According to the online resources

THE AUDITORY SETTING

and Media College (http://www.mediacollege.com/audio/ambient/), in the context of filmmaking, ambience consists of the sounds of a given location or space. This definition correlates ambience with other associated terms such as 'atmosphere', 'atmos' or 'background'. The resource-rich website FilmSound.org suggests: 'ambience pertains to the pervading atmosphere of a place'. FilmSound.org further claims that 'ambience is widely used as a synonym for ambient sound, which consists of noises present in the environment'. Drawing on these sources, these two terms appear to belong to the same family of concepts in sound practice and theory and can be used interchangeably. However, etymologically, ambient sound underscores the material and functional aspects of the term, whereas ambience emphasises social and cultural connotations.

8. 'Place' refers to generic locations that are local and governed by interpersonal, ecological or political relationships (cf. Castells in Demers 2010: 114). 'Site', on the other hand, is more specific. The latter denotes the location of an important occurrence or event; it suggests a particular place that is used for a certain activity. Therefore, in this work, the term site is used more often than place to specify the sonic depiction of a particular location. In short, in relation to sound, site is understood as being situated, inextricably bound to a particular spot, and is used here to denote the specificity of a particular place where ambient sounds are recorded.

9. 'Sound practice' is a term broadly used throughout this book. It encompasses sound recording, production mixing, dubbing, studio mixing, foley, re-recording, etc. Likewise, the term 'sound practitioner' accommodates not only artists and practitioners working with sound but also all categories of sound professionals: location sound recordists, field recording experts, directors of audiography, foley artists, sound designers, production mixers and mixing engineers, re-recording specialists, etc.

10. In film, the term 'diegetic' typically refers to the internal world created by the story that the characters themselves experience and encounter, the narrative space that includes all of the story-world's components, both those that are and those that are not actually depicted on screen. Further explanation of this crucial term will be provided in a following sub-chapter.

11. 'Best practice' is a method, technique or approach that is generally considered better than its alternatives because it produces results that are allegedly superior to those achieved by other means of production within a specific context or has become a standard way of doing things in compliance with certain aesthetic references. Best practices are used as an alternative to mandatory legislated standards to maintain quality and can be based on self-assessment or benchmarking.

12. See interview with sound practitioners in Chattopadhyay (2021). *Between the Headphones: Listening to the Sound Practitioner*. Newcastle upon Tyne: Cambridge Scholars Publishing.

13. The term 'film space' is defined as the space that the spectator encounters, a space that is organised through time (e.g., the temporal linking of shots through sound editing). According to David Sorfa (2014) and James Lastra (2000) among others, the area in front of the camera's recording field is known as the pro-filmic space. Film scholars Annette Kuhn and Guy Westwell define pro-filmic space in 'A Dictionary of Film Studies', as 'the slice of the world in front of the film camera; including protagonists and their actions, lighting, sets, props and costumes, as well as the setting itself, as opposed to what eventually appears on the cinema screen. In studio-made fiction films, the profilmic event is a set constructed for the purpose of being filmed. At the other extreme, in observational documentary forms like direct cinema, filmmakers seek, as a fundamental element of their practice, to preserve the integrity of the real-life space and time of the profilmic event. Many films occupy a

middle ground in their organization of, or relationship with, the profilmic event: as for example in the case of location-shot' (Kuhn and Westwell 2014/2015: n.p.).
14. The term 'environmental sound art' has been coined by some sound artists and incorporates processes in which the artist actively engages with the environment. See: https://global.oup.com/academic/product/environmental-sound-artists-9780190234614?cc=dk&lang=en&#
15. See: https://earroom.wordpress.com/2013/12/04/seth-kim-cohen/

2 THE AUDITORY CONTEXT AND SIGNIFICATION

2.1 FILM SOUND RESEARCH

From the very advent of sound in cinema, ambient sound has been a practical production concern. Initially, it was considered negatively, as unwanted 'background noise' from the location, and then positively, as site-specific information to be included in the film's diegesis. The latter clearly explains ambient sound's relevance and considered role within film sound production. Every site depicted in a cinematic narrative contains distinct and subtle sounds emanating from its environment. These sound sources can include, for example, wind, rain, running water, rustling leaves, distant traffic, aircraft and machinery noise, the sound of distant human movement and speech, creaks and pops from thermal contraction, air conditioners and plumbing, the noise from fans and motors, the hum of electrical machines, room tone, etc. Although film sound has received extensive academic interest, much of this attention has been invested in explaining the role of voice and music in relation to the visual image (Chion 1994, 2009; Gorbman 1987). Despite these specific layers of sound carrying the primary spatial information that constructs a site's 'presence' (Doane 1985a; Grimshaw 2011; Lombard and Ditton 1997; Reiter 2011; Skalski and Whitbred 2010) through an interplay between diegesis (Burch 1982; Percheron 1980) and mimesis[1] (Kassabian 2013a; Weiss 2011) to interlink the site and sound in a nuanced way (LaBelle 2006; LaBelle and Martinho 2011), proliferating a spatial turn (Beck 2013; Eisenberg 2015), after the advent of a digital revolutions in the cinema (Kerins 2006, 2011) often beyond a much-cited idea of the soundscape (Schafer 1994), environmental, atmospheric or ambient sounds yet have largely remained underexplored in film and media art studies and, therefore, deserve careful attention and in-depth analysis.

Little film sound research exists about the practice and implications of using location-specific ambient sounds and the specific purposes they serve. Few early writings on film sound mention the environmental or atmospheric potential of ambient sounds. But one clear exception does exist. Béla Balázs proclaims in his article 'Theory of the film: Sound' that:

> It is the business of the sound film to reveal for us our acoustic environment, the acoustic landscape in which we live, the speech of things and the intimate whisperings of nature; all that has speech beyond human speech, and speaks to us with the vast conversational powers of life and incessantly influences and directs our thoughts and emotions, from the muttering of the sea to the din of a great city, from the roar of machinery to the gentle patter of autumn rain on a windowpane. (Balázs 1985: 116)

With such urgent and ardent utterances regarding the roles of natural, environmental sounds in cinema during its formative years, prescribing which sounds should be incorporated to (re)present nature, Balázs suggests a strategy of utilising location-specific environmental sounds or ambient sounds from the early years of sound films onwards. However, his enthusiasm is not reflected in ensuing studies.

In Rick Altman's writing (1980, 1985, 1992, 2001, 2012), the technological development of sound in cinema is articulated and its impact on aesthetic choices is analysed in relation to sound-image relationships. However, ambient sound's usage is hardly addressed in his analyses and film's sound-site relationship is not discussed at all. Michel Chion's influential writings (1994, 2009) on film sound do not show considerable interest in addressing the role of ambient sound in cinema either. The next generation of scholars who address sound technology, sound practice and sonic aesthetics in cinema – such as Mark Kerins (2006, 2011), Tomlinson Holman (1997, 2002) and David Sonnenschein (2001) – do mention ambient sound as a specific layer of sound design, but their writings do not consider the complex relationship between sound and site. The following preliminary review positions *The Auditory Setting* in relation to the number of recent works that do address various aspects of film sound from synchronisation to the Dolby digital era of surround sound.

In his book *Occult Aesthetics: Synchronization in Sound Film* (2014), film scholar Kevin Donnelly offers a sustained theorisation of synchronisation in sound film. Donnelly studies how the merging of the audio and the visual generates a perceptible synergy, an aesthetic he dubs 'occult': 'a secret and esoteric effect that can dissipate in the face of an awareness of its synergetic workings.' The book examines points of synchronisation, providing 'moments of comfort in a potentially threatening environment possibly fraught with sound and image stimuli.' Correspondingly, a lack of synchrony between sound and image appear disturbing for the audience. The interplay between the two becomes central tenets of audiovisual culture, which, as Donnelly argues, provides a 'starting point for a new understanding of audiovisual interactions' (2014). This approach is discussed in theoretical and historical terms through analyses of a broad selection of film soundtracks. Nevertheless, ambient sound is hardly covered in the discussion.

In his book *Beyond Dolby (Stereo): Cinema in the Digital Sound Age*, Mark Kerins (2011) draws upon works from the last two decades and a collection of interviews with sound practitioners to uncover how digital surround sound has affected sound design in cinemas. The study includes detailed analyses of a number of American films and their soundtracks. Kerins does mention ambient sound as a specific layer of sound design in digital cinema systems, imparting more spatial information as compared to earlier sound production eras (monaural and stereophonic). But his discussion does not consider the complex relationships between sound and site.

Film sound scholar Andy Birtwistle's book *Cinesonica: Sounding Film and Video* (2010) 'explores previously neglected and undertheorised aspects of film and video sound, drawing on detailed case studies of Hollywood cinema, art cinema, animated cartoons and avant-garde film and video.' In adopting an 'interdisciplinary approach to the study of the soundtrack, breaking away from narrativity and signification, which has tended to dominate the study of film sound, the book examines how sound's materiality figures within audiovisual experience.' Through a close examination of audio-visual relations in a range of film and video examples, the book 'recasts text as the meeting point of audio and visual materialities.' The book covers topics such as deconstructive film practice, the sound of old films, electronic sounds and audiovisual synesthetic experience, and draws on theoretical resources of sound studies, musicology and post-structural theory to provide an alternative to established models of film analysis. The book underlines that film and video sound cannot be examined in isolation from the image, the book 'discusses the temporal, historical, morphological, affective and sensory dimensions of audiovisuality, and asks how sound-image relations might be considered in political terms' (2010). However, the book does not specifically explore ambient sound.

Kim-Cohen's book *Against Ambience* (2013) investigates the art world's recent turn towards ambience. As previously considered, Kim-Cohen understands ambience as the easy and comforting wash of environmental sounds that dominate recent sound art exhibitions. His discussion does not extend to film sound nor consider the roles of ambience in cinema or sound art as an essentially site-specific element.

The above-mentioned books use distinct points of entry that question audiovisual relationships (Donnelly; Birtwistle), digital/technological changes impacting aesthetic choices in film sound (Kerins) and a loose 'ambient ethos' in recent sound art (Kim-Cohen). However, none of them reads ambient sound as a potential source of site-specific evidence to be considered for in-depth analysis and further investigation. Indeed, no systematic research has been undertaken to date on ambient sound and its mediation. From this vantage point, *The Auditory Setting* offers a comprehensive understanding of the subject beyond obvious audiovisual relationships. Furthermore, the work contributes to emerging discourse in sonic research concerning the evolving relationship between site, environment, sound and mediation approached from a practice-based perspective.

2.2 The audiovisual relationship

The specialist study of film sound has only been established in recent decades. Rick Altman's and Tom Levin's early writing on the history of sound technology, examining sound's relationship to the moving image, have been instrumental in this developing field. Chion's seminal work *Audio-Vision* (1994), for example, has also contributed to the film sound canon as a corpus of developing knowledge focused on understanding the on-screen audiovisual relationship. These writings have compounded the study of sound in relation to the visual image. Sound is regarded as an element predominantly enhancing the cinematic narrative, reinforcing and/or underlining a scene's emotive potential; this scholarly stance considers the soundtrack as a secondary and one-dimensional accompaniment to visual storytelling without enacting an autonomous impact on the multi-sensory cinematic experience. However, an apparent shift seems to be occurring in more recent work. Among contemporary scholars, Giorgio Biancorosso (2009) questions the overarching comparisons of sound with image and emphasises sound's role and the potential of listening as specific and separate areas of research. The idea that sound is more than a flat, screen-centric soundtrack following the visual narrative and can be studied separately has destabilised the notion of a soundtrack. As discussed in a later chapter, soundtrack is a term that derives from its historical relationship to an optical track on the filmstrip, mixed with music, thus retaining a sense of linearity and one-dimensionality.

Following Biancorosso, this study will assert that 'soundtrack' is a restrictive term. This is particularly true for digital production methods, which utilise ambience within surround sound practices that transcend the soundtrack's linear representation and develop a spatially evocative sound environment. The effect tends to create an elaborate and fluid cinematic space in which the epistemological grounding of sounds (Branigan 1989), related to their respective screen-centric visual referents, is reordered. The wider, off-screen diegetic space available with digital cinema systems (Kerins 2006, 2011) appears to be immersive and expands towards providing an embodied experience for the listening audience; it also opens up potential multiple interpretations of sound through subjective positioning. This new setting leads to an interactive sonic space (Dyson 2009) that often appears to unfold itself beyond the visual image and on-screen constraints. Ideas about this interactive, fluid, ambient and flexible sonic space can help the listener comprehend developments in relatively independent sound art practice.

2.3 Sound studies

The sonic environment, ambience, environmental and ambient sound have gained currency as concepts in contemporary studies of sound, both in film and field recording-based sound and media art, ever since digital technology made it possible to easily record sound with high fidelity and precision from the actual location and (re)construct it in various possible spatial organisations of sound. In contemporary media scholarship, this is often called the 'spatial turn'. Andrew J. Eisenberg notes that 'the increasing recognition of the intimate links between sound and space may be attributed to a confluence of scientific and technological developments in the latter half of the twentieth century, including the development of travelling-wave models of auditory perception and the rise of multi-channel audio recording and playback' (Eisenberg 2015: 195). Sound studies scholar Jay Beck has already diagnosed an emerging sonic trope in world cinema – an increased attentiveness to the sound of real places and spaces, and the lived urban environments:

> This preference for signature sounds over dialogue shifts the audience away from semantic listening to become absorbed in the same acoustic framework as the characters. Thus, without the common set of contextual cues coming from dialogue or score music, the viewer's perceptual activity is engaged in a search for meaningful patterns and aural motifs. (Beck 2013: 740)

Beck locates this shift primarily as a digital aesthetics in film sound, after a digital revolution in the late 1990s reconfigured the production–distribution–reception chains of film and audiovisual media, connecting the different parts of the globe's sound productions in a globally dispersed, interconnected unity.

Drawing from these perspectives, this book will outline how digital sound production and its capacity for multi-channel audio recording and playback have accelerated this shift towards spatial sensibility in film sound. It will also link the emergence of field recording-based sound art related to an intellectual development in the social sciences and humanities to this shift, placing emphasis on place, space and site. Indeed, this spatial shift is the raison d'être for this book. The recent emergence and rapid establishment of sound studies as a vibrant academic field seems felicitous for these considerations. An informed critical listening enquiry and in-depth analysis of this generally ignored field will engage with pertinent spatial discourses in sound studies. Its specific context is a useful framework for analysing artistic production that uses ambient sound as its primary material. Exploration of the precise notions of sonic environment, ambience and ambient sound in film sound production studies allows the book's discussion of sound art to focus more on the intricate spatiotemporal as well as subjective means by which a site is conceptually addressed.

2.4 FILM AND MEDIA ARTS

The choice to represent both film and field recording-based sound and media artwork cases studies is twofold. Firstly, a personal trajectory formulates the passage from one medium to the other; as a practitioner, my interests can be traced from film to media arts. Secondly, and more importantly, both film sound and field recording-based sound and media artworks are developed through sound recordings made at sites for the purpose of narration and/or providing descriptive accounts of those sites. Within the context of field or location recording practices, it is the cinematic medium in particular that historically provides the scope and incentive to 'record sound from a landscape so extensively' (Chattopadhyay 2007: 110). Moreover, the art of producing and delivering spatially engaging and immersive sound experiences has recently awakened the interest of not only filmgoers but also enthusiastic contemporary media art audiences.

Technological developments that have changed how sound recording and production processes now handle the subtle, site-specific and atmospheric details of lived sonic environments and transform them into mediated environments require investigation. This book will build on existing research and look at what has not yet been discussed. It will demonstrate how sound production has been developed through the advent of digital multi-track recording and surround sound mixing in cinema, accounting for the way in which new technologies and tools have impacted the mediation of the site-specificity of sound in film and media. Therefore, the study of the production processes geared towards narrating and describing a site and reconstructing its presence by means of ambient sounds takes into account both the fields of cinema as well as sound/media art. The study explores the similarities and differences between media artworks that do not always provide a realistic (re)presentation of a site and the layers of ambient sound in film, which attempt to produce a realistic auditory setting, at least within the digital era. Both aspects will be discussed to illustrate how artistic practices can influence and substantially inform the so-called best practice for film productions while concurrently taking a critical approach towards film's use of narration and the site's presence, as well as the anthropogenic mediation of sonic environments through media technologies.

2.5 THE PHENOMENOLOGY OF AMBIENT SOUND

Whereas changes in visual elements relate both to film's diegetic world and its perceivers, changes to aural elements relate first and foremost to activities in the film's interior physical or material world (Branigan 1997; Langkjær 2000, 2006); film sound is fundamentally linked to perceptual processes that reveal the physical aspects of its fiction. Even film theorist Siegfried Kracauer, who emphasises that cinema is primarily a visual medium, notes that film sound has 'the quality of bringing the material aspects of reality into focus' (Kracauer 1960: 124). Within this reading, sound is central in providing information about the material world that unfolds in the filmic environment. It explains why sound, more than image, is able to give an embodied experience[2] of a site recorded from the pro-filmic space and carefully (re)constructed in the film space. Audiences are highly sensitive, albeit subconsciously so, to sounds included in filmic storytelling and constructed listening environments. Remove the sounds and see how the entire cinematic world collapses.

But, first of all, this assumption should be evaluated: Why is ambient sound more effective at sculpting a spatial sensation and an embodied experience of site than other layers of sound such as voice, music and sound effects? Among these layers, voice includes dialogues between characters, thus relaying primary narrative information (Bordwell and Thompson 1997). Amy Lawrence argues that in narrative cinema 'the synchronization of image and voice is sacrosanct' (Lawrence 1992: 179), emphasising the necessity of a stricter method of sound production when dealing with voice, which must be connected to an on-screen body. Mary Ann Doane affirms that dialogue or the use of voice 'engenders a network of metaphors whose nodal point appears to be the body'. She further states that the sound of the character's voice is strictly 'married to the image' (Doane 1985b: 162–163). In view of these arguments, voice in cinema is less spatial in nature, making it more creatively limited as a sound component when compared to ambient sound. The post-synchronised voice, produced by dubbing or similar practices, is 'disengaged from its "proper" space (the space conveyed by the visual image) and the credibility of that voice depends upon the technician's ability to return it to the site of its origin' (Doane 1985b: 164). This return to the original site can be achieved by the technician's creative and innovative use of ambient sounds.

Music in films usually triggers particular feelings. It is used 'largely to set mood or elicit a particular emotional response from the audience' (Kuhn and Westwell 2014/2015). Film music tracks and sound effects 'establish a particular mood' (Doane 1985b: 55) instead of providing a sense of space. Sound effects are also important for narration and creating feelings of, for example, tension and horror. In the mixing stages, the hierarchy of different sound components usually follows specific conventions: 'Sound effects and music are subservient to dialogue and it is, above all, the intelligibility of the dialogue which is at stake, together with its nuances of tone' (Doane 1985b: 55). Within this hierarchy of sonic elements, ambient sound remains fluid and malleable.

Nevertheless, ambient sound can also provide the specific atmosphere of a site produced within film space's 'reality'. It injects life and substance not only to what we see on screen but also to off-screen diegetic space for sound practitioners.[3] They use layers of ambient sound to construct the perceptual experience of reality through technological and creative means.[4] Ambient sound helps to ground the sense of a specific place[5] and secure the experience of its specific sonic environment in a way no other sound layer can. These practical considerations and creative perspectives underscore ambient sound's spatial nature when compared with other sound components. The American film theorist and audio engineer Tomlinson Holman describes ambient sounds used in film sound production from the characteristic natural environmental sounds of a given outdoor site to indoor room tone.[6] The latter is the low-frequency ambient sound of an indoor space that comes to the fore when all actors are silent; it is the sonic layer that is significantly capable of transmitting the characteristic auditory details of a particular indoor location. In this respect, Holman suggests that 'ambience most typically consists of more or less continuous sound, often with a low-frequency emphasis we associate with background noise of spaces' (Holman 1997: 177). The advent of digital recording makes it possible to record and (re)present a deep layer of low-frequency sounds (Kerins 2011).

Earlier recording media – analogue optical recording and analogue magnetic recording with limited dynamic ranges – were less capable of capturing the full spectrum of locative ambient sounds such as the elusive layer of room tone. Low-frequency content in digitally recorded ambient sound layers arguably contributes to a sense of embodiment. An embodied experience of sound in cinema is provided by a full-frequency, multi-track digital recording of site-specific, physically perceptible ambient sounds, which are diffused through a multi-channel surround sound design. As rightly argued by Kerins (2006, 2011), this sense of embodiment through perceptible, low-frequency sounds finds prominence in digital sound production – an important aspect for sound design practices, where this capacity is described as 'adding body to the sound'.[7] The concept of embodiment draws from the phenomenology of sonic perception. French philosopher Maurice Merleau-Ponty argued that perception is the product of a multi-sensory relationship between the individual's 'body' and its surroundings as a whole (Merleau-Ponty 2005: 273). Don Ihde held similar views, claiming: 'I do not merely hear with my ears, I hear with my whole body' (Ihde 2007: 44), which substantiates embodiment as a useful notion when discussing the mediation of sonic environments for entertainment and media consumption through recorded, processed and manipulated site-specific ambient sounds.

Ambient sounds are not always directly anchored to specific sources visible on screen, unlike voice and effects that usually emanate from respective characters or objects (Holman 2010; Kerins 2011), with the exception of certain non-diegetic usages such as voice-overs. This particular attribute of ambient sound gives it relative freedom over other sound components, allowing it to be perceived as an autonomous element and studied separately outside of visual constraints. It allows sound practitioners to use ambient sounds more freely and independently, exploring their spatial characteristics and site-specific associations. Therefore, sound studies perspectives regarding sound's spatial characteristics are pertinent to this research.

A recent flux of investigative scholarship in the field has resulted in two compendia: *The Routledge Sound Studies Reader* (2012) and *The Oxford Handbook of Sound Studies* (2013). They have been followed by a number of peer-reviewed journals such as the *Journal of Sonic Studies* and *Ear | Wave | Event* that are entirely dedicated to sound studies. These examples demonstrate that the subject has become a rewarding area of current academic research. Jay Beck and Tony Grajeda quote Rick Altman in their introductory chapter – 'The Future of Film Sound Studies' – of edited anthology *Lowering the Boom: Critical Studies in Film Sound* to emphasise the appropriateness and legitimacy of specialised, in-depth investigations of film sound 'within the growing field of Sound Studies' (Beck and Grajeda 2008: 1). This book's dialogue is integrated within the current sound studies discourse, albeit with a practice-based perspective that incorporates artistic research as self-reflection to compliment critical analyses.

Film scholars have already highlighted that cinema's technical advances have affected sound creation's spatial aspects (Bordwell and Thompson 1985). *The Auditory Setting* hypothesises that cinema's evolving spatiality is primarily provided by additional layers of ambient sounds, whereas other layers such as voice and sound effects have remained largely screen-centric throughout technological transitions from monaural and stereophonic to the contemporary digital surround sound environment. In certain instances, voice can carry spatial information, particularly in digital multi-track sync sound practice, as Kerins shows (2011). Instead of dubbing inside an inert studio – a practice that was standardised in many national cinemas for the larger part of the late twentieth century (1950s–2000s) – the sync track includes some spatial information directly recorded from the location. Although this process adds to the overall sense of a site-aware experience, it is the ambient sound layer that carries a film's primary spatial information and is the sound practitioner's basic tool to (re)construct the site and enhance the 'ultrafield' of the sonic environment (Holman 2010; Kerins 2011).[8] This study extends beyond research on voice and background music by focusing instead on ambient sound recording and reproducing processes that mediate the sonic environment in film and media arts.

2.6 Digital aesthetics

Historically, the voice was used to carry the primary threads of a narrative. However, its prevalence has decreased ever since other channels of sound have opened up to distribute the screen-centric appeal of films towards expanded cinemascope and surround sound (Rogers 2013). This development can be seen as a shift from the 'vococentricity' of cinema (Chion 1994) towards a more inclusive realm of digital systems. Since the 1990s a large-scale conversion has taken place from analogue recording, analogue production practices and optical film exhibition to digital technologies. The newer technology has been integrated into filmmaking production and post-production. The ramifications of these developments are far-reaching; particular evidence can be found in how the cinematic experience has changed through the use of sound technology such as multi-track synchronised sound recording and surround sound design. Most recently, digital multi-channel surround sound systems like Dolby Atmos or Auro 3D have altered the way in which the film soundtrack is rendered and reorganised. An audience's experience of film space has been reconfigured by these newer environments, which diverge considerably from earlier screen-centric mono and stereophonic settings by integrating and augmenting desired aesthetics into the surround environment through a spatial reorganisation of sound. Following these transitions, contemporary cinema facilitates specific practices involving ambient sound to create cinematic experiences that are spatially wider, more elaborate and relatively fluid when compared with the screen-centric monaural soundtrack or the flat surface of a stereophonic composite soundtrack, which is slightly wider than monaural rendering of sonic environment but still constrained to the screen's two-dimensional frame. These earlier organisations of film sound anchored the on-screen story-world by ignoring the site specificities of diegesis and evoking sound's emotive potential through post-synchronised effects and background music instead. Digitalised sound practices incorporate the multi-channel surround design of ambient sounds that handle the site in spatially perceptible ways, rather than catering for a voice- and screen-oriented audiovisual contract as postulated by Chion (1994).

Some of Chion's views of film sound (1994, 2009) need to be re-examined and questioned in relation to current sound practices that enable more layers of sound to be included in their spatial organisation. Contrary to Chion's perception, today's multi-channel film sound universe builds surround environments, which assume audiences will understand that sounds originating from surround channels are part of the same diegetic space as those on screen (Kerins 2011) that expand elaborate details beyond the screen. Innovative digital sound practices lead to new experiences in which audiences engage with cinematic sites and their mediated sonic environments through immersive listening, employing a spatially cognitive engagement with sound. New theoretical models and approaches are required for these practices to expand on existing analysis (e.g., Chion 1994, 2009). They should include studies of sound that look and listen beyond the domination of the moving image with its screen-centric tendencies. This book enables a novel framework for studying the increasingly important digital layers of sound and explores sound's spatial capacity to enrich the cinematic experience. The 'spatial turn' (Eisenberg 2015) in sound production, manifested by the use of ambient sound, is studied in relation to its development from monaural synchronised sound recording and post-synchronous dubbing to the contemporary digital multi-track synchronised or sync recording, as well as from monaural and stereophonic mixing to digital surround sound design, thus placing the studies of ambient sound within a historical context. As the knowledge pool of film sound research primarily refers to American cinema, a study of sound in other national cinemas could be considered a useful addition. Frequent references to literature on American and European cinema constitute the project's epistemological grounding on which relevant examples from world cinema (mostly Indian, other Asian, American and European films) can be compared, theorised and contextualised.

Therefore, the book investigates the capacity of ambient sound to help sculpt the site's presence and its sonic environment in film and media production, moving the complex relationship between sound, site and the environment beyond predominantly image-centric studies in film and media art. Instead of relying on traditional theories of film sound, with their typical underscoring of sound-image relationships, *The Auditory Setting* shifts emphasis towards the spatial aspects of sound production, in part by expanding its discourse towards field recording-based sound art. Concepts such as diegesis, mimesis and presence are explored from the growing theoretical corpus of sound studies, reformulating the Schaferean notion of soundscape to challenge traditional discourses regarding the site-specificity of ambient sounds. As the book develops, a number of field recording-based sound and media artworks will be discussed to illustrate sound art's technologically intersecting yet aesthetically different development when dealing with site-specific issues. This discussion will enable informed comparisons between the specifics of film sound and contemporary media art production to comprehend various differing levels of anthropogenic sonic environment mediation.

Notes

1. These crucial terms will be explained in Chapter 3, 'Key Concepts and Definitions'.
2. 'Embodied experience' is defined by digital media scholars as a state of 'being surrounded by simulated sensorimotor information in mediated environments that create the sensation of personally undergoing the experience at that moment' (Ahn 2011: iv). Within the context of this discussion, digital film sound production terminology is used to underscore the unique capacity of sync sound and surround sound design. An embodied experience of sound in the cinema is provided by site-specific sound recordings – including room tone, low-frequency rumbles and other bodily perceptible ambient sounds – dispersed in a spatial organisation following multichannel surround sound design. As argued by Mark Kerins (2006, 2011), these practices find prominence in the digital era of sound production.
3. To access in-depth conversations with prominent sound practitioners, who recount the various ways in which they use ambient sound in cinema, further reading is available in Chattopadhyay (2021).
4. See: interview with Dipankar Chaki (2020) in Chattopadhyay (2021).
5. See: interview with Dileep Subramaniam (2020) in Chattopadhyay (2021).
6. See: http://filmsound.org/QA/vocabulary.htm
7. For interviews I conducted with various renowned sound designers, production mixing specialists, mixing engineers, sound editors and location recordists, see: Chattopadhyay (2021).
8. 'Ultrafield' is an extension of the term 'superfield' that Michel Chion used to describe Dolby Stereo and refers to a new form of sound-derived spatial configuration associated with digital sound systems.

3 KEY CONCEPTS AND DEFINITIONS

3.1 Diegetic sound

The Greek notion of storytelling, diegesis, which denotes the use of a narrative process to construct the diegetic world, is often cited in film theory. Mary Ann Doane refers to it as 'the internal space' of the cinematic universe (Doane 1985b) framed and constructed by the technical tools of filmmaking. Translated to sound, this term could be understood in relation to the environmental, incidental and other location-specific sounds that are made to emanate from the story space in which events occur (Doane 1985b). Claudia Gorbman defines diegesis as 'the narratively implied spatiotemporal world of the actions and characters' (Gorbman 1987: 21). Both Doane and Gorbman use the terms 'space' and 'world' to underscore the constructed nature of film space during narrative storytelling. The term 'diegetic sound' reflects the sounds that inhabit the constructed world and whose sources are visibly present within the space of filmic events. Likewise, any sound beyond the filmic universe's interior space is called 'non-diegetic'. The most common example of non-diegetic sound is background music, which the characters do not hear and is not present within the space of filmic events; the music is not grounded in filmic reality. As previously discussed, the incorporation of location-recorded ambient sound contributes to a realistic sense of producing the site's presence. Ambient sound can be regarded as the means of reinforcing a sense of realism by enhancing a site's believability in the mediated environment. In other words, ambient 'sound is used to make the image (of the site) "credible"' (Wayne 1997: 176).

As a result, the concept of diegesis should be taken into account when examining ambient sound's roles in constructing the site's relative presence in the story-world.

Historically, diegesis has been understood as the process of illustrating the story-world with all the narrative elements that are shown or inferred within the filmic content. The process allows for a certain mediated discernment of the phenomenal world within the story, including all of the physical sites framed inside the film, be they indoor or outdoor, urban or rural, closed or open. Sites are narrated through auditory features, atmospheres and 'soundmarks'[1] (Schafer 1994) in order to establish their presence for the audience. Listeners construe a diegetic world from recorded and (re)presented sonic material by taking in tiny aural hints and interpreting the contours of sites and their sonic environments from the relative volumes and spatial matrixing of these ambient sounds. Noël Burch (1982) asserts that diegesis describes narrative action, including places, people, clothing and sounds. As Edward Branigan sees it, diegesis is the 'implied spatial [. . .] system of a character – a collection of sense data which is represented as being at least potentially accessible to a character' (Branigan 1992: 35). Both scholars point to the necessary spatial component within narrative sound practice (location-specific recording and spatial design of ambient sounds as sense data) in the (re)creation and (re)construction of pro-filmic space.

Shifting sound practices that impact diegesis are known phenomena in cinema, which have been studied within the theoretical corpus on narration and storytelling. When writing about the specifics of narration in digitally produced American cinema using DSS (digital sound systems), Kerins argues that:

> [F]ilmmakers have taken advantage of DSS's expansion of the cinematic soundfield beyond the screen. To some degree this represents a simple acceleration of established narrative strategies – filmmakers have [. . .] relied on ambient sound in the 'surrounds' to set up diegetic spaces, and this trend has certainly continued with movies employing DSS. The difference here is that DSS has encouraged the construction of complex multichannel sound mixes, where the different sounds in each speaker channel together create a seemingly realistic and complete aural environment in a way difficult (if not impossible) with monophonic or Dolby Stereo sound. (Kerins 2006: 44)

Kerins's discourse reflects the practitioner who embraces digital systems as a narrative strategy. However, he is not particularly interested in ambient sound as a component within this strategy. Nevertheless, his insights provide an idea about the concept of presence. As Kerins argues, the apparent completeness of the constructed aural environment in cinema suggests the relatively high (or arguably highest) degree of the cinematic site's presence (re)presented in the story-world. This story-world is considered diegetic if the elements that belong to the film's narrative universe are included in the storytelling.

There is a question of mediation in diegesis in relation to sound. This capacity to mediate allows the narrator (e.g., the filmmaker, sound practitioner or sound artist) to control how much is revealed in the film's narration – places, environs, objects, situations, spaces and characters that inhabit the story-world. The process of mediation follows two sound production stages: (1) the recording of sounds from the site itself; and (2) studio sound design or composition to (re)produce the site and its environment. From his moral and ideological stance against the mediation of sounds recorded from the site, Schafer states that 'we have split the sound from the maker of the sound' (Schafer 1994: 90). Material gathered in this book will show how torn and ruptured sound recordings can be processed and spatially organised through sound art practices to create new diegetic worlds that are often only minimally abstracted from their site of recording. Within this strategy, ambient sounds contribute to the construction of the auditory setting through artistic intervention and transformation.

3.2 Mimesis

Theorists of early cinema have argued that, 'since film is always framed by the camera (and sound recorder), it is therefore a diegetic form and not a mimetic one' (Prince, in Kassabian 2013a). Mimesis, as opposed to the basic tenets of diegesis (i.e., narration and depiction), suggests imitation or representation (Dumouchel 2015; Weiss 2011). While diegesis narrates the action, mimesis shows said action (Kassabian 2013a). Kassabian suggests that cinematic narration through sound combines both strategies to a certain degree: 'Surely all realist film forms are both diegetic and mimetic in significant proportions, and it might be more interesting to consider how, when, and why those proportions shift in one direction or another' (Kassabian 2013a: n.p.). How these proportions have shifted in the move from analogue to digital production will be discussed. Particular attention will be given to how contemporary digital sound techniques render sites more present and how digitally reproduced sites are spatially wider, more elaborate and fluid when compared with the screen-centric monaural soundtrack or the stereophonic composite sounding space's flatness. Digital practices incorporate ambient sounds as multi-track synchronised sound recordings and surround spatialisation in a more mimetic process of representation, which describe sites in intricate detail instead of employing other overtly controlled ways of narrating, as if 'holding a mirror to the nature' (Dumouchel 2015: 51). It is no surprise that sites appear more mimetically present in the digital era than in previous eras of sound production; it has become possible to render 'sounds with an increased exactness' (Beck 2008: 72). In other words, a shift has occurred from the diegetic to the mimetic through the move from analogue to digital cinematic sound production.

3.3 Presence

The conceptualisation of 'presence' concerns the degree to which a medium can generate a seemingly accurate reproduction of objects, events, environs and space – representations that look, sound and/or feel like the 'real thing'. In film-related sound studies, Doane claims that

> concomitant with the demand for a lifelike representation is the desire for 'presence', a concept which is not specific to the cinematic soundtrack but acts as a standard to measure quality in the sound recording industry as a whole. The term 'presence' offers a certain legitimacy to the wish for pure reproduction. (Doane 1985b: 163)

The word 'pure' is particularly significant here – it denotes the search for a recording that provides a natural, complete registration of sound. Doane made this reflection on presence before the arrival of digital technology; her conceptualisation of presence was drawn from analogue optical or magnetic sound recording practices. Presence gains added currency through the digital capacity to produce a 'complete sonic environment' (Kerins 2006) that presents detailed sonic information from the location and surrounds its audience in a spatially rich aural perspective and depth of (sonic) field, an 'immersion in the filmic environment – audiences are, [. . .] aurally, literally placed in the middle of the action' (Kerins 2006: 44). In contemporary digital media studies, presence is defined as the 'feeling of being present' (Reiter 2011: 174) – even in an artificially constructed environment – or, in broader terms, as the 'perceptual illusion of nonmediation' (Lombard and Ditton 1997: 9). These definitions and concepts of presence suggest a tendency towards the mimetic representation of sound; in the digitally produced cinematic environment, the pro-filmic space provides an intensified 'sensation of reality' and 'completeness'. This notion of presence helps to explain how audiences experience a feeling of bodily 'being there'. Subsequent reflections on digital sound practice will demonstrate how an aesthetic of 'spatial fidelity' (Kerins 2011) pervades the digital realm. This notion of spatial fidelity operates closer to 'spatial realism' (Altman 1994) than the term as used by Jonathan Sterne in *The Audible Past* (2003).[2]

Whereas Sterne is primarily concerned with the 'social circulation' of digital audio reproduction, this study centres on the inherent technical characteristics of digital audio recordings such as a high-definition, wide headroom and broad dynamic range, an improved signal-to-noise ratio and multi-channel spatialisation – aspects that enable digital audio to reproduce reality in a spatially plausible way. As with Kerins, Sergi and Holman, attention is drawn to the inherent spatial fidelity of digital recording technologies, while placing fresh emphasis on ambience or environmental sounds.[3] This sense of spatial realism, as David Neumeyer suggests, utilises a system of narrative processes that draws upon the plausibility of physical worlds, accomplished through digital recording and design (Neumeyer 1997: 16).

Despite the conducive creative freedom of digital sound production, the question still remains whether or not the subtler aspects of acoustic worlds from urban and rural sites are mimetically and faithfully narrated. On many occasions, noisy elements of ambient sound recordings are controlled and sanitised through editing processes and advanced noise reduction to provide cleaner sonic environments.[4] For example, the typically syncretic, chaotic and inchoate structure of Indian cities is reflected in multiple layered sounds from pre-industrial, industrial and post-industrial eras, simultaneously active in mere juxtaposition or in intricate contrapuntal relation to one another. The urban sound environment is thus sonically overwhelming and potentially disorienting for the listener (Chattopadhyay 2014b: 140). More often than not this sonic intensity does not manifest fully in Indian films that present more aestheticised sonic accounts of their sites. In either case, this spatial atmosphere can no longer be understood as a linear and one-dimensional soundtrack; rather, it might be called a 'cinematic soundscape'.[5] Here, reference is made to R. Murray Schafer's original formulation of the term 'soundscape', indicative of 'an acoustic environment as a field of study just as we can study the characteristics of a given landscape' (Schafer 1994: 7). This formulation 'seems to offer a way of describing the relationship between sound and place. It evokes the sonic counterpart of the landscape' (Kelman 2010: 215). However, the Schaferean soundscape's particular aim simultaneously 'draw[s] attention to imbalances which may have unhealthy or inimical effects' (Schafer 1994: 271). This moralising tendency (LaBelle 2006: 203) applied to the control of incoming ambience by means of acoustic design strongly corresponds with sound design deployed in contemporary films, which involves editing processes and advanced noise reduction. The underlying intention is to transform lo-fi sounds into hi-fi sounds by removing noise content and prioritising potential audience entertainment and enjoyment. According to Schafer, lo-fi sounds are 'overcrowded, resulting in masking or lack of clarity' (Schafer 1994: 272); they have a lower signal-to-noise ratio and tend to impose 'an increased level of disturbance upon the body, society and the environment' (LaBelle 2006: 202). Hi-fi sounds, on the contrary, are defined as 'the quiet ambiance' (Schafer 1994: 43), having 'a low ambient noise level and discrete sounds emerge with clarity' (Rodaway in LaBelle 2006: 202). The compulsion to achieve cinematic soundscape clarity often leads the sound practitioner to use soundmarks[6] instead of accurately capturing the complete ambience of sites. This tendency to underline a particular sound, often at the expense of many other ambient sounds emanating from a specific site and its rich sonic environment, intends to sonically compensate for the noise reduction and editing of many sync sound layers in post-production.[7] These 'industrial' norms, practical rules and creative regulations embedded in the essentially 'functional' aspects of film sound production often tend to thwart the sound practitioner's artistic potential, keeping it from flourishing and further enriching the film's spatial experience of the auditory setting.

3.4 Rendering

'Rendering' is important film and videomaker terminology. It denotes a film production process whereby a digital system (e.g., a computer workstation) administers information from a coded data source and uses that information to produce and display a simulated image. The process can be compared to an artist's rendering of a scene from a realistic source. With the increasing sophistication of computer graphics since the 1990s, rendering has become a distinct technical process of film and media production editing. Rendering also connotes reducing, suggesting that reality is condensed in this process.

In sound production, rendering is the use of sound to convey feelings or effects associated with the onscreen situation, which are often in opposition to a faithful reproduction of sounds that might be heard in a realistic situation (Chion 1994). Rendering aims to convey a feeling associated with the sound source. Rendered sounds translate tactile sensations into auditory sensations. The sounds suggest a narrative associated with composite sensations rather than an event's auditory reality – the filmmaker or media practitioner modulates the sound according to the narrative. For example, a car chase is often accompanied by a shrill screech of tyres, conveying tension. The filmmaker intends to render the scene by the sole means of sound modulation, which systematically exaggerates its contrast or intensity. This cinematic and medial device of exaggerating contrast and intensity is a narrative trope for attention and emotive engagement at the excuse of sonic realism. The audience recognises these sounds to be truthful, effective and fitting not so much because they are reproduced the way they would be heard in reality; instead, the sounds are rendered to convey or express the feelings, moods and emotions associated with the situation, thus making the work's atmosphere consistent.

In his book *Ecology without Nature* (2009), Timothy Morton further unpacks the term:

> Rendering is technically what visual- and sonic-effects artists do to a film to generate a more or less consistent sense of atmosphere or world.

> After the action has been shot and the computer and other effects pasted into the film, the entire shot is 'rendered', so that all the filmic elements will simulate, say, a sunny day in the Alps, rather than a wet night in the tropics. This rendering, like Jean Baudrillard's idea of the simulacrum, pertains to a copy without an original. (Morton 2009: 34)

In light of this perspective, rendering appears to be not only an immensely important tool for the sound practitioner but also a significant concept. It is a principle means of reducing, mediating and manipulating sound to produce a sensation that is material and physical, though somewhat intangible, in order to surround a film's audience with a make-believe atmosphere, more or less palpable, yet ethereal and subtle.

3.5 Soundscape and the soundmark

Meanwhile, in audiovisual media art or sound art, the mimetic representation of a site in the form of field recordings tends to develop more into unrestrained, idiosyncratic, playful and often subjective constructs. These constructs, as will be shown in ensuing chapters, are typically a result of the intricate interplay between the site's recognition and its abstraction in compositional stages, utilising ambient sounds extensively recorded in the field as compositional ingredients or raw material. Field recording-based sound artworks often transcend the Schaferean notion of soundscape. These works neither give substantial importance to underscoring stereotypical soundmarks of the site nor do they intend to enhance the ecological discourse of differentiating between lo-fi and hi-fi environments. They encourage a subjective interaction with the site. As Brandon LaBelle articulates, 'artistic production is but a mirror of the artist's own image: mimesis depicting interior states, psychological anxieties, euphoric hopes, and ecstatic dreams. Art represents life at its most poignant, its most dramatic, and its most memorable' (LaBelle 2006: 212). The artist's own image of the site as derived from interaction with the site while making field recording frames the selfhood inscribed in these sound artworks. The artist's subjectivity is also reflected in how these works are composed. Interviews with field recording artists from *In the Field: The Art of Field Recording* (Lane and Carlyle 2013) reveal current discourse regarding field recording as an artistic practice. Said discourse reveals and contributes to a larger debate between the realistic presentation and artistic intervention, transformation, mediation and manipulation of environmental sounds. This tension often challenges and dictates the artistic decision as to whether the field recording is processed or presented in its raw form with as little post-production editing as possible. This decision largely depends on the artist's intentions when approaching a specific site as a subject of artistic intervention and aesthetic transformation.

Many listeners and artists alike tend to appreciate works that are unprocessed. Likewise, the deliberate choice of medium and methodology for particular recordings may contribute to a perceived compositional structure without the need for artistic transformation. Needless to say, this choice of preserving the rawness of sound material for the potential listener's interpretation essentially arises from the artist's sonic preference for purity. Within this debate, it can be argued that the choice of method largely depends on the specific narrative the artist wants to convey by intervening in the site. In most cases, the site-specificity of the recorded sounds is deliberately altered through further compositional mediation, whether entirely based on recordings or involving studio processing. However, I will show that sound artworks that go through an artistic transformation via compositional mediation using sound recording and spatialisation techniques might appeal to a wider range of listeners than a purely documentary approach to field recording. Through artistic intervention and transformation of the sonic environment, sites are rendered and nuanced for the ear.

This study explores how discourse on 'acoustic ecology' is reconfigured in the shift from ambient sounds recorded onsite to the production of what is termed 'soundscape composition'. It takes Schaferean terminology (Kelman 2010) as its point of departure, underscoring artistic freedom and aesthetic sensibilities. Sound studies scholar Joanna Demers relates this particular term to compositions developed from field recordings and argues that the field recording as 'audio footage ties a soundscape composition to the ecological, social, historical, or cultural dynamics of a specific location, which both personalises and politicises the act of listening' (Demers 2010: 120). Indeed, the material layers of ambient sound collected through field recording from a particular site always carry some documentary evidence. The composition also allows the listener to co-create how the site is perceived. The artist might choose to intervene and artistically transform field recordings so that they could be considered works of sound art rather than pure documents to give the listener a fertile space or open-ended situation in which to listen in an engaged, embodied and subjective manner.

The capacity of ambient sound to provide site-specific evidence in sound art does not differ from that of ambient sounds in film production. The artistic form's unique characteristic derives from the distance achieved through an ontologically-driven approach to the site, weaving it, rather, into an ambivalent reproduction that is open to multiple contingent interpretations 'by bringing place out of place and toward another' (LaBelle 2006: 213). It is no surprise that Demers finds sound in an artistic context 'a tantalizing phenomenon that simultaneously discloses and hides a great deal about its origin' (Demers 2010: 115). The artist's preference for avoiding the presentation of field recordings as purely documentary works can be substantiated by John Drever's essay

'Soundscape Composition: The Convergence of Ethnography and Acousmatic Music' (2002). In this essay, Drever describes soundscape composition as the juxtaposition of site-specific ethnography and musical composition, incorporating ambient sound as its key ingredient. This articulation takes into account aspects of convergence between the site-based evidence embedded in field recordings and the sonic abstraction that manifests through the artistic practice of recording and/or composing. Both Demers's and Drever's formulations depart from the Schaferean notion of soundscape embedded with ideas of clean rural and urban sites to embrace the artistic and compositional possibilities of field recording.

Notes

1. 'Soundmark', inspired by the word 'landmark', was coined by Schafer to refer to a site-specific sound that is unique or possesses location-related qualities that make it noteworthy.
2. For Sterne, sound fidelity relates to social construct and social choice. While he questions whether 'the old vacuum-tube equipment sounds better', Sterne also suggests that 'nobody disputes the clarity of digital reproduction' (Sterne 2003: 277). This preference for 'better' sound hinges on predominantly social and cultural aspects of sound reproduction. In 'The death and life of digital audio' (2006), he latterly questions the 'metaphysical assumptions' that digital audio recordings lack life and naturalness, arguing that 'digital recordings have as legitimate a claim on sonic experience as their analogue counterparts'; based on their social lives, he considers that 'digital recordings are at least as lively as analogue recordings ever were' (Sterne 2006: 338).
3. Digital sound recording and production frameworks have introduced a number of creative possibilities, including a significantly larger dynamic range, which is a fourfold improvement over the monophonic and almost double that of the stereophonic format: larger headroom, which is a major improvement over both monophonic and stereophonic formats; discreet channels for multi-channel systems such as Atmos; wider panning for sound spatialisation; and full-frequency channels with a consistently flatter response than any analogue counterparts. These technical improvements contribute to faithful recordings made on location and faithful-to-original sound design deployed in the studio.
4. For further elaboration of this statement, please refer to the interviews with sound editors such as Bobby John in Chattopadhyay (2021).
5. See: Chattopadhyay (2013).
6. According to Schafer, a soundmark is 'a community sound which is unique or possesses qualities which make it specially regarded or noticed by the people of that community' (Schafer 1994: 10).
7. Post-production is work done on a film (or recording) after filming or recording has taken place. Editing, processing, designing, spatial organisation and sound mixing are all performed in post-production.

4 APPROACH AND METHOD

4.1 Historical overview

The Auditory Setting takes a practice-based approach to its investigation of how ambient sound recorded from particular sites as sonic material contributes to the production of mediated environments in films and media artworks. Places are studied for their specific sonic environment and as sites recorded and (re)presented, firstly, in a number of films and, secondly, in a few sound and media artworks developed from field recordings made at specific sites. Methodologically, five primary tracks are followed that open dialogue with one another: a historical overview; ethnographic research and fieldwork; personal input, including interviews with artists and practitioners; artistic research; and self-reflective analysis.

As explained above, ambient sounds used in cinematic narration relate directly to sites portrayed onscreen. The relationship between site and sound is constructed according to the narrative strategy undertaken by the filmmakers/directors and depends largely on the sound practitioner's ability. Therefore, it is necessary to understand how ambient sound is conceptualised before embarking on any enquiry into its capacity for providing site-specific evidence. Notions of atmosphere and ambience as spatial elements intrinsic to the diegetic universe and processes that transform the pro-filmic space into film space via onsite recording and studio-based sound organisation are employed to explore how choices and arrangements of sound substantially effect the spatial dynamics of mise-en-scène and its sonorous space.

The neologism mise-en-sonore is introduced to describe an auditory setting that in effect influences the verisimilitude or believability of a filmic work in the ears of its audience. As the sonic equivalent of mise-en-scène, mise-en-sonore can be understood as the mediated atmosphere designed to provide a specific sensation of the site through ambient sound. This term's invention and playful formulation expands upon film theorist James Lastra's conceptualisation of film space and pro-filmic space. It also draws upon the definition of the same terms by film historians Annette Kuhn and Guy Westwell, who declare that one role of ambient sound in the process of narration and description is 'to preserve the integrity of the real-life space' (Kuhn and Westwell 2012: 333). For instance, the soaring sound of wind mid-shot during the depiction of a room can suggest the presence of a nearby sea or the arrival of a stormy upheaval; the dense sound of traffic in a similar shot may suggest the presence of a mundane, urban milieu. Aesthetic choices that determine the quality, volume, texture, design and spatialisation of these ambient sound layers will impact the presence of specific sites in the cinematic story-world. Therefore, the nature of ambient sound usage and the mediation of sonic environments in various corresponding and intercepting phases of sound production will be examined as: (1) direct or synchronised sound (optical recording or electro-mechanical recording), monaural mixing; (2) analogue magnetic recording, dubbing, stereophonic mixing; and (3) digital sync recording and surround sound design. A top-down approach has been used within the study's historical, critical listening and self-reflective analyses.

4.2 Ethnographic research

The historical evolution of the sonic environment of a place is entangled with its social fabric, which may not be a linear process necessarily but a multi-layered, multi-linear or plural development open to multiple influences and peripheral interventions. The idea of social formation emerges from this perspective (Althusser et al.) and refers to a society – a social structure at any level such as a nation, city or specific area – with all of its historically constituted complexities. In this contemporary moment, a society or state is often seen as a static and inflexible idea with nationalistic inclinations (e.g., in many parts of the world, including Europe and the US). The emergent and contingent sonic environment of a site, understood from a position of social awareness, constitutes multiple social influences, including but not limited to neighbouring and socially diffused music and site-specific sounds that are part of everyday ambience, which in itself is not static but historically transformative. Likewise, social music (LaBelle 2002) and sounds diffused in urban or rural environments (e.g., Azaan or street demonstrations) generate site-specific associations that emanate from and reflect within a specific setting (e.g., a locale or geographical area). These innate elements require critical listening and investigation not only to understand the atmospheric layers they suggest but also to speculate their historical constituents and contribution to or influences from the processes of social formation. Often such an inclusive idea of atmosphere proliferates a sense of plurality and multiplicity embedded in the public and social life of a site engaging sociality in a more affective way.

This study's use of the term 'site' denotes a source of actual sonic attributes, which are collected as material during onsite recordings and, as art critic and curator Miwon Kwon argues, are 'based in a phenomenological or experiential understanding of the site, defined primarily as an agglomeration of the actual physical attributes of a particular location' (Kwon 2002: 3). The wide and often indiscreet use of the term 'site-specificity' is problematic in the arts, as Kwon points out. Following her cautionary suggestions, the term 'site-referenced' is underscored here as it refers the listener back to the site where material was originally collected and considers sound as a 'signifier and the Site as that which is signified' (Alloway 1981: 42). Within the context of film and (media) art production, Joanna Demers defines site more specifically in relation to sound art and field recording: 'Site [. . .] entails not only the environments in which sound propagates but also those that listeners physically and metaphorically occupy' (Demers 2010: 113). For this study, site connects the 'physical conditions of a particular location as integral to the production, presentation, and reception of art' (Kwon 2002: 1). For this reason, focus will be placed on certain generic sites (e.g., grasslands, woods, beaches or riverbanks, street/public square, airport, train compartment, room, corridor, rooftop, basement, train or bus station, industrial site, abandoned location and ruins) for critical listening from a sonic ethnography approach. Field recording from sample sites will also be used to hint at the mediation process of recording. With these recordings as reference, a number of films or film sequences and passages of media artworks – where similar or related sites are recorded and designed as part of the narrative or descriptive auditory setting – will be considered. This specific ethnographic approach to research will not only ground the book in the real world but also allow a critical comparative analysis of the recording, mediation and production of the sonic environment in films and media artworks. Ethnography has its own tradition of field recording, as do other disciplines such as ornithology, anthropology and archival research. Although aware of these and other disciplines in which field recordings are used, this book concentrates on sonic ethnography based on 'location study',[1] which gathers extensive information from a specific site through ethnographic means before and during the actual recordings take place.

4.3 Personal inputs

Correspondingly, learning about the nitty-gritty of sound production through in-depth conversations with established sound practitioners is a prerequisite to understanding how the auditory setting is produced in cinema. First-hand documentation is an invaluable resource for unravelling what has historically transpired in the use of sound. A discussion of current practice and the claim that digital sound production has impacted the mediation of sonic environments require complementary empirical evidence. Personal input from sound practitioners constitutes the bottom-up approach of this book.

Interviews and ongoing conversations with practitioners over many years, which are compiled in two separate publications,[2] provide references to this complementary approach. Practitioner input is based on a specific set of semi-structured and open-ended questions about how ambient tracks are handled from recording to design and how media technology impacts these processes.[3] According to social science qualitative research scholars Jody Miller and Barry Glassner, semi-structured and open-ended interviews may solicit 'authentic accounts of subjective experience' (Miller and Glassner 2011: 131). Interviews conducted with sound practitioners to extract empirical evidence have enabled them 'to speak in their own voices about their art and craft' (LoBrutto 1994: 1). Sound studies scholar Mark Grimshaw asserts that a questionnaire-based qualitative approach involving semi-structured interviews 'allows the interviewer a certain level of control which directs the interviewee down particular paths. Equally it allows the interviewee to expand on themes outside the limits of the questions, which can reveal unexpected information' (Grimshaw 2011: 54). Dialectics between the top-down approach of historical mapping, critical listening and reflective analyses, and the bottom-up approach of consulting artists and practitioners for their personal input (as an evidential basis of arguments presented) form the backbone of this book, ensuring that 'even the more abstract notions about filmmaking and cinema remain grounded in real-world practices' (Kerins 2011: 10).

4.4 Artistic research

Artistic research is based on the assumption that artistic practice can make epistemic claims (Borgdorff 2009, 2012; Schwab 2014). However, little academic investigation considers artistic practice as a significant mode of knowledge production. Only recently has artistic research gained currency through gradual academic recognition (Biggs and Karlsson 2011; Schwab 2014; Schwab and Borgdorff 2014). But most of the academics cited above are not artists themselves; the process of knowledge production and transmission still commonly remains in the hand of non-practitioners. Actual artists are marginalised in academia's institutional hierarchy. As a core principle, this book advocates for change, arguing that more artists should claim their work as research creation in the arts, thereby contributing to the production of new knowledge. The growing need for artists to actively intervene in arts-based research (and pedagogy) and add real-world knowledge and processual understanding of spaces, sites, environs, materials and objects to debate is addressed in this book with adequate and sustained attention to artistic research through a number of original artworks. These sound pieces are presented on a complementary website, which can be experienced while reading the book. This dedicated website that supplements this book hosts these pieces and other listening and viewing examples discussed. The website can be accessed directly via the QR codes that are on the rear cover of the book.

4.5 SELF-REFLECTIVE ANALYSIS

In my work, some of these sites are exposed in field recording. A number of these personal sound works that are based on field recording at specific urban and rural sites ingrained in site-specific cultural traditions will also be discussed. Within the artworks developed from field recordings, these sites tend to be artistically mediated and transformed via the creative process of recording and the ensuing production process. This process is examined in order to better understand the nature of (re)presenting sonic environmental and onsite actualities in sound art. My own artistic practice forms a response to the pertinent site-specific issues. However, having been trained in filmmaking before becoming a sound art practitioner, as several other emerging sound artists from India,[4] I will first establish the historical context of film sound production. From there, self-reflective analysis of my own practice provides a more in-depth understanding of the tendencies that address specific sites through artistic transformation. This understanding will help in critically engaging with the portrayal of the sites and mediation of their sonic environments in sound-based media artworks. It will then be easier to take a critical look at my own artworks as representative of sound art practices and help construct new knowledge that should prove thought-provoking for film sound practitioners. The aim is to develop a better understanding of the artistic processes not only in relation to innovative and cutting-edge better practices in sound production but also to encourage more mindful practice when recording sound. Among others, the following artworks will be discussed:

Landscape in Metamorphoses (2008) is a stereo soundscape composition developed from field recordings made at an area called Tumbani in India between February and April 2007. Published by Gruenrekorder (Germany) on a limited-edition CD-R, the piece captures the transformation of Tumbani from a tribal-dominated pastoral landscape into an industrial zone. The auditory setting slowly changes from a rich natural environment into a monolithic industrial soundscape. As an audio essay, the work studies the trajectory of metamorphoses through unprocessed field recordings. Based on the motivation to return and revisit, having spent my childhood there, I realised while undertaking the recording that the topography of my childhood had already disappeared into nostalgia. Not merely a sonic representation of a transforming landscape, this work is also a lament for the personal loss of a place.

Elegy for Bangalore (2013) is a stereo and multi-channel format soundscape composition premiered at Klangkunst, Deutschlandradio, Berlin and released on CD by Gruenrekorder. The piece stems from the sound/video installation-project *Eye Contact with the City*, the result of an artist residency in Bangalore between 2010 and 2011. The primary material used in the installation is formed from extensive field recordings that were made at various construction sites in Bangalore and retrieved sounds from archival reel-to-reel tapes found at the city's flea markets. The repository of field recordings and other audio materials eventually took the form of this elegiac composition during a subsequent artist residency at the School of Music, Bangor University, in the summer and autumn of 2011.

Decomposing Landscape (2015) is an award-winning sound work that offers in-depth listening to the transfiguration of rural landscapes in India undergoing environmental decay and destruction. The work, which uses field recordings made on the site and diffuse sounds in third-order Ambisonics B-format, is a multi-channel sound composition. The work was developed through the process of meticulously collecting ambient sounds from an SEZ (special economic zone) in India during extensive fieldwork over several years. The collection forms a digital archive that was instrumental in realising the work, which was composed, mixed and produced at ICST, Zurich University of the Arts, during an artist residency in 2014. The work was released in 2015 by Touch (UK) as both Binaural and Ambisonics mixes.

4.6 STRUCTURE OF THE BOOK

The book is divided into four main parts. The first, this introductory part, consists of four chapters that present a framework for understanding the topic, namely the mediation of the sonic environment, and defines ambient sound and ambience through their various connotations and associations. These introductory chapters examine the book's context through a review of existing literature on research in the field. The book's conceptual approach is clarified in terms of an historical analysis of relevant works; the book's structure and methodology are also explained.

The second part consists of three chapters that investigate the technological trajectories of sound practices, and conceptualises the use of ambient sound from optical recording to the digital realm. By historicising developments in the use of ambient sound through different intersecting phases of optical recording and monaural mixing, magnetic recording and stereophonic mixing, digital sync recording and surround design, Part 2 demarcates, rationalises and historicises the primary eras of sound production.

The third part consists of nine smaller chapters that discuss relevant sequences from film and sound/media artworks where generic sites (land, field, meadow; forest, jungle; village, rural environment; indoors; riverbank, beach, island; street, public squares, urban neighbourhood; public transport; airport; underwater, outer space) are the specific settings for narration or the select sites for recording and documenting sound for site-aware artwork. Critical listening is employed to analyse relevant passages from a number of films and representative artworks developed from specific sites. The critical listening and reflective analysis of these artworks shed light on the artistic transformation of ambient sounds recorded from select sites producing what will be termed 'manufactured presence' and 'poetic presence' in the spatial experiences of films and media artworks, respectively. These works are studied thoroughly to understand the strategies employed in their production of ambient sound as a specific component evoking a sense of presence and embodied experience, whereby the rich sonic environments of the sites are mediated, transformed and modified to form augmented atmospheres that satisfy different storytelling and artistic production tastes and approaches.

The fourth part is a reflection on the book's findings regarding presence, rendering and sonic reality presented across three chapters. In listening critically to the trajectories of sound production within world cinema and audio-visual media arts, it is observed that sites have been irregularly rendered and produced through various phases of sound production. Three primary historical markers are underscored that seem useful when locating and mapping prominent technological shifts. These developmental stages have manifested as aesthetic choices embraced by sound practitioners. Part 4 details how these principles are reflected in the production of a site's sonic presence. In other words, the various forms and formats of technological innovations and transformation have informed the degree of site-specific presence produced through the use of ambient sound components. Therefore, the central concern of this final part is the study of specific uses of ambient sound through corresponding and intercepting recording and sound production phases that have composed the auditory setting in film and media arts. These phases are divided as follows: (1) analogue monaural synchronised sound recording (direct sound by optical recording on location a.k.a. sound-on-film) and monaural mixing; (2) dubbing, studio-based analogue processing and stereophonic mixing; and (3) digital multi-track synchronised recording (a.k.a. sync sound) and surround sound design. Critical listening, reflection and analysis of the passages of sound from representative films, specifically depicting select generic sites and sonic environments in film and media works, qualify the evidential account of this research. The book's final part also hints at future directions for film and media sound production.

Notes

1. See: http://nemeton.org.uk/other/soundscape-composition/ and the interview with sound recordist Lasse-Marc Riek (Lane and Carlyle 2013: 171–179).
2. Chattopadhyay (2022), a collection of interviews with sound artists and practitioners from the Global Souths. Chattopadhyay (2021), a collection of interviews with film sound technicians from India.
3. The questionnaire's basic format is represented in Chattopadhyay (2021), a collection of interviews with film sound technicians from India.
4. I refer here to Indian sound artists such as Navin Thomas and Sukanta Majumdar who work with recorded sound. Most directly or indirectly draw inspiration from Indian cinema and many are trained in film, since it is the cinematic medium that provides the impetus to 'record sound from a landscape so extensively' (Chattopadhyay 2007: 110).

PART 2

SONIC TRAJECTORIES

And now more and more I use less and less music, because I can use the improved mixing facilities (sic), and I can use [a] more creative soundtrack, whereby one can use actual sounds almost as you use music to suggest moods and things like that [. . .] For instance, in a city [-based] story the city itself provides the noise of traffic, and it provides the mood building soundtrack you know [. . .] In *Ashani Sanket* one could well have used folk music in abundance, but I preferred to use bird noises; I preferred to use the sound on *Dheki*, you know, that sort of thing, and I preferred to use wind sound [. . .] I used one particular bird – the woodpecker, which I recorded, I was lucky to be able to record one. And it comes at a very crucial point when Moti dies [. . .] one can hear the woodpecker, which is a very shrill and rather alarming kind of, rather eerie sort of sound. I felt the use of music would sentimentalize the scene. So I decided to use this, which was also a realistic sound. (Satyajit Ray 1979[1])

Figure 5.1 Direct recording outside of Melies Studio

5 MONAURAL SOUNDTRACKS AND RECORDING (SONIC) REALITY

5.1 MECHANICAL AND OPTICAL RECORDINGS, SOUND FILM AND DIRECT SOUND

The earliest sound recordings, made on a mechanical phonograph cylinder invented by Thomas Alva Edison in 1877–1878, captured the sound of a cornet and his rendition of the nursery rhyme 'Mary Had a Little Lamb', ending with laughter.[2] Irrespective of the focus on Edison's voice, it is possible to imagine that the room tone of the space where this recording was made was also registered in the process – even if this first recording of ambient sound cannot actually be heard due to the recording's low resolution and playback. Around the same time, Édouard-Léon Scott de Martinville devised the phonautograph in Paris. As more sound recordings were made, Edison's cylinders quickly became the primary media for commercial recording, sales and distribution, enabling a global industry for music and other businesses. Sound's arrival in cinema took longer due to the resistance of silent era filmmakers. They feared the disruption and demise of cinematic reality as constructed by silent moving images. Meanwhile, Edison believed that a truly comprehensive cinematic experience was only possible when moving images were synchronised with sound. The first public exhibition of projected sound films was made in Paris in 1900. It then took few years before sound films were deemed commercially viable. Sound's reliable synchronisation with the moving image was difficult to achieve with early sound-on-disc systems. The amplification and quality of recordings were also compromised, which rendered the intricate layers of site-specific ambient sounds to a negligible register. Innovations in the sound-on-film technique (direct optical recording on film) led to the first commercial screening of sound films in the 1920s. In his book *Occult Aesthetics: Synchronization in Sound Film* (2014) Professor Kevin Donnelly shows that the synchronisation of sound and image brought about a revolution in the audience perception of cinematic reality. Audiences began demanding a more realistic and cogent cinema experience.

Emile Berliner's invention of the gramophone record (1887) and the existence of even earlier disk media (most notably by Alexander Graham Bell) gradually led to a sustainable recording format for music (e.g., 78 RPM shellac discs and the vinyl LP). Electrical recording methods were developed and mastered with the advent of valves and later the transistor, which revolutionised sound recording. Outside the US and the UK, the practice of sound recording arrived in many non-Western cultures mainly through the West's colonial pursuits in Asia and Africa. Imperial powers travelled with technologies such as recording devices for measuring, inspecting and mapping people and places that they intended to rule. For example, early sound recordings in India were made by British colonial officers as part of a massive effort to study hundreds of different languages and dialects spoken in India at that time, but most of their recordings were aimed at quantifying a vast and inexhaustible source of local sounds into a few minute's of recording on discs. Gradually, their practices began sporadically including field recordings of traditional music and folksongs from India's great cultural landscape. However, Indian classical music practitioners were deeply sceptical about the recording of their performances rendered on media (e.g., cylinders and shellac discs). In particular, fundamental incompatibilities between the transcendental and 'timeless' improvisational nature of Indian classical music, and the temporal, durational and technological constraints of a three-minute-long recording (Kinnear 1994) on cylinders or disc led to mistrust. They turned down offers to record their voices for many years. In contrast, Indian filmmaking embraced the technology and assimilated it, as will be examined later. Other film industries such as those in China, Hong Kong and Japan were slow to sonify their cinemas, predominantly for cultural reasons: silent film and traditional performing arts (e.g., Kabuki, Bensi, Noh theatre) in these regions shared many similarities, whereas sound film would project a more concrete and tangible sense of reality.

The primary steps in sound film's commercialisation were taken in the mid- to late 1920s. Sound films, which included synchronised dialogue, known as 'talking pictures', or 'talkies', were produced via an optical recording of sound made directly onto the film during shooting. This method required actors to perform live on location. Therefore, the earliest feature-length sound film with directly recorded sound included only music and sound effects. The first actual, feature-length talkie is widely considered to be *The Jazz Singer* (Alan Crosland

1927), which was made with Vitaphone, then the leading brand of sound-on-disc technology involving a meticulous process of recording all sounds directly onto a single phonographic record that was then synced in real time with the projection. However, the romantic adventure film *Don Juan* (Alan Crosland 1926) was made a year earlier with the same Vitaphone sound-on-disc system; the film's soundtrack consisted of a musical score along with incidental sounds and sound effects, including wild takes of non-specific vocals and ambient sounds in a couple of crowd scenes. Although it didn't have any spoken dialogue, *Don Juan* was the first feature-length film to assemble a synchronised soundtrack that importantly included ambient sounds.

Sound in cinema generated a lot of debate and not all filmmakers were keen to incorporate it. For example, Chaplin resisted talkies for a long time. Eventually, he first used sound effects in *Modern Times* (1936) and is heard singing in a climactic sequence that utilised direct sound recording. His fully-fledged talkie was his next film *The Great Dictator* (1940). Before making his first sound film, he deliberated on his future as an essentially silent filmmaker in the new world of talkies. At that time, he was toying with ideas about the role of dialogue and other sounds in film while working on an ultimately unfinished script with the working title *Bali* (1932) that mocked colonialism and European self-importance in Asia. The manuscript reveals his cautionary steps in the world of sound, which considered the medium as a tool to delineate reality, particularly the political and social realities of his time.

A few other filmmakers such as Rouben Mamoulian were far more steadfast and advanced in exploring the capacity of direct sound. For his film *Applause* (1929) Mamoulian insisted on using two microphones on location and later mixing the recorded sounds, which was an innovative use of direct sound at the time. Mamoulian's later work *Love Me Tonight* (1932) was recorded directly in a studio but begins with rhythmic sounds of a Parisian morning produced via monaural mixing of 'unexpected sound effects that made a dropped vase turn into a sonic boom' as Richard Barrios writes in the Library of Congress[3]. Such works are precursors to the complex sound design incorporated in films that have emerged in later eras of sound production. With time, gradually, a more advanced and easy-to-realise sound-on-film method was developed beyond sound-on-disc technique to become one of the main standards for direct monaural sound in cinema.

Direct sound generally refers to the technique of recording music, voice (dialogue and otherwise), as well as ambient and incidental sounds at the same time that a pro-filmic space is being captured on film. In a well-known sequence of the legendary Indian film *Devdas* (P. C. Barua 1935–1936), the eponymous protagonist Devdas is languishing over his initial arrival at a brothel in Calcutta following his recent break-up with Paro, a childhood sweetheart from his native village. Devdas's fateful interaction with the prostitute Chandra leaves him in a state of perpetual melancholia, claustrophobia and remorse from which he never recovers. The mise-en-scène indicates that the story is taking place in an indoor location within a closed building. But the incidental sound of a birdcall appears and continues throughout the sequence alongside the actors' directly recorded voices and an abundant, background musical score. Typically, Indian films from this era used the camera to establish shots, which the sound recording device followed to capture a limited sound field within the visual frame. Attention was paid to available sound-producing objects in accordance with the mise-en-scène and story-world. In most cases, the director and cameraperson determined microphone placement. Within the given space and time of a shot, a scattering of different sound sources, most of which are not related to the sound script, are considered unwanted noise. In a vococentric script, the microphone's liberal use is reduced, as the recording's directionality is forced to focus on 'almost always the voice' (Chion 1994). Within the limited scope of recording, available sound sources are narrowed down to the bare minimum on recording media. Despite direct sound recordings being suppressed to a limited dynamic range, some stray elements intrude onto the film's predetermined soundtrack, which may be capable of carrying meaning and developing understanding about the nature of the site and the auditory setting. The off-screen birdcall in *Devdas* holds distinct documentary evidence and is a slice of the sonic environment's actual reality. Even if the direct sound recorded on the film's soundtrack is incidental, off screen and not deliberate, it enhances an aurally 'realistic' pro-filmic space (Kania 2009). Direct sound recording hints at the existence of a vibrant world that, if used, might have enlivened the mediated universe of a film. Despite a high level of control and musical masking, many vococentric Indian films made with direct sound exemplify the occasional recording of incidental ambient sounds from the natural auditory setting due to on-site recording with actors who performed live in front of the camera.

Therefore, in direct sound practice, films captured the setting's sonic environment relatively realistically. There was little chance of manipulating the sounds for narrative purposes. Many European filmmakers, particularly in France and Germany, embraced such possibilities. Jean Renoir, who believed passionately in direct sound, shot his second sound film, *La Chienne* (1931), in the noisy Parisian streets of Montmartre, producing a real, phenomenal sonic environment. René Clair's *Sous les toits de Paris* (Under the Roofs of Paris) (1930) used recorded street sounds and songs that even compromised the voice and musical film score, those more revered components within the monaural soundtrack's hierarchical order.

5.2 The monaural aesthetics

After the introduction of synchronised and direct sound to cinema in the late 1920s, sound practice became monaural from recording to production stages and to reproduction, meaning that 'a single channel of sound was played from a loudspeaker placed behind the screen, creating the illusion that the sound of the film was emanating from the projected images' (Kuhn and Westwell 2014/2015). As early as 1928, Rudolf Arnheim recognised that the significant interplay between the picture and three-dimensional movement within space was problematically invalidated by the single-source and screen-centric practice of synchronised sound (Bloom 2014). Arnheim meant that 'synchronised sound distracts from the significant play of visual interpretation among all the elements of the image and instead locks the viewer into the space' (Bloom 2014: 431). Such criticism is perhaps due to the overarching emphasis on the moving image and sound source's 'marriage'[4] in one speaker behind the screen, which was then the standard in monaural sound production. Today's surround sound environment allows the source more freedom of movement outside the screen-centric coupling between sound and image, as Arnheim had hoped. The free-floating three-dimensional sensibility he looked for in cinema would perhaps be realised today in the spatial environment of Dolby Atmos.[5] Arnheim's resistance to synchronised sound with monaural aesthetics emphasises 'the differences between film and reality as a key artistic quality of film form' (Arnheim quoted in Bloom 2014: 431). Clearly, Arnheim was concerned that synchronised sound practice reduces three-dimensional objects onto a two-dimensional screen, disturbing film's relationship to reality.

As Peter J. Bloom (2014) points out, Béla Balázs's ideas on sound film starkly contrasted with those of his contemporary, Arnheim. His defence of synchronised sound and monaural aesthetics suggests an extension of cinema's narrative capacities as sound provided a more spatially defined experience. Bloom refers to Balázs:

> By contrast with a two-dimensional image, the temporal nature of sound becomes related to the hearing subject's own location in any given space. The potentially spatial characteristics of sound, which Altman (1992) has further described as the 'material heterogeneity' of sound, may then be better guided, Balázs insists, through a visual representation. The image assists in disentangling the location of voices speaking or a place sounding, for example, as attached to different speakers appearing on screen with their own distinct qualities and physiognomies of expression.[6]

James Lastra interprets these different viewpoints in his description of two corresponding 'models' operating within the Hollywood classical narrative:

The first, heir to metaphors of human simulation and described in terms of perceptual fidelity, emphasizes the literal duplication of a real and embodied (but invisible) auditor's experience of an acoustic event. Its watch-words are presence and immediacy [...] Aesthetic perfection entails the absolute re-presentation of the original, while the other model emphasizes the mediacy, constructedness, and derived character of representation.[7]

These opposing stances frame the tension in many national cinemas: between providing narrative pleasure in storytelling via a sonically modulated, musical and verbose representation of sound, and the realistic re-presentation of actual sites, actors and social situations in direct recording and synchronised sound practice. The former is exemplified by many Hollywood fantasy films (indebted to Georges Méliès), religious and devotional films from the 1940s and 1950s in India, early Hollywood musicals, gothic horror films from Universal Pictures such as *Dracula* (Tod Browning 1931) and *Frankenstein* (James Whale 1931), and 'monster' films such as *King Kong* (Merian C. Cooper and Ernest B. Schoedsack 1933). The latter, aligned with work by the Lumière brothers, is illustrated by neorealist Italian films such as *Bicycle Thieves* (De Sica 1948) and social realist Indian films of the 1950s such as *Neecha Nagar* (Lowly City, Chetan Anand 1946) and *Do Bigha Zamin* (Two Thirds of an Acre of Land, Bimal Roy 1953). These two polarities defined many national cinemas at the time. The latter approach was practised by a new breed of social realist filmmakers: for example, Vittorio De Sica, Luciano Visconti, Frederico Fellini and Michelangelo Antonioni in Italy; Robert Bresson, François Truffaut, Jean-Luc Godard in France; and Satyajit Ray, Bimal Roy, Chetan Anand and Guru Dutt in India. La Nouvelle Vague in France and neorealism in Italy evolved as new wave filmmakers' authorial choices advocated for the later model. Meanwhile, many Russian filmmakers maintained the former approach (following the asynchronous model prescribed by Pudovkin[8]), as exampled by Dziga Vertov's *Entuziazm* (1930) with its post-synchronised experimental soundtrack. Most European filmmakers continued to practise the latter approach of direct sound, with the exception of studio-dominated film productions in Italy, in Denmark between the 1930s–1960s (Bondebjerg 2005), and elsewhere. French filmmaker René Clair's example also deviates, as he made surreal use of sounds in comedy films such as *Under the Roofs of Paris* (1930) and *Le Million* (1931) otherwise influenced by the previous model of producing narrative pleasure. This trajectory was later revived by filmmakers such as Jacques Tati.

Such a reading of European cinema helps us to understand the primacy of auditory details that many Italian neorealist and French New Wave films offer through direct recording and synchronised sound. The result is a sonic experience that relies on perceptual fidelity and aesthetic perfection for a faithful re-presentation of the pro-filmic space in terms of a screen-centric use of location-specific ambient sound with monaural aesthetics (Lastra 2000). With this context in mind, it is important to recognise the site's presence in the diegesis produced by the keen observation of a location primarily through synchronised sound recording and the monaural organisation of ambient sound – a practice that has created a precedence for the perceptually realistic auditory settings in later European cinemas, where a predominantly direct sound aesthetic has been perfected.

Central here is the question of framing the site in cinema through the spatial organisation of ambient sound in a monaural soundtrack to create a screen-centric mise-en-sonore or auditory setting 'to place the auditor as literally as possible in the pro-filmic space' (Lastra 2000: 181–182). Monaural reproduction and practices of rendering ambient sound into a soundtrack result in film space actions and events occurring at a frontal distance from the viewer; the auditory setting behind the screen presents itself as if a window to a mediated world. The use of synchronised sound and methods of monaural mixing informed by an ethos of direct and synchronised sound enable the auditor to experience sites through direct sonic information (Birtwistle 2010; Burch 1985). This adds to the verisimilitude of the story-world and fosters a familiarity with places. The auditor is informed about the site's presence in the narration of the diegetic story-world by 'letting the camera be the eye, and the microphone the ear of an imaginary person viewing the scene' (Maxfield quoted in Lastra 2000: 183).

5.3 Magnetic recording

Magnetic recording's extensive use in cinema began in the 1950s. The arrival of magnetic tapes made sound recording seemingly easier and of relatively higher quality. When magnetic tape-based recording machines became portable, the ability to copy, store and erase tracks whenever required was embraced, even if it was at the expense of asynchronous modes[9] because magnetic tapes were not coupled with the camera. Unlike the previous direct optical recording system, this development created the scope for mixing and re-recording beyond the location. James Buhler, David Neumeyer and Rob Deemer comment on the advantages of analogue magnetic sound recording in film: 'The introduction of magnetic tape likewise allowed an efficient and relatively inexpensive way to record and mix sound into a number of channels. This also provided an efficient way to provide a variety of mixes' (Buhler, Neumeyer and Deemer 2010: 338). Likewise, the advent of magnetic tape made better-quality recording possible in cinema, with a higher dynamic range than direct optical recording.[10] Such sound recording flexibility also paved the way for parallel artistic sound practices, which would later be termed 'sound art'. In Paris, Pierre Schaeffer and Pierre Henry were inspired to experiment with recorded sound on splices of tape, joining them together, combining and recombining them for artistic purposes. A few artworks that delineate the trajectory of this practice will be described later.

In the context of filmmaking, Hollywood saw a 'frozen revolution' with the advent of magnetic tapes (Belton 1992). In India, film writer Gautam Pemmaraju observed that magnetic tape's revolutionary effect on sound recording and production had a significant impact: 'Sound captured analogously on tape with magnetic emulsion on it was of far better quality (and dynamics) than that on optical film' (2013: 80).

In-house sound studios became popular for the post-production of magnetic tape instead of direct recording on location. As a result, film sound became increasingly distanced from the real site narrated on screen. Gradually, an analogue studio-centric technique of film sound design emerged as the dominant mode of practice. Dubbing and Foley followed technological advancements made possible by the Nagra[11] portable recorder (utilising quarter-inch magnetic tape) and the MagnaTech Rock-and-Roll mixing console.[12] The studio system invited more investment in sound post-production. Tools and techniques like looping, multi-track mixing and track-laying opened up the possibility of using parallel resources to reconstruct sound, which made any remaining dependence on direct, on-location sound recording obsolete. Stock sounds were shared or became commercially available as a bank of 'sound objects' from which raw material could be selected and mixed to create ambience and sound effects, even though, in most cases, ambience was a minor concern in sound organisation. With the rise of new technologies such as analogue magnetic recording, sound objects recorded on magnetic tape were no longer referred to as a site-specific sound source (Demers 2009). The practice of recording sound on tape enhanced sound's materiality, making it possible to decouple sound from the site as raw material. At this point, various sources of raw material could be brought into the studio and re-coupled with the image through analogue post-synchronisation processes. Films were increasingly shot on a pre-designed set inside studios instead of in real locations and film sound became a mere dialogue-background, score-sync effect scheme. Industry-dependent and technologically informed sound technicians were employed to design a soundtrack for a film out of asynchronous sound sources, using pre-recorded sound materials. In most cases, these technicians did not pay much attention to ambience, which would otherwise demand closer attention to the location or the sound's source in its recording and design stages. Song and dance sequences and loud background music were used merely to mask these shortcomings.[13] Many sound practitioners admitted that the use of a loud mix in the background score limited the possibility of including any substantial ambient sound layers in the soundtrack. This lack of a subtle and sensitive presence of ambient sounds meant a lack of information about the pro-filmic space in the narration (Burch 1982). Studio-centric sound production gradually approached the relative abstraction of the film's story-world, exemplified in Hollywood films from the late 1960s, 1970s and 1980s, and Indian and other Asian films from the same time (e.g., the popular films in Hong Kong and Korea). However, films made by neorealist filmmakers in Italy, new wave filmmakers in France and social realist filmmakers in India such as Satyajit Ray continued to present a more grounded and nuanced use of sound, which was marked by a direct sound aesthetic created with environmental sounds recorded on location using portable magnetic tape recorders such as Nagra and reel-to-reel machines.

5.4 Audiographic realism

As magnetic tape replaced optical film and techniques of direct sound were replaced by tape-based editing and mixing in the studio, the sense that the reality of the site and site-specific sonic environments could be better constructed and manufactured inside the studio than captured on site became prevalent. Irrespective of this growing dependence on sound studios, some of the films in the magnetic recording era tended to 'simulate the perceptions of an observer located on the film set, whose eyes and ears (camera and microphone) are joined as inseparably as those of a real head' (Maxfield quoted in Lastra 2000: 183). These production aesthetics were based on the sustaining tenets and extension of synchronised sound. In many realist independent films such as those authored by Robert Bresson[14], Vittorio De Sica, Satyajit Ray and Jean Renoir, 'we perceive the sound not only in temporal sync, but also in correct spatial placement, as our brains create the bridge to reestablish a normality to the situation' (Sonnenschein 2001: 47). Bresson, De Sica, Ray and Renoir seemingly chose to use specific ambient sound layers, among a multitude of other recorded sound components, as storytelling devices to produce a spatial sensation and reproduce the site's realistic presence in the film space, in contrast to the studio-centric films embedded with an escapist overtone.

These filmmakers' strong belief in the ability of ambient sounds to carry narrative creates the premise of what I term 'audiographic realism' in cinema. By this coinage, I intend the synchronised use of sound without significant sound synthesis, retaining the materiality or the objecthood of documented sound with perceptual fidelity representational of the original site and its sonic environment in a monaural, screen-centric use of site-specific and site-aware sound recordings. This is analogous to photographic realism's determination not to affect the appearance of a photographic object (Kania 2009: 240). In choosing to maintain a realist paradigm in cinema, the authors of independent and auteurist films made sound as a synchronised documentation of reality their cinematic ethos: 'the main contribution of sound was an enormous advance towards realism, and a consequent enrichment of the medium as an expression of the ethos' (S. Ray 2011: 5). Here, the definition of 'realism' refers back to the tradition of observational cinema, which represents reality by recording vision and sound that come 'from within the world of the film' (Kania 2009: 244). For example, Satyajit Ray, one of South Asia's most influential filmmakers for whom the realist paradigm was an authorial choice, continued to use ambient sound as a site-specific documentation of reality as part of his cinematic signature – one that expands the practice of his predecessors to a higher degree of precision, creating a benchmark in Indian cinema. As will be further discussed in the next chapter, this is a sound practice that provides a detailed depiction of site and creates a mode of situated listening, where the auditor finds ample information to relate to the places framed within the narrative and the specific sonic environments of these places depicted on film.

Often discussed under the rubric of social realism and realist filmmaking, La Nouvelle Vague, the French New Wave gave birth to sound experimentations such as unexpected editing of outdoor recordings. *400 Blows* (Truffaut 1959) and *Breathless* (Godard 1960) demonstrate these refreshing attitudes that broke away from conventional narratives exemplified by Hollywood. Their work was inspired by the realist aesthetics of Robert Bresson, who is often considered a precursor to the French New Wave. *400 Blows* and *Breathless* are reference points for studying the trajectory of synchronised sound and monaural aesthetics – they exploit the technique's scope and push the boundaries of aesthetic choices. The mode of ambient sound's use in these films is a benchmark in practising audiographic realism by giving thorough consideration of the site and deep respect for the pro-filmic space and its sonic environment. This creative approach helps shape up a locative embodied sonic experience derived from the reality of life, not in any way escapist or fantastical – a tendency that was common with many contemporaries in global cinema. In 1951 Ray wrote: 'For a popular medium, the best kind of inspiration should derive from life and have its roots in it. No amount of technical polish can make up for artificiality of theme and dishonesty of treatment. The Indian filmmaker must turn to life, to reality' (Ray 1976: 127). This statement aptly frames Ray's realist aesthetic as different from most of his contemporaries of popular Indian mainstream filmmaking. They also used the same monaural system as a standard format but deployed it differently, using a primarily vococentric model of narration dominated by the rhetoric of narrative pleasure and a normative structure of song and dance sequences celebrating the non-diegetic fantasy space in cinema.

5.5 Dubbing

Many film industries worldwide rarely recorded sound on location from the 1950s onwards. Dubbing and re-recording gained momentum and became common practice in mainstream film. Film soundtracks were also mostly created (or re-created) in the studio. Actors would recite and re-record their lines as their images appeared on the studio screen in a process known as 'looping'[15] or ADR (Automatic Dialogue Replacement). Background music, along with lavish song and dance sequences at regular intervals, followed these practices and various sound effects, known as Foley,[16] entirely made in post-synchronisation within the studio's close confines, were added later as secondary or tertiary layers of sound organisation.

However, the typical use of post-synchronisation in any popular mainstream cinema of the time created several aesthetic problems. Most relevant to this analysis is the lack of actual spatial information in recorded and designed sounds rendered by this technique and the inability of this style of sound organisation to provide site-specific evidence of the pro-filmic space in the film space (Lastra 2000).[17] Actors had to perform twice: once on location in front of the camera and again in the studio in front of the studio microphone, where real situations on location would be impossible to recreate. Most actual location sound recordings (e.g., pilot or guide track) were completely replaced in the studio. Technical shortcomings were masked by highly processed Foley and sound effects that were inordinately loud and high-pitched. Ambient sounds were often neglected.

ADR became a regular practice from the 1960s onwards with the arrival of Arriflex 35 IIC and Arriflex 35 III cameras, which required a blimp (a soundproof cover) to shield its notorious motor noise during location shooting.[18] Such distracting camera noise required all sound to be recreated in the studio. Eventually, this became the standard. Dubbing, which emerged alongside analogue magnetic recording and mixing, was facilitated by multi-track re-recording in the studio. The ensuing phase of sound production became known as the 'dubbing era' (roughly between the 1950s and 1990s) in many film industries, including Italian and Indian filmmaking. This significant stretch of time illustrates what was a growing interest in the controlled deployment of a few sound elements as design material in films, keeping the voice's primacy along with prominent usage of dubbing, post-synchronisation, background music, song or dance sequences and processed sound effects. Ambient sounds were missing from this hierarchy of sound organisation. Why were ambient sounds scarcely used in this era of sound production? What was the nature of diegesis undertaken in this specific practice of ambient sounds (or a lack thereof)? How was the sonic environment's presence re-produced? In order to address these questions attention is drawn to the specific sound practice of 'dubbing' as a narrative strategy.

'Dubbing', according to writer Jorge Luis Borges, is 'a perverse artifice' contributing to 'ingenious audio-visual deformation' (Borges 1999: 262–263). His indignation regarding dubbing is perhaps based on voice replacement practices by foreign exhibitors who converted American films from English into respective, regional languages. However, in India and Italy the replacement was only spatial and temporal, and generally not linguistic, since the same actors would eventually replace their own in-sync voices (from the pilot or guide track) and 'dub' in the same language. The question, then, was not only what film scholar Nataša Ďurovičová terms as 'voice-body duplication in post-synchronicity' (Ďurovičová 2003)[19] but also one of a more asynchronous nature. Actors were divided in space and time while performing their lines of speech twice – on location and again inside the studio – resulting in little or no audible information about the cinematic site narrated in the story. This process of voice replacement 'privileges one aspect of speech, namely comprehension, at the expense of all of its other aspects' (Ďurovičová 2003). In order to compensate for this and counter what Borges poses as 'perverse artifice' and 'audio-visual deformation', voice, music and sound effects were mixed loudly and in an overly expressionistic style, alongside frequent interruptions (Gopalan 2002) of song and dance, particularly in post-synchronised popular mainstream Indian films and Chinese martial art films. This aesthetic strategy maintained a primarily non-diegetic film space where site-specific ambient sound would not easily fit (Chattopadhyay 2017a).

Commercial Indian and Italian films during this era were indeed known for their poor sound design quality and lack of ambient sounds. As such, there was an apparent deficiency in the industry personnel's sonic sensibility to create an aurally perceivable film space and convincing sonic environments, perhaps symptomatic of the 'peculiar inability of these films to produce a persuasive relationship with live location sound, the only proper sound resource actually available to the cinema' (Rajadhyaksha 2007: 14). Indeed, it is crucial to study this peculiar trend in sound practice that removed the site's presence within the diegesis as a narrative strategy if the developments of sound production towards the digital realm are to be traced.

Realist films also used dubbing but predominantly aimed to provide spatial verisimilitude not only through the elaborate use of site-specific ambient sounds but also in the recording and re-presentation of voices. In an interview, Satyajit Ray's sound mixer, Jyoti Chatterjee, speaks about the director's use of 'straight or direct dubbing' to avoid certain camera and production noises. Unlike the standard loop dubbing used in Indian cinema from the 1960s onwards, this method captures the actor's voice immediately after the shot is taken.[20] 'Direct or straight dubbing' is done in the same place and under similar circumstances to retain the site's spatial authenticity and the sited performance of the actors – something that could not be recreated in the studio in front of looped visual images. Evidence of such innovative dubbing can be found in

Ray's films *Nayak* (The Hero, 1966) and *Aranyer Din Ratri* (Days and Nights in the Forest, 1970). This practice of random dubbing on location[21] shows a staunchly realist filmmaker like Ray's commitment to creating the site's presence in diegesis, expanding the possibilities of forming a cinematic reality as close to experientially real, site-aware and lived sonic environments.

Notes

1. Ray said this in an interview with Samik Bandyopadhyay on Kolkata Doordarshan.
2. Available at https://time.com/5084599/first-recorded-sound/
3. See: <https://www.loc.gov/static/programs/national-film-preservation-board/documents/love_me_tonight.pdf>
4. 'Married print' is a standard term in many film industries to denote the combination of sound and image on a single irreversible optical print.
5. Dolby Atmos specifications available at <http://www.dolby.com/us/en/brands/dolby-atmos.html>
6. Bloom (2014: 433).
7. Lastra (2000: 181).
8. In an essay from 1928, Sergei Eisenstein and Vsevolod Pudovkin advocated for an asynchronous rather than synchronous mode of sound production in order to sustain the dynamic montage of silent era cinema as a narrative strategy.
9. Separately recording various film sound components almost entirely inside a studio.
10. See: personal interviews with practitioners in project 'Audible absence: Searching for the site in sound production' (Chattopadhyay 2017a).
11. Mostly battery-operated and 'phantom' (48 v) powered, portable, professional audio tape recorders produced by Kudelski SA, based in Switzerland. The Nagra II model was the most popular of the series for use in the Indian film industry.
12. Sound designer Dipankar Chaki speaks of the early years of the MagnaTech Rock-and-Roll mixing console in the Bengali film industry and how it improved sound quality. See personal interview in Chattopadhyay (2021).
13. See: personal interview with Dev in Chattopadhyay (2021).
14. Bresson's realism can be considered to be more of a subdued kind and is inclined towards minimalism.
15. See: personal interview with Anup Mukherjee in Chattopadhyay (2021).
16. 'Foley' is a technique used in the sound post-production stages of filmmaking to recreate the sound effects of a scene for post-synchronisation with the image. It allows for the clean recording of effects made synthetically inside a studio since production mics would include unwanted locational noises, which are, of course, almost entirely absent in the studio. Foley is traditionally used to provide the actor's footsteps, movements and other 'personal' sounds, all made post-synchronously.
17. 'Pro-filmic space' is defined by film sound scholar James Lastra (2000) as the space of the fictitious site in front of the camera, a space that is reconstructed in the film space as a cinematic experience by recording, layering and designing sound.
18. Paragraph on sync sound in Asia available at <https://en.wikipedia.org/wiki/Sync_sound>
19. Available at <http://epa.oszk.hu/00300/00375/00001/durovicova.htm>
20. See: personal interview with Jyoti Chatterjee in Chattopadhyay (2021), a collection of interviews with film sound technicians from India.
21. To retain site-specific details and the ambience, when direct synchronised recording confronts logistic hindrance.

Figure 6.1 Inside a sound studio

6 STEREO SOUND AND THE EXPANDED SPACE

6.1 STUDIO-CENTRIC SOUND

As I have shown in the previous chapter, 'dubbing' was introduced in cinema in order to avoid camera noise emanating from the popular and affordable Arriflex 35 III cameras along with other incidental background noises from the location of shooting. Dubbing, like 'looping', quickly became a norm in the sound techniques of producing the auditory setting primarily inside sound studios. Such sound practices in the dubbing era, with an emphasis on post-synchronisation, effectively destroyed perspective in cinema as argued by many film writers like Pemmaraju (2013), in the sense that the physical reality of the sites with their spatial details and natural auditory situations from the location could not be recreated inside the sound studio. A critical landmark in the history of cinema is the separation of the production of the sound, including voice, from the image. In India, this led to the 'playback' and, later, the 'dubbing' era. [. . .] the production of the dialogue also came to be separated from the filming on a set or a location. This was driven by a technological imperative: the noise made by the moving parts of the camera' (Pemmaraju 2013: 80). The effects of recording the dialogue inside the studio made the voice sounding 'unsitely'[1] and unnatural.

Indian films such as *Dharmatma* (Khan 1975), *Johny Mera Naam* (Johny My Name, Anand 1970), *Deewaar* (The Wall, Chopra 1975) and *Lahu Ke Do Rang* (Blood Has Two Colours, Bhatt 1979) are representative of the dubbing that was also used in Italy and Hong Kong in the 1970s and 1980s. Actors' voices were processed with studio reverb even when they were depicted in natural, outdoor settings. In one particular sequence from *Dharmatma*,[2] the tribal woman Reshma and the main protagonist Ranbir, who has fallen in love with her, speak in an open clearing in the middle of a forest (according to the storyline, the site is in the distant land of Afghanistan).[3] The dialogue is processed clean, polished and crisp; a sound compressor was used to accentuate its intelligibility. Neither the ambience of the forest nor the sound perspectives of the actors' – their respective standing positions as they face one another on either side of a tree there – is audible. Furthermore, when the villain, Jankura, arrives, envious of their amorous proximity, he shouts in anger and his voice emerges with the acoustic processing of a reverberant room rather than the openness of a forest. Similarly, in an early sequence from *Deewaar*, a character makes a speech in an exterior courtyard in front of a number of factory workers. However, his voice appears cleanly recorded by a method of 'close miking' (Lastra 2000) with applied studio reverb for an interior location, without the slightest sign of the sound perspective his position in an open field would need in order to provide a believable auditory setting. James Lastra describes how in American film sound, studio-based dubbing's use of the 'close frontal miking of actors, which minimizes reflected and indirect sound, became the norm for dialogue' (Lastra 2000: 142). He acknowledges the lack of sound perspective this specific practice creates: 'Despite changes in shot scale, the sound recordist has maintained "close-up" sounds in order to ensure intelligibility, thereby violating the presumed norms of "sound perspective"'(Lastra 2000: 143). It is no surprise that these Hollywood norms influenced popular films from India, Italy and Hong Kong, exporting similar studio-dominated sound production aesthetics into their contexts.

6.2 Hyper-real sound effects

The car-chase sequence in *Deewaar* (1975) and the fight sequence in *Dharmatma* (1975) exemplify the use of sound effects in an overly enhanced and dramatically modulated style rendered with hyper-real textures. In the first example, when Bijay's car reaches the end of its fateful journey at the top of the temple stairs, its tyres make a loud and unnatural screeching sound that would not occur in a real situation, as the car had already scaled the concrete stairs. In the second, the fighting actors' punches and pistol shots are processed with extra reverb, time-stretching[4] and compression[5] to render the sounds histrionic; they do not sound 'real' at all. A hyper-real environment of suspended disbelief and emotive tension is created that does not realistically relate the sound to the 'sitely' source depicted in the cinematic universe. Narration in these films 'creates a specific emotional tension' (Tan 2011: 35) via studio manipulation and the abstraction and modulation of recorded sound materials as processed audio effects, producing a suspended and unsightly reality.

Indian music writer Rajiv Vijayakar, in his book *The History of Indian Film Music* (2009: 53), comments on Indian film sound practices suggesting that hyper-processed sonic modulations were commonplace in both Indian soundtrack production and music production:

> The foremost changes that came in this decade were probably the advent of consciousness in sound and the beginning of change in the old order, and both these factors were also interconnected [. . .] As a kind of compensation, echo or reverb was added to [. . .] film soundtracks.

In New Hollywood and post-classical cinema (from the 1960s to the 1980s), filmmakers began experimenting with sound. The sound editor's specific role emerged – splicing, combining and modulating sounds recorded on malleable magnetic tape, which produced a new kind of nonlinear storytelling that broke away from the clean and linear classical narrative. Emily Thompson in her book *The Soundscape of Modernity* articulates such practice as 'a fundamental compulsion to control the behavior of sound' (2004: 2) in the context of American cinema.

Thus, in the dubbing era of much world cinema, the processing of sound effects, namely echo or reverb, used both in film sound and music productions, was the result of consciously working with sound to control and compensate for the lack of realistic sonic representations. This can be understood as film's asynchronous tendencies, separating sound from its real site-specific sources added to enhance dramatic and spectacular qualities. In his book *Beyond Dolby (Stereo)* (2011) Mark Kerins shows how these new experiments during the 1960s and 1970s made film soundtracks louder and more high-pitched due to the inherent characteristics and frequency response of magnetic tape. Consciously processing sounds later led to expanding cinematic space and recorded reality through the stereophonic mixing of ambient sound.

Sound production's gradual standardisation during the heydays of dubbing led to popular and syncretic forms like 'Bollywood' or 'Nollywood' in global cinema that associated film industries with domestic cultural production (e.g., Hollywood). Such industrial nomenclatures and norms helped to proliferate studio-centric control via the manipulation of sounds recorded on magnetic strip for post-synchronisation. This industrial process predominantly instigated the dramatisation of sound design to enhance sound's emotional and affective qualities, playing on the fringes of audience imagination. The aim was to create popular mass appeal by exploiting melodramatic overtones through over-processed voices and modulated sound effects, etc. For example, the specific sonic representation of an antagonistic character was constructed using vocal manipulation tools like compressors and extending the reverb of footsteps and other gestures to instil visceral responses in the audience through affective mimicry – physically affecting the spectator with 'auditory entrainment' (Plantinga 2009: 94). These production aesthetics became accepted modes of developing the cinematic spectacle and its scope in the transition from monaural to stereophonic mixing, though the latter practice was relatively short-lived.

6.3 Stereophonic space

Monaural mixing was deemed inadequate for handling elaborate spatial information and sonic environments in some films. Many filmmakers endeavoured to push technological limits and develop the craft of sound production to realise more ambitious film projects. One of the main figures from this experimental and innovational phase was George Lucas. When working on a sci-fi film called *Star Wars* (1977), Lucas thought that monaural mixing[6] would not do this film creative justice. Lucas teamed up with Dolby and together they developed Dolby Stereo. Following this innovation, sounds emanated from a pair of two plus one speakers placed behind and outside the screen with four channels, considerably expanding the mise-en-sonore. Previously ignored sound components like ambience found a place in this expanded space for their ability to manoeuvre spatiality and impact the viewer/listener.

American cinema gradually embraced this development in stereophonic production and reproduction. As film scholar Eric Dienstfrey argues (2016), Dolby Stereo developments 'were not revolutions but extensions of surround-sound practices that Hollywood codified in prior decades' (2016: 167). While he calls such historical attribution the 'Dolby myth', there is no doubt that the stereo mixing technique generally opened up the sonorous space or 'superfield' (Chion 1994) around the visual screen.

Certain genres of films were more inclined to the development such as Westerns, action-oriented, high-budget martial arts films and sci-fi dramas. As Buhler, Neumeyer and Deemer state: 'Although stereo sound was commercially feasible by 1940 [. . .] it would not be systematically exploited by the industry until the introduction of Cinemascope in the early 1950s' (Buhler, Neumeyer and Deemer 2010: 336). In other film industries, including Italian, Chinese and Indian cinema, stereophonic mixing was introduced years later due to its slow adoption – limited competency in the studio was met by issues regarding the changeover from monaural sound systems to stereo mixing and reproduction in cinemas. However, by the early 1980s, most cinema worldwide started producing stereophonic films. *Disco Dancer* (1982) provides one of the earliest examples of stereophonic mixing in Asian films. The use of sound helped to augment film's spectacle beyond the constraint of the screen;

audiences gradually started to shift their attitude towards the cinematic site, from looking at it to living in it.

The advent of stereophonic technology in cinema led to an emergent sense of spatiality in film as the sound palette extended, allowing ambient sound to find importance in the scheme. According to film sound scholar Gianluca Sergi, stereophonic mixing made it possible to create an extra off-screen space in which part of the focus was left to the viewer. Stereo sound also made it possible for the viewer to engage with sound's directionality. This enhanced the audience's spatial orientation towards the fictional space over its monophonic counterparts. It also created the possibility of a dynamic sonic experience in which the sound could move around and beyond the screen (Sergi 2004). Thus, unlike monophonic sound, it became possible to make use of the off-screen space without having to link it to something on screen. Both Sergi and other film sound scholars have pointed out the specific nature of early stereophonic sound production: 'Over the course of the 1950s, however, more and more films emphasised spectacle and grandeur, and the introduction of the widescreen format and stereo sound furthered this goal' (Buhler, Neumeyer and Deemer 2010: 339).

In dubbing-dominated films, the relatively higher dynamic range available within magnetic sound recording and wider headroom in stereophonic mixing enlarged the possibilities of studio-centric sound production. Music and sound effects were placed on separate channels to spread the sound across the screen. This practice created spectacular effects for an expanded fantasy-like experience, augmented with martial arts and action in Chinese films, and lavish song and dance routines in foreign locations in Indian films. Action sequences were packed with echo and reverb, dislocating sounds even further from their realistic sources. Indian popular film *Sholay* (Sippy 1975) was India's first film with a four-track stereophonic sound having spectacular effects.[7] *Sholay* achieved cult status and remains a reference point for both Hindi-language cinema audiences and the Indian film industry as a whole, not only because of its technological achievements but also for its substantial emotional and affective appeal to a mass audience through its use of sound. This mass appeal is exemplified by Indian audiences, who repeat lines, copy the tone and texture of voices, and buy sound recordings of the film's villain Gabbar Singh even today (Shankar 2009: 168). The character's specific sonic representation was constructed using vocal manipulation and the extended reverb of his footsteps and other postures and gestures. This narrative strategy was aimed at triggering visceral responses from the audience (Plantinga 2009), leading to its mass appeal. The technically synthesised cinematic hyper-reality achieved through studio processing and stereophonic mixing was centred on manipulating the audience's emotional engagement with the spatially expanded cinematic spectacle (Sergi 2004). The narrative strategy, which *Sholay* used to construct a fictional site in the spectacularly colourful and eventful film space, was adopted throughout Indian cinema during the 1980s. Film historians Wimal Dissanayake and Malti Sahai observe that:

> Sholay clearly is not a realistic film, there is very little social specificity inscribed in the filmic text. The narrative codes employed in the film serve to construct a metaphoric view of Indian society and its manifold problems. A metaphoric representation displaces accuracy. (Dissanayake and Sahai 1992)

The synthetically reconstructed, fictitious location (the village Ramgarh in *Sholay*), highly processed sound effects in brutally violent scenes, elaborate fight sequences and deliberately arranged folk-rhythmic song sequences intricately contribute to the film's affective intensity and emotional appeal (Shankar 2009: 168). They engage audience members in the filmic world of a spectacular fantasy – a metaphoric and displaced representation of the Indian society.

The wider popularity of these films, however, was linked to stereophonic mixing that 'foregrounded the spectacular experience' (Kerin 2011: 28) for public consumption.

6.4 Sounding media arts

With the advent and adoption of magnetic tape recording and stereophonic mixing, musicians, artists and composers started to enjoy creative freedom. The ability to capture sounds from environments and manipulate recorded sound as raw material – editing and splicing, playing backwards, recombining and then mixing them in stereo – allowed artists the flexibility to realise their artistic imagination with sound. Sound studios began to experiment with tapes, allowing multiple 'tracks' to be recorded at the same time for greater flexibility. A growing trend of artistic sound media practice emerged around tape culture parallel to film. The works of Pierre Schaeffer and Pierre Henry in Paris, taking tape recordings of ambient sound and turning them into objects for composition, have already been mentioned. In America, artist Alvin Lucier realised *I am Sitting in a Room* (1969) by recording his voice in the same room over and over again until all that remained were the ambient sounds and the resonant frequencies of the room itself. Around the same time, artist Max Neuhaus built sound installation *Times Square* (1977), engaging with the ambient sounds of a traffic island. Hildegard Westerkamp's *Kits Beach Soundwalk* (1989) – a composition with spoken words – was produced by recording ambient sounds of Vancouver's Kitsilano Beach. These experiments were precursors to what would become known as sound art.

There is some confusion and uncertainty about how to define sound art. The question concerns whether sound art derives from an experimental music tradition or stems from the visual arts. The issue problematises the position of sound art in aesthetic practices at large. As a result, the somewhat complementary attitudes reflected in many artists', critics' and curators' commentaries explain why the current state of sound art triggers serious thoughts about the term's taxonomies and structure. From the Western art historical tradition, early examples of sound art include Luigi Russolo's noise intoners and subsequent experiments by Dadaists, Surrealists, the Situationist International and artists from Fluxus, which have influenced a trajectory that leads to what Seth Kim-Cohen terms 'the conceptual turn' (Kim-Cohen 2009). Because of the diverging approaches to the term, debates often occur as to whether sound art falls in between the categories. Other artistic lineages from which sound art arguably emerges include: conceptual art, minimalism, site-specific art, sound poetry, spoken word, avant-garde and experimental cinema. Sound scholar Christoph Cox suggests: 'At its best, "sound art" opens up or calls attention to an auditory unconscious, a transcendental or virtual domain of sound that has steadily come to prominence over the course of the twentieth century' (Cox 2009: 19). It is apparent that sound art has taken a definitive surge in aesthetic practice, production and dissemination and gained major attention in recent years, but such developments occur rather 'tentatively and ambivalently' (LaBelle 2006). Kim-Cohen has described sound art as the unwanted child of music (2009). Indeed, many artists working with sound media employ sounds not typically associated with music. They may have used everyday sounds, such as site-specific ambient sounds, for instance, but their selection of sounds encourages the experience of listening – not merely hearing sounds as white noise in the background but as an art experience in and of itself. Kim-Cohen has pointed out the boundaries, tendencies and specific shifts in post-war sound art practice after Pierre Schaeffer's experiments with *musique concrète* and John Cage's experiments with silence (Kim-Cohen 2009).[8] Following traditional scholarship on sound and site, such as Canadian composer R. Murray Shaefer's work at the Simon Fraser University, particularly the World Soundscape Project (WSP),[9] terms such as 'soundscape' and 'acoustic ecology' now describe specific sound practices embedded with strict ecological fixations. It can be argued that these practices were inherently constrained within predominantly objective and linear structures of electroacoustic music. I have already taken a critical position in respect to the Shaeferian idea of the soundscape in the book's introduction. I will further discuss this issue in Part 3, showing that a set idea of the soundscape may not fully explain sonic flux of cities vis-à-vis rural sites – a more situationist and poetic approach is necessary.

Music writer Geeta Dayal argues that sound art seems 'less esoteric' in the contemporary 'new media' environment because of our 'newfound comfort with the immaterial world of pure data and information flowing through the cyberspace' (2013).[10] Drawing on this perspective, it would be useful and perhaps better to read sound art within the domain of media arts when conceptualising and historicising its emergence.

Notes

1. Synonymous to 'site-unspecific', the term has been used in Miranda (2013).
2. Film available at <https://www.youtube.com/watch?v=Upc4w_WDy_k> (last accessed May 2020).
3. IMDb film listing available at <https://www.imdb.com/title/tt0361505/>
4. See: personal interviews with sound practitioners in Chattopadhyay (2021), a collection of interviews with film sound technicians from India.
5. 'Time-stretching' is used to make sound effects appear dramatic and temporally intriguing, whereas 'compression' is employed to smooth out sound's rough edges.
6. Lucas was aware of this limitation, as in monaural mixing sound is directed through a single channel from a single speaker behind the screen positioned at the screen's centre or in the front of the theatre – which I have discussed in the previous chapter.
7. See: personal interview with the film's sound mixer Hitendra Ghosh in Chattopadhyay (2021).
8. Kim-Cohen diagnoses this conceptual turn in sound art after the groundbreaking intervention of Marcel Duchamp. He states, '[...] since the 1960s, art has foregrounded the conceptual, concerning itself with questions that the eye alone cannot answer, questions regarding the conditions of art's own possibility. The conceptual turn is not intrinsically an inward turn from gaze to navel gaze. Instead, conceptualism allows art to volunteer its own corpus, its own ontology, as a test case for the definition of categories [...] A conceptual sonic art would necessarily engage both the non-cochlear and the cochlear, and the constituting trace of each in the other' (2009: xxi).
9. Along with Hildegard Westerkamp and Barry Truax as colleagues, among others.
10. See: Dayal, G. (2013).

7 DIGITAL SURROUND SOUND AND THE MIMETIC SITE

7.1 THE STATE OF THE DIGITAL

Since the early 1990s, a large-scale conversion from analogue recording and production practices to digital technologies has taken place in cinemas.[1] Digital technology has been integrated into the production and post-production stages of filmmaking as well as reproduction and projection formats. The ramification of this development has been far-reaching and particularly evident in the way filmmaking has changed through novel digital sound practices (Holman 2002; Kerins 2011). Production practices and techniques such as location-based multi-track sync recording and surround sound spatialisation have altered the notion of the film soundtrack[2] in cinema's imminently digital realm. This process of digitalisation has had a substantial impact on narrative strategies and aesthetic choices made with cinematic sound production, informing the creation of the site's presence[3] in pro-filmic space[4] by innovative modes of diegesis.[5] Likewise, the mise-en-sonore or auditory setting[6] has also been reconfigured, contrasting considerably with earlier monaural and stereophonic cinematic experiences, especially in terms of ambience. Therefore, it is necessary to consider these transformations in light of the aesthetic choices and strategies of working with environmental sounds in the digital era and the new kind of spatial experiences they have triggered. This will help in reaching a thorough understanding of digital technology's implications on modes of sound production that alter sound-site relationships. Given the complex, rich and layered sound environments of urban and rural sites, the desire to evolve

Figure 7.1 Digital sound recording on location

sound production to attend to them is evident in film practices. In the digital era, these aspirations are recognised.

Scholars of sound production Tomlinson Holman (2002) and Mark Kerins (2006, 2011) posit that digital sound systems (DSS) have introduced a number of possibilities, including significantly larger dynamic ranges of over 100 dB (a fourfold improvement over its monophonic predecessor and almost double that of the stereophonic format) (Holman 2002; Kerins 2011), larger headroom[7] of 20 dB (a major improvement to the 6 and 12 dB headroom of monophonic sound), six discreet channels (5.1 surround sound) and more channels in other multi-channel formats such as Dolby Atmos, wider panning for sound spatialisation and full-frequency channels (20 Hz–20 KHz) with a flatter response. These capacities have made new production practices possible, including wider dynamic range, increased mixing complexity and spatial fidelity (Kerins 2011), while recording and processing the available depth, perspective and width[8] of ambient sounds collected on location. Digital multi-track synchronised or 'sync'[9] recording and multi-channel surround sound mixing offer a wider palette of sound materials including, among others, previously ignored ambient sounds for designing a spatially elaborate mise-en-sonore. With the advent of digital technology, broadly available and easy-to-handle recording devices, applications and facilities have made various options and formats available to sound practitioners.[10]

What is aesthetically different in this new trend as compared with earlier production practices (e.g., optical direct recording, monaural mixing, magnetic recording, dubbing and stereophonic mixing)? Gianluca Sergi (2004) asserted that early digital surround sound mixing practices relied on 'the same screen-centric notion of cinema sound as their mono and Dolby stereo predecessors' (Kerins 2011: 5). But he also pointed out 'a reassessment of the relationship between screen sound and surround sound' (Kerins 2011: 5) in later surround sound innovation. These statements suggest that surround sound technology shifted the preconceived idea of screen-centric sound (mono as well as stereo) towards an extensive area of diffused sounds surrounding the cinema screen. Film scholar Vivian Sobchack expresses these transformations as 'shifts of emphasis and attention in both sound technology and our sensorium' (Sobchack 2005: 2), leading towards what Rick Altman has noted as 'greater realism' (Altman 1992: 159), predicting the future of sound production in cinema in terms of technological innovations that support mimetically more realistic and cogent representations of place and its sonic environments in the sensorium.

As a matter of course, the emergence of any new technology in cinema generates a great deal of discussion and deliberation about its potential use or abuse. The question of how 'stereo' should sound has been much debated since the advent of stereophonic sound in the 1950s, when, as discussed, cinematic sound was already standardised in accordance with the monophonic recording-production-reproduction chain, from direct sound recording to its monaural projection in cinema theatres throughout most parts of the globe. Gianluca Sergi has described this transition as the change from a low-quality, optical, monaural soundtrack to a relatively cleaner and better-quality Dolby stereo soundtrack via tape-based magnetic recording with greater dynamic range, depth and signal-to-noise ratio but with problems in sound localisation still at the fore, raising serious questions about the contribution of stereo to cinema. He states:

> This design (i.e. early Dolby stereo) follows the principle that audiences should be offered directional sound (i.e. sound whose direction could easily be identifiable) only from one wall of the auditorium, namely that where the screen is placed. The notion at the core of this thinking is that sound emanating from somewhere other than an onscreen source would cause the audience to get distracted in an attempt to locate the origin of that sound, hence disrupting the narrative flow. Thus, the implied suggestion is that the surround channel be employed only in a diffuse, non-directional manner so as not to 'disturb' the narrative. Despite implicitly suggesting that primary information ought to originate from the screen, the one-wall principle did away with the need to deal with complicated alternatives, like additional surround channels, that would have meant a serious rethink of the meaning of stereo in the cinema.[11]

From what Sergi writes, it is evident that more channels meant rethinking and reordering the existing set-up to achieve a new spatial organisation of sound in cinema. With explicit reference to practical and experiential accounts, noted sound designer David Sonnenschein writes in the book *Sound Design: The Expressive Power of Music, Voice and Sound Effects in Cinema* (2001) about the addition of channels to the existing normative structures of routing and mixing sounds in order to design different soundtrack elements for an emerging surround sound design:

> In the LCRS [left, centre, right and surround channels] (Dolby SR and Ultra-stereo) system, the dialogue normally projects from the center with effects and music coming from the left, right, and surround speakers. Ambiance and music can take advantage of the multiple sources to create a space within which the audience can be enveloped [...] With the addition of other speakers beyond the basic four LCRS, the variables increase and more discrete placement can be made with the sounds.[12]

Sonnenschein suggests that stereophonic cinema makes it possible to create an extra off-screen space allowing the audience to engage with sound's directionality. This capacity opens up a new spatial orientation towards the fictional space, creating the possibility of a dynamic sonic experience in which the sound can move around and beyond the screen (Sergi 2004). Mark Kerins claims that the stereophonic system's off-screen diffusion of sound is limited (2006: 43). Indeed, the 'off-screen space' has now been expanded with added channels in the digital surround sound system, which emphasises a spatially-evocative sound environment instead of offering a linear, one-dimensional soundtrack with voice, effects and background music mixed into a single track. Mark Kerins has argued that in comparison to the screen-centric monaural and stereophonic soundtrack, digital surround systems 'spread out into the theatres as their makers see fit' (2006: 43), granting the sound practitioner more creative freedom in the narrative strategy. Kerins has also argued for the 'spatial fidelity' that is provided by the digital surround system. The sound practitioner uses digital systems to put forward 'more perceptible sounds' in the surround channels 'to build multi-channel environments. They assume that audiences will understand sounds originating in the surround channels to be part of the same diegetic space as those originating onscreen' (Kerins 2011: 70), spatially expanding and substantially enriching the sound environment.

Film sound scholar Giorgio Biancorosso also placed emphasis on the spatial reordering of sound in order to produce a more convincing diegetic space in cinema, with the shift from monaural to stereophonic and to the digital surround system:

> After all, sounds whose sources remain unseen not only reach us at all times, but are also crucial in guiding our sense of inhabiting a certain kind of space, specifying its properties and suggesting the kinds of activities taking place therein. It is fair to assume that we bring this ability to perceive the space around us through sound to bear on the construction of a diegetic space. Digital Surround Sound depends on it.[13]

The growing digitalisation of filmmaking all over the world post-1990 allows for the appreciation and construction of a diegetic space to which previous sound practices, in mono and stereophonic frameworks, paid lesser attention. The increased importance of authenticity in diegesis led to more site-specific spatial details being included in recording and reproduction aimed at generating an embodied experience. The spatial organisation of sound makes audiences believe in the site's presence within the story-world's narrative, which is achieved through the treatment of ambient sounds in the multi-channel sonic environment of contemporary global cinema.

Apart from adding more audio channels in the digital surround realm, an emergent fascination with real locations over sets and more detailed and accurate evidence – noticeable in production practices such as location recordings of synchronised sound in films – suggests a rediscovery of cinema's original search for realism.[14] For example, in recent mainstream Indian films, the preceding practices of dubbing, stock sound effects and studio Foley are gradually being replaced by authentic, site-specific location sync sounds. These sound layers incorporate a wider dissemination of naturalistic and site-specific auditory artefacts into the construction of the filmic space, adding depth, texture and sonic perspective in the ambience. This reordering of the film space has been gaining momentum with the increasing amount of direct participation of sound technicians in the filmmaking process through their involvement in location-based sync recording, production mixing and surround sound design. Digital multi-track synchronised sound has been accepted as a highly precise, artistically demanding and skilled recording technique practised by sound technicians, involving the use of original dialogue, which was previously replaced in the studio as pilot or guide track, thereby lessening the dependence on tedious post-production processes such as dubbing and studio Foley.

7.2 Sync sound

During the early 2000s, a major upgrade followed in the form of emergent digital technology, which introduced sync sound recording techniques and surround sound formats to many cinemas, accelerating the process of globalisation and the corporatisation of local film industries. A significant shift in focus, redefining the aesthetics within sound production, led to the emergence of sophisticated terms such as 'sound design'. New approaches have helped reconstruct the site's spatial presence within the diegetic story-world, evoked by site-specific digital recording and surround sound design. Although in most European cinemas (with a few exceptions, including Italian cinema) sync sound was already in practice, in many other national cinemas, where dubbing and post-synchronisation were the predominant mode of sound production, on-location sync sound recording techniques have been revolutionary. Such practice is a direct result of recent trends in digital innovation. In the widely used term in the industry – 'sync' – the emphasis is on the 'synchronisation' aspect of recording sound on digital multi-track formats, pointing to the fact that the practice qualitatively not only differs from earlier post-synchronised dubbing but also from monaural direct sound, therefore triggering a completely different set of narrative methodologies in approaching the pro-filmic space and composing the presence of the site in the cinematic story-world (Chattopadhyay 2017a).

The multiple options for organising different digital tracks have opened up possibilities for recording and utilising a larger number of sound elements, including ambient sounds, sync effects, dialogue and background musical scores. The increased storage space of digital formats also allows for recording and mixing additional ambient sounds on location after shooting in order to capture the intricate details of a sonic environment – layers that can be added later during sound design. These extensive recordings of site-specific ambient sounds have incorporated actual material into post-production without the need to reuse stock sounds and pre-recorded ambience that obviously were previously gathered from somewhere else. A variety of digital applications are available in the studio to manipulate and restructure the site-based characteristics of recorded ambient sounds to fit the cinematic narrative.

Contemporary cinema in the digital realm facilitates deliberate sound practices to create cinematic experiences that are 'spatially present' (Grimshaw 2011; Lombard and Ditton 1997; Skalski and Whitbred 2010). This mode of sound production differs considerably from earlier productions.[15] Digital sound practices, such as multi-track synchronised recording and surround sound design, impact the organisation of ambient sound to produce mediated sonic environments that sound more perceptually and spatiotemporally real. Drawing on works in film sound production (Holman 2002; Kerins 2011; Sergi 2004; Sonnenschein 2001), in light of narrative strategies of diegesis (Burch 1982; Percheron 1980) and considering notions of presence (Grimshaw 2011; Lombard and Ditton 1997), it can be said that current digital practice tends to construct spatially evocative sonic environments as opposed to the linear soundtrack of earlier cinema. When it comes to Indian song and dance social dramas, Chinese martial arts films or popular Korean and Hong Kong action films, escapist, spectacular, narratively and diegetically interrupting sequences such as song and dance routines (Gopalan 2002; Rajadhyaksha 2009) are also challenged by the audience's demand to experience a more realistic auditory setting. The digital era's creative and innovative ambient sound practices lead to a new realm in which audiences can increasingly connect with the site's presence through spatial perception (Waller and Nadel 2013) and auditory cognition (McAdams and Bigand 1993). Crafted from multiple ambient sound layers recorded at actual sites, these layers can provide audiences with an embodied experience of sound. The resultant effect can be playfully termed a 'cinematic soundscape' if we consider the notion of soundscape (Drever 2002) as a point of departure for studying a site-aware evocation of sound in cinema through an ethnographic interest in environmental sounds on location, as opposed to the linear and spatially-limiting notion of the film soundtrack.

7.3 Sound design and deconstruction of the soundtrack

Scholarly perspectives on sound production (Kerins 2006, 2011; Sergi 2004; Sonnenschein 2001) and the aesthetic impacts of production practices on cinematic experience – described as 'real' (Altman 1992), 'sensorial' (Sobchack 2005) or 'authentic' (Biancorosso 2009) – cannot be evenly applied to all national cinemas, as exemplified by India cinema's historical trajectory. It is not difficult to maintain that the site in cinema has been inconstantly rendered and produced due to evolving phases of production practices affected by technological innovations and shifts. There have been phases of sound practice such as the entire dubbing era that cared less about the site, giving more importance to typical narrative tropes such as music and song. However, as noted earlier, certain phases such as the digital era reflect a more concrete representation of site. In this light, the advent of sync sound and digital surround sound is significant, at least within the context of film sound's developments through its earlier phases of production practices (i.e., monaural and stereophonic frameworks). In my other writings (Chattopadhyay 2016, 2017b, 2018b) and in my doctoral dissertation (Chattopadhyay 2017a), I have discussed mainstream Indian film's general tendency to ignore subtleties while constructing the filmic space and mediating the sonic environment of many sites. These observations resonate with Indian film scholar Asish Rajadhyaksha's reflections when he points to the 'peculiar inability of Indian cinema to produce a persuasive relationship with live location sound' (2007: 1). He elaborates:

> To point to the inability of music to become sound, thus providing one context, and even a key explanation, for the peculiar inability of Indian cinema to produce a persuasive relationship with live location sound, the only proper sound resource actually available to the cinema [. . .] this in fact echoes the lament of all location recordists at the Indian cinema's curious resistance to live sound: both in the end questioning the dubious antecedents of the content of a film's soundtrack.[16]

However, the location sound recordist's lament tends to fade away with the use of contemporary digital tools and techniques, allowing for multiple sound layers, especially ambient sounds, to be directly captured from shooting locations and incorporated into the sound design's multi-channel environment. The result is the site's significant presence in the spatiotemporally constructed story-world, using ambience as the primary element. In an interview with Dipankar Chaki, the practitioner clarifies, 'ambience [becomes] an extremely artistic aspect of the film sound [. . .] it is probably one of the most behind-the-scene things which is constantly colouring up[17] the whole [. . .] treatment of the film'.[18] How is the construction of the pro-filmic space in Indian cinema 'coloured' or affected by the use of ambient sound in the narrative process of diegesis? Rajadhyaksha points out the overwhelming desire of an Indian audience to believe in the filmic reality, which leads to convergence in the viewer's/listener's mind with a delineated narrative based on the conventional protocols of verisimilitude. He quotes Chion to support his point:

The convergence – in which 'ambient sounds, which are often the product of multiple specific and local sources' do not recognize the hierarchy between a 'space inhabited by the sound' and its multisource origin – hinges on a confusion that is 'at the very heart of our experience itself, like an unsettled knot of problems'. This confusion has had significant technical consequences where the desire to read in the sound its origin has run counter to the conventional protocols of verisimilitude.[19]

This convergence expects the audience to delineate a story-world and make sense of the site's presence narrated through the conventional protocols of verisimilitude. This sense of verisimilitude is provided by the qualitative attributes of sounds, namely textural richness, depth, perspective, volume, dynamic range and spatialisation of ambient sounds recorded on location and incorporated into digital sound post-production. These qualities help the audience to relate to the site as lived experience, as part of the phenomenal world (Bordwell 2009). Earlier in this book,[20] the notion of ambient sounds recorded from the controlled environment of direct or locational synchronised sound recording and the monaural production-reproduction chain was explored in relation to the reconstruction of reality and site using a strictly screen-centric projection of sonic information. The subsequent phase of magnetic recording, dubbing and studio-centric re-recording instigated a distance and abstraction from the film's location, the sonic process thus escaping the site altogether. Stereophonic mixing and reproduction rendered this abstraction as something spectacular (Kerins 2011; Sergi 2004), as if an expanded fantasy-like experience located far away from the site's reality. I have shown in 'The auditory spectacle: Designing sound for the 'dubbing era' of Indian cinema' (2015c) and in my doctoral dissertation (Chattopadhyay 2017a) that mainly studio-centric technicians tended to construct the pro-filmic space by synthetic means, typically paying little attention to any site-specific sounds and using music and hyperreal sound effects as aural masking during this period of sound production.

However, the advent of digital sound production has challenged these previous limitations of sonic realism in cinema, offering a wider and more flexible milieu of sound recording and design practice with more freedom for the practitioner. Kerins writes of emergent digital technologies in Hollywood:

> When 5.1-channel digital surround sound (DSS) first appeared in the early 1990s, it offered filmmakers better dynamic range, more channels, and greater flexibility for placement of sounds within the multichannel environment.[21]

To a certain degree, this argument is also valid for digital technologies incorporated into world cinema. The 35 mm filmstrip had a dynamic range of 78 dB

(Kerins 2011: 54) limiting the signal-to-noise ratio in optical sound recording. Within this narrower dynamic range, monaural synchronised recording was restricted in the amount of ambient sound content that would be optimal for a film soundtrack, putting emphasis on the voice. In the magnetic recording era, sound recording's dynamic range was around 98 dB, depending on the tape material's quality. The digital equivalent, on the other hand, offers a dynamic range of over 100 dB, which means that sounds include more breadth and depth of recording (i.e., retaining high-volume capabilities alongside the transmission of very soft and minute sounds). This wider headroom[22] provides an inclusive capacity for recording, layering, designing and mixing sounds, which have gradually replaced dubbing, Foley and stock ambient sounds to include more aspects of the actor's live performance, sync sound effects and location-based ambient sounds. When audiences experience these 'actual' sounds – through a spatially wider, digitally cleaned, multi-channel surround design by film-school-educated sound designers – they can trigger a subjective sense of the site's presence in the listener's auditory perception and cognition, exploring the immersive and embodied potential of ambient sounds. This mode of production inherently engages with ambient sound's corporeally immersive potential. As Mark Grimshaw argues, ambient sounds 'can create a sense of physical presence' (Grimshaw 2011: 38). This immersive sense of the site's presence in the cinematic universe is constructed with the surround spatialisation of site-specific ambient sounds, enveloping the audience beyond the screen but diegetically connected to the story-world. This experience of sound surrounding the audience produces the perception of being there as if in reality. This process of diegesis brings into play a 'coherent representation of the sound world' (McAdams and Bigand 1993) in the spatially organised sonic environment by unfolding and spatially widening the linear and one-dimensional soundtrack of previous production eras into a circumambient auditory setting of a digital film space.

7.4 SURROUND SOUND

As the new trend of digital multi-track synchronised sound recording and surround design became widely accepted in filmmaking, sound production incorporated newly available digital technological innovations to its existing set-up. Post-production techniques – editing, designing and mixing in the studio – became faster and the projection of sound in theatres and multiplexes moved toward Dolby 7.1, Auro 3D, Barco and Dolby Atmos systems. Pixar's *Brave* (2012) is widely recognised as the first Hollywood film to have fully used Dolby Atmos technology in surround sound mixing. However, the aesthetic potential of Dolby Atmos matured in several later films such as *Gravity* (Alfonso Cuarón 2013) and *Blade Runner 2049* (Denis Villeneuve 2017). The voices of characters in *Gravity* fly past the audience and move around the theatre in direct and sometimes indirect coordination with the screen; such spatial experimentation with sound was radical at the time and effective in construing a sense of gravity's absence as an existential position in outer space. Flying vehicles were heard overhead as well as seen on screen in *Blade Runner 2049*. The first Indian film to be released in the Dolby Atmos format was *Sivaji 3D* (Shankar 2012). Currently, Dolby is set to face an opponent in Auro 3D, which entered Indian cinemas with *Vishwaroopam* (Kamal Hasan 2013). Both companies have developed and offer audio technologies that digitalise, split and route sounds into multiple, surrounding speakers. Veteran sound practitioner Anup Dev states, 'The difference in sound quality between 5.1, 7.1 and Dolby 3D is almost imperceptible [. . .] However, the same cannot be said about Dolby Atmos. The difference in sound quality is huge.'[23] A few other films outside of Hollywood and popular Indian cinema should be mentioned for their creative sound work within Dolby Atmos-led sonic environments, such as the South Korean film *Parasite* (Bong Joon-ho 2019) and Mexican film *Roma* (Alfonso Cuarón 2018). Both films, with other notable works, will be discussed within this context in a later chapter.

As it stands, contemporary cinema in the digital realm holds six distinct benefits: (1) multi-channel recording capabilities; (2) an enormous dynamic range from the softest sound to the loudest; (3) discrete, full-frequency channels and their complex routing options; (4) the ability of the digital multi-track digital recorder to capture sounds from all corners of a location in synchronisation with the visuals of live performances, movement and effects; (5) extra storage for recording stray ambience such as environmental soundmarks, room tone and other characteristic sounds from the location after shooting; and, finally, (6) the digital sound studio's capacity to employ surround sound design with numerous tracks holding layered, location-specific ambient sounds in creative ways. How do these new technical capabilities influence the production of the sonic environment in film space and how is this new practice reflected in the audience's experience of the site? Expressions used in reviews of films made with digital surround sound technology such as 'real', 'familiar', 'authentic', 'immersive' and 'great sense of place' indicate shifts within sound experiences and the proliferation of a new trend, with audiences increasingly feeling the need to relate to convincingly real and believable sites in the mediated sonic environment. Audience expectations have led filmmakers and sound practitioners to instigate a shift from overdependence on 'telling' the story of a place to potentially 'showing' the sites of pro-filmic space. Likewise, the diegetic universe has become more mimetic.

In relation to surround sound, Mark Kerins states that the digital sound system 'is engineered to model a "true" 360-degree multichannel environment where the focal point of the soundscape can be anywhere in the theater'

(2006: 43). The emphasis on 'true' in this statement underlines the 'lifelikeness' (Rogers 2013: 56) of the acoustic environment created by a narrative strategy for which ambient sounds are organised and spatially rendered so that they 'construct for us a sense of the material world which the characters inhabit' (Fischer 1985: 239). For Kerins, this practice engenders an 'expansion of the cinematic soundfield beyond the screen' (2006: 43). He adds:

> To some degree this represents a simple acceleration of established narrative strategies – filmmakers have long relied on ambient sound in the "surrounds" to set up diegetic spaces, and this trend has certainly continued with movies employing DSS. The difference here is that DSS has encouraged the construction of complex multichannel sound mixes, where the different sounds in each speaker channel together create a seemingly realistic and complete aural environment in a way difficult (if not impossible) with monophonic or Dolby stereo sound.[24]

How do audiences relate to the site and further orient themselves in this mimetic, perceptually realistic and spatially enveloping sonic environment? As Kerins shows, DSS's use of ambience can be considered as an expansion of established practice in the sense that it:

> [. . .] centers on a strategy of immersion in the filmic environment – audiences are, visually and aurally, literally placed in the middle of the action [. . .] in which the narrative processes of cinema [. . .] communicate complex perspectives, and dependence on a complex interplay between sound and image to orient audiences.[25]

An understanding of how audiences orient themselves in this surrounding sonic environment by 'being there' relates to processes of spatial perception and cognition. Betty J. Mohler, Massimiliano Di Luca and Heinrich H. Bulthoff theorise spatial perception and cognition in terms of careful navigation through multiple modalities, including audition:

> When an observer moves, the sensory systems capture multiple signals: The retinal projections of the environment change, the vestibular organs sense acceleration, environmental sounds move with respect to the body, and so forth [. . .] Information from multiple sense modalities is often necessary to navigate successfully. Vision, touch, and audition can provide contextual information to vestibular signals for a more robust and stable representation of perceived head orientation and movement.[26]

If we consider the observer to be stationary and their surrounding environment to be moving, as in the case of a DSS experience, the same orienting process leads to the perceptual and cognitive appeal of cinematic sound. Audiences are invited to orient themselves within the film's narrative world; the process essentially involves capturing sensory signals from the environment and performing an internal, mental computation that can be divided into early or low-level perception and advanced or higher-level mental processing or cognition. Sense modalities provide sensory information (Bordwell 2009) – for example, ambient sounds from any given environment of a film – and process them accordingly for the perception of spatial properties such as distance, direction, depth, etc. In the case of audition, as one of the sense modalities, air vibration in the cinematic environment provides information that human ears, due to their slight yet perceptually significant difference of being on the right and left sides of the head, can capture: interaural time and interaural intensity differences (Waller and Nadel 2013). Spatial information is recovered from ambient sounds that come from the cinematic environment and audiences locate themselves within it as lived experience (Bordwell 2009). Ontological questions such as 'Where am I?' and epistemological questions such as 'What can I hear?' relate directly to the site of the story-world via the spatially constructed soundfield that the audience interprets (McAdams and Bigand 1993; Mohler, Di Luca and Bülthoff 2013). Here, Béla Balázs's key statement from the introduction on sound in cinema is worth reiterating, as the careful inclusion and spatial organisation of ambient sounds in contemporary films reveal to audiences the 'acoustic environment, the acoustic landscape in which we live' (1985: 116), adding to the site's presence in the mediated sonic environment and the produced film space.

It is no surprise that in many post-2000 Hollywood, European and Asian films site-specific details are included in the sound design. For example, in recent Indian films such as *Delhi-6* (Rakeysh Omprakash Mehra 2009), *Love Sex aur Dhokha* (Love Sex and Betrayal, Dibakar Banerjee 2010), *Dhobi Ghat* (Mumbai Diaries, Kiran Rao 2011) and *Kahani* (The Story, Sujoy Ghosh 2012), spatial arrangements of ambient sounds trigger strong cognitive associations with the site, facilitated by inventive strategies of sync recording and surround design. Multi-layered and richly evocative aural information plays out a spatial topography of the locations where the films were shot in the minds of the audience, creating a sonic recognition of the sites in the story-world from lived, everyday experiences. With reference to believability and cognition in cinema, Bordwell describes audiences as active information seekers (2009: 360) in the way they extract information from the phenomena of the natural environment (2009: 363). In contemporary films, site-specific ambient sound brings a wider diffusion of auditory information into the filmic space, adding depth, texture and auditory perspective, so the audience can develop a spatially oriented, enveloping and expanded sonic environment beyond the screen. These possibilities motivated film scholar Ranjani Mazumdar to claim that in contemporary films even '[t]he city's wastelands saturate the mise-en-scène' (2009: 238). The practice of digital sound and surround sound design in contemporary world cinema apparently manifests in paying due attention to the sonic environment of urban as well as rural sites and landscapes.

7.5 Digital technology, field recording and multi-channel sound artworks

With the advent of digital technology in the field of sound art practices, widely available and easy-to-handle recording devices, applications and facilities have made various options and formats available to artists and practitioners. As discussed earlier, scholars of sound production Tomlinson Holman and Mark Kerins consider that the DSS has introduced a number of creative possibilities, including significantly larger dynamic ranges in sound recording, larger headroom, multi-channel formats, wider panning for sound spatialisation, and full-frequency channels (20 Hz–20 KHz) with a flatter response (Holman 2002; Kerins 2011). These capacities have made new production practices possible – a wider range of dynamics in sound as well as increased complexity in mixing and spatial fidelity (Kerins 2011) – while recording and processing the available depth, perspective and width of sound. Film scholar Vivian Sobchack expresses this as '[. . .] shifts of emphasis and attention in both sound technology and our sensorium', predicting the future of sound production in terms of digital technological innovations, producing works rich in spatial dimensions that stimulate a sonic sensorium (2005: 2). Creative practices using sound in the digital realm lead to new experiences in which audiences engage with sites and objects often through immersive listening, involving novel spatial engagements with sound.

As is clear from these practical and conceptual considerations, sound phenomena and the so-called sonic object or site often disentangle from each other in the digital realm, making sound's materiality a case for artistic intervention and transformation, a virtual mode of spatial experience where the sensorium of the listener is triggered. Indeed, sound is more easily 'torn' (Schafer 1994) from its objects, sites and sources in the digital realm and this condition contributes to the often uncanny and uneasy 'object-disorientation' of sound beyond geographical and sociocultural sites. In the hand of the artists, sound can be reconfigured into a new 'unsitely spatiality'. Moreover, digital communication devices and technologies facilitate the extensive nomadism of agents attuned to the psychogeographic evocation of physical locations and corporeal places in the post-globalised universe of intense mobility. In this universe, we encounter an immediate place and situate ourselves within it in ways that are intertwined; they are not only discreet physical experiences but sometimes appear as hybrid and syncretic environments. For example, smartphones can record sound from one place and send it elsewhere to someone else via applications such as WhatsApp; one place becomes merged with another as a distant place is heard through a Skype chat, thus enabling the listener to move, migrate and navigate from one place to another mentally more than physically. The sonic interactions with multiple sites that are moved through and the expanded objects dispersed in the cyber network that are encountered tend to be unfixed and evolving rather than having a concrete structure.

With the introduction of high-quality portable recording technologies after the digital revolution in the 1990s, 'field recording' practices have become an independent and evocative art form in themselves within the realm of media arts. Generally, field recording employs the methodology of recording site-specific ambient sounds outside of the studio. The current form of field recording practices often involve capturing environmental sounds that vary between animal sounds from the remote corners of the wilderness to everyday urban sounds subliminal in volume and low frequency in content; therefore they tend to be complex in texture, tone and characteristics.[27] In response, artists have often pushed the technical limits of sound recording, demanding low noise and extended frequency response in portable, easy-to-use recording formats, ranging from high-resolution, multi-track recording gadgets to DIY contact microphones.[28] Digital technology's emergence has made such recording techniques and methods possible. As a sprawling practice in the contemporary realm, field recording-based sonic media art facilitates the recording of sound on location with intricate detail: greater depth of field and wider, dynamic frequencies produce more precise, controlled and accurate documentary evidence of sites. These recording capacities allow artists to reach out towards uncharted territories e.g. locations under water, below ground, in the Amazonian forests, arctic landscapes and even into outer space.[29] Contemporary practices with sound are acclimatised to the saturation of digital technology in recording, production and reproduction. This condition gives birth to a new context that is termed the 'post-digital', marked by intensifying technological convergence, aesthetic inclusivity and artistic freedom (Chattopadhyay 2014a; Cramer 2014). In this post-digital territory, field recording is clearly advantaged by greater flexibility, access to the farthest corners of locations and applications with precise control over each recorded audio clip. Options for retaining numerous tracks open possibilities for recording a larger number of sound elements and working with multiple layers of sound captured from a given location. In the studio, there are also plenty of choices for processing sounds digitally or with retro-aesthetic means (e.g., analogue) towards spatialisation and multi-channel diffusion.

The spatial organisation of field recordings of ambient sounds in multi-channel surround spatialisation (e.g., Ambisonics format) creates a spatially augmented sonic environment realised through the artwork's narrative progression. The extent to which audiences associate with the sites and how engaged they become while following the artistic transformation of field recordings in multichannel surround, both in terms of compositional techniques and the intricate spatialisation of ambient sounds, depends on the framing of this constructive interplay between absence and presence or between abstraction and recognition of site-specific evidence through sounding media art's spatiotemporal development.

Notes

1. See: interviews with Aloke Dey and Anup Mukherjee in Chattopadhyay, B. (2021). (Collection of interviews with film sound technicians from India.)
2. The term 'soundtrack' is widely debated in film sound studies due largely to its usage, denoting a linear optical track on the filmstrip mixed with an accompanying music track, thus transmitting a sense of linearity and one-dimensionality. I argue elsewhere (Chattopadhyay 2013, 2015c, 2016) that 'soundtrack' can be a limiting term in cinematic sound studies; shaped by the methodologies of the digital realm, sound in cinema transcends the linear representation of a fixed 'track' and moves towards an elaborate and fluid spatial environment.
3. 'Place' is a generic term. 'Site' is more specific. Site is used more often than place here to describe the narrative depiction of specific locations in cinema.
4. 'Pro-filmic space' is defined by film sound scholar James Lastra (2000) as the fictional space, the area in front of the camera and sound device's recording field, which is reconstructed later in the cinematic experience through the recording and designing of sound.
5. Claudia Gorbman defines diegesis as 'the narratively implied spatiotemporal world of the actions and characters' (1987).
6. The term 'film space' is defined as the space that the spectator encounters, a space that is organised and constructed (e.g., linking shots through sound editing and sound design). On the other hand, the area in front of the camera and sound device's recording field is known as the 'pro-filmic space', as discussed earlier in the book. In combination, these two concepts reflect a situation whereby the choice and arrangement of pro-filmic space substantially affect the spatial dynamics of the mise-en-scène of sound – I have taken the liberty of using an unofficial but useful coinage, mise-en-sonore or the auditory setting, the actual sonorous environment, spatial organisation of ambient sounds that the listener experiences – a setting that in turn influences the verisimilitude or believability of a film that the audience hears.
7. 'Headroom' means the amplitude above a designated reference level that a sound signal can handle before it distorts or clips.
8. See: interview with Aloke Dey in Chattopadhyay (2021), a collection of interviews with film sound technicians from India.)
9. This term is widely used in the South Asian film industry. It is an abbreviation of synchronised sound recording made on location during shooting. This, as I discuss later, meant that sounds were recorded in synchronisation with the image on site.
10. See: interview with Anup Deb in Chattopadhyay (2021), a collection of interviews with film sound technicians from India.)

DIGITAL SURROUND SOUND AND THE MIMETIC SITE

11. Sergi (2004: 20–21).
12. Sonnenschein (2001: 47).
13. Biancorosso (2009: 263).
14. Referring to the direct sound recordings made in cinema between the 1930s and the 1950s.
15. The analogue monophonic sound production era conveyed some observed and recorded evidence of the fictional site through synchronised means with an aesthetic of realism and later the dubbing era induced the somewhat remote and site-unspecific conditions in the auditory setting via dubbing and sound processing, as well as the non-inclusion of ambient sounds into the scheme of sound organisation.
16. Rajadhyaksha (2007: 1).
17. This perspective on 'colouring up' with ambience resonates with Brian Eno's conceptualisation of ambience as 'a tint'. See: *Music for Airports* liner notes available at http://music.hyperreal.org/artists/brian_eno/MFA-txt.html
18. See: interview with Dipankar Chaki in Chattopadhyay (2021), a collection of interviews with film sound technicians from India.
19. Rajadhyaksha (2009: 10).
20. Part 2, Chapter 5.
21. Kerins (2011: 53).
22. See: interview with Bishwadeep Chatterjee in Chattopadhyay (2021), a collection of interviews with film sound technicians from India.
23. See: interview with Anup Dev in Chattopadhyay (2021), a collection of interviews with film sound technicians from India.
24. Kerins (2006: 44).
25. Kerins (2006: 44).
26. Mohler, Di Luca and Bulthoff (2013: 90).
27. See: interviews with field recording artists in Lane and Carlyle (2013).
28. As an example, American sound artist Bill Fontana uses Accelerometer and Danish sound artist Jacob Kirkegaard uses various kinds of contact mics.
29. Examples include the field recording works of Andrea Polli and the NASA sound archive.

PART 3

ON LOCATION AND OTHER STORIES

Basically anything seen through a camera limits the view of a spectator to what's visible through the lens, which is always much less than what we can see with our own eyes. No matter how wide we make the screen, it still doesn't compare with what our eyes can see of life. And the only way out of this dilemma is sound [. . .] The viewer always has this curiosity to imagine what's outside the field of vision; it's used all the time in everyday life. But when people come to a theatre, they've been trained to stop being curious and imaginative and simply take what's given to them. That's what I am trying to change. (Abbas Kiarostami in an interview with Jonathan Rosembaum (Saeed-Vafa and Rosenbaum 2003: 114))

PART 3

ON LOCATION AND OTHER STORIES

8 LAND, FIELD, MEADOW

In my childhood, my family had a house in the countryside beside a seemingly endless expanse of land. The area broadened as it lengthened until it reached the Jharkhand peninsula in eastern India. Where the land touched the hills, the borders between grassland, hills and clouds merged into a layered landscape. This enormous, empty space in front of the house sounded different throughout the day. Mornings were occupied by birds. I would wake up to their symphony, finding their vibrant song cathartic. This collective sounding, spanning the greener areas, continued for hours until midday. How many birds were there? Numerous, I would guess. Many of them were local and acclimatised to this rural hinterland and its inhabitants. Others were less known, their communicative calls those of countless migratory birds. Alongside the birds, cattle were also prominent. They would call to one another over a patch of breakfast pasture. As they moved, enthusiastic for the morning, their sounds merged with those from the small metallic bells tied around their necks that rang in tune. Anyone standing in the vicinity would hear the cowbell orchestra extending to the horizon. As the morning aged, various machinery and traffic noises joined the transitory landscape of sound. Rickshaws and bicycles run by daily labourers peddling for work added their high-pitched, navigational bicycle bells to this evolving auditory setting. In the afternoon, when working women returned home from the factory, they would sing in chorus, their traditional songs merging with cricket sounds rising from the darker edges of grassland. As night fell, the landscape would become mysterious, its apparent silence interrupted by frogs, insects and the distant drums of tribal villages.

These shifts in the sound environment were simultaneously dynamic and constant.

A few of the later sequences from Indian filmmaker Ritwik Ghatak's swansong *Jukti Takko Aar Gappo* (Reason, Debate and a Story, 1974) were shot in this region on the tribal-dominated Bengal-Jharkhand border. A rich combination of crow, cricket and insect sounds were captured and reflect Ghatak's socio-politically sensate ears towards the then dying ultra-leftwing 'naxalite' movement. As the protagonist Nilkantha Bagchi – played by Ghatak himself – unleashes a drunken monologue about the country's and region's political crisis, his voice reverberates in the open, waiting landscape, reflected by the silent hills surrounding the grassland. Later, police gunshots engulf the setting, assassinating both the main protagonists, Nilkantha and the naxalite activists, who had been hiding in outlying trees, and the meditative landscape. After the loaded conversation between Nilkantha and the naxalite leader is abruptly ended by the violent encounter, the two surviving lovers, who were nomadic Nilkantha's companions, communicate through their intense breathing that joins other ambient sound from the grassland and forest.

Landscape in Metamorphoses (2008), my sound artwork, draws on recordings made in the same region – more precisely in the Tumbani area near the Bengal-Jharkhand border – between 2005 and 2007. The project focuses on the complex, socio-politically laden natural landscape, where pockets of tribal populations had once settled. The area has recently and rapidly developed into an industrial zone, which has transformed the picturesque environment into a wasteland. This profit-making industrialisation of the grasslands, fields and meadows has destroyed the integrity of the people who were connected to their landscape and dependent on it for their livelihood. *Landscape in Metamorphoses* records and reconstructs this dying landscape within a soundscape composition, combining phonographic recordings from the area and subsequent creative sound design into 'musically' constructed ambient sound layers and samples. The extensive phonographic material, collected over several visits, forms a digital archive that was used as the composition's source material. The work is primarily an auditory mediation of place created through the artistic transformation of an acoustic landscape into an electroacoustic environment.

Tumbani has undergone gradual transition over time. After the Second World War, the area has been affected by several notable changes: India's urban expansion; the construction of inter-state roads, a new residential school and an airbase; and the depletion of natural granite resources. Since then, this small region has been designated a special economic zone (SEZ), which produces a large amount of stone chips for the concrete industry, employing both the landscape and local people in this industrialisation and development process. In being transformed from verdant pastures into an SEZ, Tumbani is representative of many other similar localities in India that are slowly yet inevitably succumbing to a fast-changing, globalised world. Tumbani's cultural roots and traditions have been displaced and replaced by the homogenised appearance of a typical industrial zone. The area is an interesting case of cross-fertilisation – industrial development has changed the land yet seemingly improved the livelihood of what Raymond Dasmann calls 'ecosystem people' (Dasmann 2002), who traditionally relied on the natural environment for their everyday sustenance and material needs. However, the holistic idea that both land and livelihoods can be developed is debatable; questions need to be raised about how and in what way the landscape and indigenous people are adapting to industrialisation processes and what the likely consequences will be. Moreover, the effect of development in Tumbani is not homogeneous – change is not evenly distributed nor evident throughout the entire region and evidence of change from earlier times and more recent transformations are simultaneously apparent. For example, traditional tribal practices are gradually fading away under the pressure of changes to livelihoods. Only fragmented parts of the community still perform ritual chants within the overwhelming soundscape context of popular film soundtracks on the radio, smartphones' caller tunes, or in TV soap operas. School buildings remain empty most days while a thriving marketplace indicates a developing transaction-based culture.

Landscape in Metamorphoses is not only a sonic representation of a transfiguring landscape but also a commentary on the decomposition of personal, location-based memory-associations; I grew up in Tumbani. As a boy, I was part of the group of 'outsiders' to the area influenced by urban development. I could have easily been described as one of the 'biosphere people' (Dasmann 2002), living within a culture that explored and exploited natural resources for development and profit. This gamut of people found its own place within the landscape, with a warm and sincere yet shaky and ultimately futile interaction with the indigenous community – the outcome has been the slow urbanisation of grassland pasture, which has left behind significant sonic memories.

Throughout my formative years, I experienced a comparably slow and intrinsic transformation of my personal relationship with the location; as an adult outsider to the land and ecosystem, I observed how the audiovisual environment of the place is continuously being reshaped under industrial, urban and global influences. At the same time, I experienced my role shift from participation to performance. These experiences were qualitative rather than quantitative and, in this manner, catalysed my development as a sound practitioner, phonographer and field recording artist. I felt motivated to return, revisit and rediscover the area. My visit felt nostalgic. I missed the songs that the tribal workers used to sing on their way to work that were no longer performed. I noticed the earth-grinding machinery from a stone factory reverberating in the 'background' of the landscape, engulfing the breathing sound of endangered insects. From the very moment I started to make field recordings, I felt it was my artistic responsibility to recreate the 'experiential location' I remembered from my childhood. The phonographic expedition and artistic process therefore sought to investigate how the topography of my childhood had been transfigured into a different ecosystem, which in turn questioned the social and political issues embedded in the current land use. This was the very question that had driven the region's ultra-left movements historically. These same complexities sensitised my work, driving the field recording to be not just posited here and now but derived from a historical consciousness around the site. The pro-active gathering of environmental field recording in remaining natural habitat was attuned to the passing of time, where traces of manifold realities were listened to. Land and environmental art critics and curators Jeffrey Kastner and Brian Wallis note: 'Among the many relationships that define the human condition, the individual's connection to the environment is primary [...] We aspire to leave our mark, inscribing our observations and gestures within the landscape, attempting to translate and transgress the space within which we find ourselves' (Kastner and Wallis 1998: 11). Resonating with them, noted historian Jacob Bronowski in *The Ascent of Man* (1973) underscores that as humans, we are indeed ingrained in our landscapes, knowingly or unknowingly. Whether field, meadow or grassland, these locations function as sites for human intrusion. They are spaces we occupy, perceive, transform and personalise through the agency of cultural practices. The media art project *Landscape in Metamorphoses* responds directly to this idea of inclusive listening to the essence of a place by attending to the locative ambient sounds.

Many film sequences use open fields, meadows and grassland as auditory settings for narrative to unfold. Often the depth of sound that would be present naturally in such sites is not considered part of the filmic space. Only a few elements are usually allowed to enter through a rigorous process of noise reduction and filtering. Master filmmakers struggle to compensate for this loss. Sergei Eisenstein's first sound film *Bezhin Meadow* (1937) was banned by the Russian authorities for its daring formal experiments. Later, its final print was destroyed by bombs during the Second World War. Looking at the still images shot during the making of the film and other surviving materials gives a sense of Eisenstein's mystical and poetic realism that he wanted to delineate by using direct sound. His approach was chosen to explore the detailed description of the eponymous meadow where the principal narrative takes place in Ivan Turgenev's original short story that inspired the film. Sixty years later, Russian filmmaker Alexander Sokurov made *Mother and Son* shot on location in another meadow setting. The outdoor sequences of this film are literally blowing in the wind. A complex and resonant layer of ambient sounds – interweaving a number of site-specific elements such as wind through the meadow, birds flying by, distant bells and a passing train – makes the sonic experience enriching and emotionally compelling. Such an affective atmosphere is constructed by the sheer presence of the meadow as a sonic environment, in all its detail and depth. The auditory setting resonates with the emotional concern that the son has for his ailing mother, who both live in a cottage by the meadow. The audiovisual relationship can be understood as contrapuntal, since the nature in the meadow is vibrating with life – wind blows powerfully through the meadow carrying a number of sonic traces of the locality such as church bells and forest murmurs, while the view of the dilapidated house and two characters are laden with a sense of devotion, and surrender. The depth of field in the ambient sound charges the setting with deep sadness and loss due to the mother's ensuing death. Simultaneously, the spatial dynamics of these environmental sounds leave the auditory situation open for transcendence beyond loss by connecting the here and now with the ethereal and eternal. The density of ambient sounds keeps the frames open, which are often distorted by deliberate reflections that make the image precariously unsharp and mysterious. The asynchronous and contrapuntal relationship between ambient sounds (natural, mimetic, deep, dense, layered and alive) and the sparse and unnatural moving images (diegetic with characters apparently oblivious to the lush, green nature and movement of life) makes the audiovisual synthesis mysterious and poetic. The meadow as a sensitive, lyrical auditory setting allows the narrative of death to be transcended, making the film deeply emotive and moving.

9 FOREST, JUNGLE

When I was seven years old, I once got lost in the forest. I had been following my father, who walked faster than me, on our way through the trees behind our house to meet someone in the tribal village. At a certain point, I realised that I couldn't hear my father's footsteps in front of me – sounds that I had been tracing while looking around in curiosity. I had been taken by the sunlight as it played on the leaves and butterflies as they passed by in solemn unison with the green leaves and dark tree branches. Then, I found myself alone. The murmurs of wind blowing through leaves and the friction between movement and stasis had already drowned out my father's footsteps – my lone sonic navigational tool in the forest. Their absence accentuated other sounds. The intimate whispering wind carrying news of fallen leaves, its intensity and proximity suddenly sounded ominous and dreadful. Surrounded by this maze of sound, I lost my sense of orientation and security. I wanted to escape this estranging sonic immersion to find familiar voices that would ground me. By retracing my footsteps, I gradually found a way out of the vibrating forest. My guiding force had been a heightened relationship with the forest's sound world and my isolation. Ambient sounds and the reflection of my own anxious voice among the dense trees had allowed me to navigate through the labyrinthine green and escape.

Much later, I went back and recorded the forest. The recordings recalled my childhood memories of a maze-like space. This time, however, clarity prevailed. The leaves still moved at their own pace and the murmurs still whispered in my ears, the tree branches still cried out in pain while moving in the gentle breeze, but they didn't sound oppressive. They sounded present and assuring. Perhaps, my listening has come of age, bringing with it maturity in sonic navigation through forest-like sites.

Some early examples of films set in the forest or jungle are Merian C. Cooper and Ernest B. Schoedsack's *King Kong* (1933) and Cedric Gibbons's *Tarzan and His Mate* (1934). Both of these films were shot on location, mostly with direct sound mixed in monaural, which was a production norm at the time. However, site-specific sounds were rarely used in these films. Likewise, the sites – as in the jungle, for example – have not contributed much to the construction of the auditory setting within the filmic space, which is dominated by a focus on the protagonists and their voicing bodies. In *King Kong*, it is the animated beast and its overemphasised roars accompanied by a continuous dramatic musical score, and companion voices in *Tarzan*, that are central to the diegesis.

In Satyajit Ray's *Apur Sansar* (The World of Apu, 1959), the protagonist, Apu, sets out into the world after the sudden passing of his dearly beloved wife. The pain of his loss makes him numb. He attempts suicide, stops talking and taking care of himself, withdraws from society and leaves his job, his house and familiar city for a nomadic existence for many years. In his wandering, he passes a roaring sea and encounters an unknown forest. He aimlessly roams through the dense array of trees as the smaller details of flora and fauna appear in front of his lost, melancholic eyes and reluctant, tired ears. Unseen birds continue chirping, portraying the impenetrable trees as reverberant and transcendental. A musical score consisting of flute and other wind instruments lifts the scene to a level of mystic realism. However, the music does not drown out the birdsong and forest murmurs. The musical refrain is grounded in the here and now by accompanying natural sounds, which provide a glimpse into the protagonist's state of mind while going through a very difficult and slow healing process. The auditory setting of the forest with the birds, insects and otherworldly murmurs is constructed in monaural sound. The production has a direct sound ethos that keeps much of the pro-filmic space's pilot or guide track from the forest site as film space elements for its mise-en-sonore, representative of the protagonist's outside reality. This reality, as perceived by an emotionally traumatised Apu, vibrates incessantly with the full force of life and its many mysteries. The uplifting flutes in the musical score merge with this reality. Apu responds by opening up his tormented soul for reconciliation with nature. When Apu finally arrives at the edge of the forest, he finds a valley between three mountains. There, he sits down in silence. His face looks relatively absolved though still sad. As the bird and insect sounds from the forest die down, a distant breeze carries them to the horizon where the sun is setting; the musical score recedes to strings and a few wind instruments. Apu takes out his unfinished novel from a worn bag. He tosses the novel's loose pages one by one down the valley. The paper flies away silently accompanied by the sounds of a gentle breeze. Apu has completed a phase of his life, freeing himself from painful memories, hopes and youthful dreams towards greater acceptance.

Francis Ford Coppola's magnum opus *Apocalypse Now* (1979) was shot in Vietnam's jungles. Unlike the makers of a typical, popular Hollywood war film, Coppola and the film's sound designer Walter Murch transformed their tropical jungle site into a nightmarish auditory setting that critically comments on war and its horror rather than relying on a simple, straightforward narrative delivery. Murch used a palette of recorded ambient sounds to create a stereophonic sound environment that at times appears hyper-real and at others surreal as it suggests the trauma faced by American soldiers in the Vietnam War. In order to treat these ambient sound layers as vehicles for generating fear and trauma in situ, Murch strips them of their realistic associations to restructure them like *musique concrète* – the musical treatment of environmental sounds. He 'took those realistic sounds and deconstructed them on synthesizers'[1] in order to engage the audience on a visceral and sensorial level, much attuned to subconscious fears and uneasiness. This affective quality is achieved by stereophonic mixing that helps radically widen the mise-en-sonore's scope; Murch admitted his excitement at moving from the monaural mixing in his earlier works to stereo sound for the first time in this film. In a number of jungle sequences, this kind of quintaphonic or six-track stereo mixing can be heard, which was novel at the time. Like a grid, a complex layer of ambient sounds – such as the wing beats of a bird flying away, distant birdcalls, insects at close proximity, continuous cricket sounds, an intruding wind and distant, human-like voices – are mixed with low-frequency rumbles like music, which surround the ears from two sides. Through this evocative auditory setting, the jungle emerges as a primeval creature, much like the tiger ready to pounce that suddenly appears from the jungle in a sequence reminiscent of a panic attack – distilled personification of the horror that is.

In Alexander Sokurov's *Mother and Son* (1997), a grieving son is waiting for the imminent death of his mother. After feeding his bed-ridden mother for the last time, he leaves the cottage, crosses a field and then walks into the forest. There, he roams aimlessly and then lies down on the ground. The surrounding forest creates an auditory setting for solace: the intense wind blowing through the silent trees sounds like a comforting murmur; a stream of water, flowing through the forest, takes away his pain; a few birds pass by asking after his well-being; a friendly fly appears from a distance. The horn of a distant train intrudes on this setting, marking the presence of human civilisation with anthropogenic life and death. The sound of a bell follows. The wind intensifies. He comes closer to a tree and leans on its trunk. In this diegetic sublime auditory setting, a non-diegetic musical score intervenes – a lullaby of his mother's, which blows like the ethereal and ephemeral wind, moves sonically up and down, appearing and disappearing. Enclosing his face with his hands on the tree, the son starts to cry. The sound of his crying is posited centrally within the mise-en-sonore alongside the stereo wind and off-screen lullaby, softly embracing the frame. The son's deep and ineffable sadness is accommodated by the larger scheme of things, the passing of the world, of time and of nature as is.

In a sequence from the second segment of Apichatpong Weerasethakul's *Tropical Malady* (2004), a soldier lost in the forest encounters a tiger representative of a shaman legend of the forest in the depths of night. A tension situation develops through this contact, which according to the author of this cinematic experience is sexual, since the tiger is the alter ego of the soldier's lover, Tong. This sense of ineffable tension is complemented by high-resolution, unrestrained, synchronised recordings of ambient sound from the forest, including shrill, high-frequency insect and cricket sounds that underscore the auditory setting's sense of sensuality and bewilderment. As Philippa Lovatt writes, 'the sound of the environment is often so dominant that it dismantles our reliance on the verbal or the linguistic to ground our understanding of what is happening in the narrative, and instead encourages (or rather insists upon) an embodied, phenomenological, engagement with the sensuality of the scene' (2013).

Lars von Trier's *Antichrist* (2009) uses a similar strategy that deploys ambient sounds mixed with drone-like music to create a sense of unease, which is almost like a horror soundtrack as Kristian Eidnes Andersen, the film's sound designer, states in an interview.[2] I invited Andersen to give a master class on my course 'Sound Design for Film and Video' at the University of Copenhagen in 2013.[3] He presented a number of clips from the film and informed my students that he and von Trier had gone to the forest locations a few months before they began shooting the film. They had gathered organic material, such as dry wood and fallen leaves, from the location itself and site-specific sounds to compile an eerie sound design that suggests things are going wrong in the constructed auditory setting. The placement of ambient sounds in the surround sound environment was crucial, as they often appeared from the rear channels to envelop the audience from an unusual position creating disquiet and trepidation.

In the realm of sound art, there are a handful of works based on field recordings made in the forest, woods or jungle. Marc Namblard's *F. Guyana* (Gruenrekorder 2017) was realised using recordings made in forests from coastal regions of French Guiana in November and December 2014, 2015 and 2016. The environmental sounds gathered are not ordinary, nor mundane. They are rich with the focused study of a single location unhindered by any interference from the outside world or the artist himself. These recordings are infused with the spirit of a pure form of phonography without any editing and post-production. The captured auditory setting of French Guiana is well defined and full of vivid detail. The intricacies of the location are revealed through rigorous concentration on particular elements of the forest, including bees, cicadas, monkeys and crickets, along with the cumulative forest drone that roars throughout the work.

Chris Watson's *Stepping into the Dark* (Touch 1996) is an engrossing collection of field recordings made in rainforests. Watson recorded diverse auditory settings in the South American rainforest, Kenya's Mara River and at Moray Firth 'in all their complicated, occasionally abrasive glory' (Cooper 1996).[4] Watson states in the note on his Bandcamp page of the release:

> In recent years I have noticed that some of the locations I visited as a sound recordist displayed remarkable and particular characteristics. These may be sparkling acoustics, a special timbre, sometimes rhythmic, percussive or transient animal sounds. Without a doubt, playing a recording made at one of these sites can recreate a detailed memory of the original event. Also, as others have described, there is an intangible sense of being in a special place – somewhere that has a spirit – a place that has an 'atmosphere'. These recordings avoid background noise, human disturbance and editing. They are made using sensitive microphones camouflaged and fixed in position usually well in advance of any recording or animal behaviour. The mics are then cabled back on very long leads to a hide or concealed recording point, the aim being to capture the actual sound within each particular location without external influence. Sites are discovered by researching local natural or social history, by interpreting features on a map or through anecdote and conversation with people about their feelings for or against particular places. This also includes flora and fauna, local time of day, the weather and the season. The recordings are the atmospheres of special places.[5]

Likewise, the release's twelve unedited tracks capture the natural setting of the dense jungles and the tropical rainforests in raw field recordings, which focus on the layered overtones made by flies, tree frogs, moths, fishing bats and other lively actors of a typical tropical rainforest that orchestrate the collective sounding of such natural locations.

Notes

1. See: http://designingsound.org/2009/10/09/walter-murch-special-apocalypse-now/
2. See: https://www.youtube.com/watch?v=-UTEVJHnxk0
3. The courseware is available here: http://budhaditya.org/teaching/
4. See: https://www.allmusic.com/album/stepping-into-the-dark-mw0000189394
5. Watson 1996, further reading: https://chriswatsonreleases.bandcamp.com/album/stepping-into-the-dark

10 VILLAGE, RURAL ENVIRONMENT

The village and rural environment are traditionally recognised as the cohabitation of nature and culture based on a sustainable ecological relationship between humans and non-human entities, flora and fauna, and humans and animals. In villages, humans don't live as estranged from natural environments as they do in cities. However, we have arguably entered the Anthropocene epoch, a new geologic era defined by unprecedented man-made disturbances of earth's ecologies (Morton 2013). In this era, the ecological integrity of rural environments and village surroundings is endangered, primarily in re-emerging economies of the Global South, due to governmental pressure for rapid growth and development. Massive structural and geological transformations impact the sonic environments of rural sites and villages. For example, Asia is undergoing increasingly intense land development to facilitate rapid urbanisation (McKinsey 2010). As a result of this speedy man-made growth, many of the greener pastures around South Asian, Chinese and Southeast Asian village areas and rural hinterlands are becoming post-industrial zones, whose environmental and sociocultural ambiance is being heavily affected. As a consequence, rural sites are transmuting into homogenised wastelands. Such complex, unfolding transitions affect traditionally rich cultures. In South Asia, numerous rural sites are undergoing such intense, multi-layered, developmental processes that their unique sonic environments are being suffused with mutating character. Some of these village sites have been appropriated as fertile sites for film and media artworks.

Decomposing Landscape (2015) is one personal example. I developed this particular media art project by recording extensively at specific rural sites in eastern India. The work creates a discursive auditory setting to facilitate a contemplative and in-depth observation of rural habitats and their sonic environments, which are in transition due to economic development; as corporations profit from this arrangement, villages and indigenous communities are displaced and dispossessed. The outcome of the project includes an Ambisonics composition – site-specific, phonographic field recordings arranged and diffused through multi-channel spatialisation, a multi-channel sound and video installation, and a virtual reality piece. The collected recordings form a digital archive, which was used to realise the work. The project aims to share an aesthetic interpretation of the gradual transfiguration of developing societies to the wider public. It employs: post-digital[1] music technology and hybrid methodology using old and new audio applications and tools; aesthetic inclusivity, combining retro and current techniques of sound processing; and artistic freedom in arranging sound in an Ambisonics surround sound spatial environment.[2] The work's sonic representation of specific rural sites reconstitutes the actual environment of the landscape through the creative spatial composition process that followed a longer process of attentive site-specific listening and gathering field recordings of environmental sounds. The compositional strategy consists of artistic interventions: taking intricate site-specific multi-track field recordings and transforming these recognisable environmental sounds through studio processing. The sounds are spatially diffused into a blurry area between musical abstraction and recognisable sonic evidence of the ecologically affected rural site. The question is how much spatial information, in terms of the recorded environmental sounds, is retained and how much artistic abstraction and mediation is deployed during production practice? This process needs to be examined in order to better understand mediation in field recording-based media artworks that intend to register and recount rural sites endangered by anthropogenic intervention.

The same question is valid for films that develop a cinematic soundscape of a rural site via a chosen method or combination of methods: location-based recording (called a pilot or guide track), direct sound, sync sound in the digital era or more asynchronous studio-based sound production, using a sound bank of ambient sounds and Foley. Each selected sound element forms part of the film's site-specific auditory setting. However, the actual rural site's sonic environment and auditory situation is much more detailed and diverse. The film track doesn't take everything but creates its own soundscape, which is reproduced when screened. Each filmic reproduction plays with the fringes of memory, invariably shifted from the aural experience of actual sites.

A vast sonorous space continuously surrounds us. For example, as I write this chapter during my extended residency at Copper Leg in rural Estonia,[3] cut off from the outside world during the COVID-19 lockdown, the most prevalent sound comes from my laptop fan blowing out air. It is mixed with the ambience of a morning breeze entering the window of my cottage accommodation. These are the closest, immediate sounds, other than my own breathing and the occasional keyboard hammer. Further away, as I extend my hearing's depth of field, I can discern the distant sounds of traffic on the main road in this otherwise silent village location. And yet no space is ever truly silent, as the lower frequency of the room's tone itself, disguised beneath the sound of my laptop fan, can testify. Sound sources need to be located through active effort, otherwise they remain hidden from our conscious level of hearing. As I continue listening, I pick up more discrete sound fields: birdsong, grass being mown in front of the cottage, an airplane moving through the clouds and so on. With a subjective approach, my hearing will discount some ambient sounds while paying attention to only a few sounds. If an omnidirectional or binaural microphone with a given depth of field closer to human audition replaces my hearing, it will record all sources to form an inclusive sonic environment of this rural location. While re-listening, I will be able to hear the details from the surrounding auditory setting and will be surprised to find such aural depth. Andrei Tarkovsky's seminal work, and a cult classic of world cinema, *Stalker* (1979) was made around this rural area of Estonia, not far from Tallinn. River Jägala and the Joa village are just a few minutes' drive from my residency – these are the sites where large parts of the Zone sequences of this highly regarded allegorical science-fiction film were shot.[4] In a field recording expedition on this site, now in 2020, I could locate deep drones of unseen grasshoppers, and the sharper sounds from the river entering the secluded and abandoned location of a former hydropower plant. The movements of the water through pipes and tunnels, and through the pebbles, merging with the vibrations of the insects, and the omnipresent air as passing through the sprouts and weedy annual grass, cumulatively sound like an ever-growing composition. There is also a deep and ominous murmuring of absence – as if something was there but doesn't exist anymore. Or was it my imaginary construct of the ambience following the film's composed sonic environment? In one of the most cited and discussed sequences from *Stalker*, electronic composer Eduard Artemiev's atmospheric score accompanies the blurry transition from natural environment to an augmented one on the indolent journey to the Zone. In this transition, almost symptomatic of the treatment, mediation and rendering of environmental sounds generally found in cinema in varied degree, the natural ambiences like the ones I listen to and describe above, and the incidental sounds, such as the rail itself, turn syncopated under an electronic modulation. I wonder, what would it sound like if no such compositional treatment was employed, rather there was an intensive and attentive focus on the intriguing natural atmospheres already existing on the location? As the film's sound mixer Vladimir Sharun speaks of the self-indulgence Tarkovsky used to exercise in his method of filmmaking,[5] it is perhaps no surprise that the site-specific ambient sounds and their aural range and dynamics are slowly replaced by a deeply personal interpretation of the site, and such artistic position renders the film both poetic and prophetic towards the subjects of the post-apocalyptic collapse, human destiny, faith and the capacity for redemption.

Although such aural range is often suppressed in film, some stray sound elements can intrude into the medium's highly mediated sonic environment, carrying evocative narrative meaning. Let us recall the village sequence where Indir Thakrun dies in *Pather Panchali* (Ray 1955): the sound of tree-branches crossing in a low breeze at the village's edge vibrate at high and mid frequencies. Although the sounding object is off screen, the unassuming diegetic effect of its aural texture adds to the ominous death. On the one hand, the sound functions as a kind of prayer for death, a sublime lament to life's end, like a requiem. And on the other, it signifies nature's indifference to death – dry, non-lyrical and unavoidable. At the time of recording, the optical recorder picked up this sound element as stray ambience, which may be perceived as environmental noise to some extent, but at the monaural mixing stages the sound was useful as a means to reconstruct the auditory setting of a death sequence in a village.

In *Ashani Sanket* (Distant Thunder, Satyajit Ray 1973) it is the quintessentially opulent environmental sounds of a Bengali village that contrast with and simultaneously amplify the man-made[6] famine's abject hunger and deprivation. One particular sound keeps permeating the ambience – the sound of *Dheki*, the conventional rice-husking device used in rural India. The sound remains suspended in the air and reverberates throughout the village's mud houses as the demand for rice increases and it becomes unavailable. Tons and tons of rice and other essential commodities were withdrawn from the Bengal region and sent to British soldiers fighting in the Second World War, often when there was excess of food stock. The vain hope of eating one meagre meal a day in rural Bengal is ridiculed by the sound.

Indian filmmaker G. Aravindan's *Oridathu* (1987) examines the arrival of electricity in a rural setting of Kerala. The film focuses on the cultural shock, resistance and general reactions in the village to the slow and devastating processes of modernisation. This development gradually wipes out traditional and ritual sounds such as conch shells played in the evenings from the typical auditory setting of village households. They are replaced with the sounds of electrical lamp switches and lamp-posts. As crows are electrocuted, the village's ambience is absorbed by their fearful cries. The traditional acoustic ecology, therefore, begins to fall apart and is replaced with new sounds. As sensitive filmmaker Aravindan listened carefully to the transformation, his film has become a critique of technological modernity's effects that disturb intricate systems of tradition.

Hungarian film-author Béla Tarr's *Sátántangó* (1994) and *The Turin Horse* (2011) are set in rural environments. In *Sátántangó*, a desolate village and its inhabitants are confronted with displacement and dispossession through endless suffering. The opening long-take with a duration of about nine minutes depicts a large herd of village cattle wandering through the derelict village houses and the muddy road without a direction and then vanishing in the distance, occasionally trying mindless intercourse with each other. Their cry of desperation is lost within an ambient sound of incessant and gloomy drift of wind through the village and a distant sound of church bells, time-stretched – indicating a sense of doom. The shot establishes a bleak auditory setting of hopelessness and the emptiness of the human condition in a post-communist-era East European village. More than this premise, the film questions the idea of leadership, and betrayal of the political saviours stuck in their egotic world. Tarr presents a microcosmic view of the social, political and spiritual collapse of humans.

Is it his deeply sensitive, emotionally and intellectually honest, penetrating and sincere vision that prompts Béla Tarr to stop filmmaking after *The Turin Horse*? In his last film, the paralysing misery and vague foreboding of the human condition is unpacked in another barren village auditory setting. In a crumbling house at the corner of the village, a father and daughter and their prescient horse struggle to survive the days, which seem to be leading towards an impending doom. The almost constant ambience of punishing wind envelops their meagre existence, waiting for nothing. The village receives news about an approaching apocalyptic catastrophe. In this sparse auditory setting of a village, Tarr announces the breakdown of the cohabitation of nature and culture, and the cracks in the ecological relationship between humans and non-human entities and animals, at a point of no return.

Notes

1. I will explain this term in Chapter 20 ('Emerging Trends and Future Directions'), but here it will suffice to state that 'post-digital' is a condition in contemporary creative sound practice within which older mono- and stereophonic practices are converged with, and absorbed within, the three-dimensional surround sound environments.
2. The multi-channel sound artwork was developed during an artists' residency at ICST, Zurich University of the Arts, and, upon completion, was awarded first prize in the Computer and Electronic Music category of the Computer Space festival, Sofia, in 2014. It was subsequently released by Touch, London, in 2015. For further reading, see: http://budhaditya.org/projects/decomposing-landscape/
3. See: https://copperleg.rae.ee/1st-open-call-winter-spring-2020-2/
4. See a BFI article exploring these locations: https://www.bfi.org.uk/news-opinion/news-bfi/features/andrei-tarkovsky-stalker-locations
5. See: http://www.nostalghia.com/TheTopics/Stalker/sharun.html
6. Professor Amartya Sen argued about the British Empire's racially biased colonial policies in India in many of his research publications, such as Sen, A. (1981). *Poverty and Famines: An Essay on Entitlement and Deprivation*. New York: Oxford University Press.

11 INDOORS

As I am back in an indoor urban location, I look for freedom inside the close confines of a room; the walls slowly move towards me, the geometry of my environment remains in flux. The intruding wind and its muffled diffusion of sound through the porous windowpane take over and enhance fragments of silence, even those left over from yesterday. I have nothing to say to the objects within my indoor environment while the car horn disperses outside across the neighbourhood; outdoor sounds provide an essential sense of place for an indoor setting. Reflections of the sound inside the room and its fading residues underscore the nature of interactions with lived and remembered experiences of the outdoors. As a car horn dissipates into the construction sounds of houses being built in the urban neighbourhood, I appreciate how my indoor ambience reflects a conflict between private and public spaces as their sounds intermingle and subtly coalesce within a fertile room tone. I can listen to my desire for freedom inside the close confines of this room and let my thoughts regain their innocence. The walls merge with my skin and the built environment closely surrounds my body. As I search for an exit, another car horn rings out. The moving and static, and the distance between them grow beyond a known arithmetic. They merge into one another and replace my search for freedom. My confinement is defined by the sense of domesticity within this enclosed space. I embrace the sonically approaching walls and enhanced silences to feel secure and tend to ignore the muffled sounds of wind. The window divides the safety and privacy of the room tone from the outdoor ambience of a thriving urban environment, as if the windowpane is the architecturally built border between inside and outside realities. Windows and walls, separating the outdoors from the indoors, are often made soundproof or covered by heavy curtains that sometimes act as soundproofing. Why are ambient sounds considered unwanted noise in a household auditory setting? Is it because the sanctity of the private has a margin of acceptance whereas the public sphere needs to be held back? When someone opens a window and leans down to see and hear what's happening on the street corner, his or her curiosity crosses this margin. This is a moment when outdoor sounds enter the domestic sphere and deliver news, perspectives and views. Is this intrusion unwanted? Does it imply sonic disruption? Or is it part of a sonic flux outlining the transformative ambience of rooms and other indoor sites such as corridors and staircases?

In 2007 I was commissioned to develop a series of sound works by the Calcutta Art Research Foundation.[1] One of these works was based on listening to the indoor sonic environments of Kolkata's middle-class households. I was still a film student at the time and eager to undertake the job as my first freelance assignment. While doing research on everyday household situations in a number of accessible joint families, I discovered that there are differences between the sonic world of households whether they are in north or south Kolkata – the sounds of daily chores, room tone and Bengali accents differ – and yet, as a whole, they represent the soundscape of an intimate and insular indoor life and its dynamics with the vibrant city outside. In recording sounds from early morning to the nighttime, I observed that a certain linearity is maintained from day to day. The sounds in a typical Kolkata household interior are generally generated from the kitchen, spoken words/voices, room ambience, sounds from electrical devices and the intrusion of exterior city sounds. For the project, these sounds were recorded, collated and reproduced as a composition of the sound environment and its dynamics within a changing cityscape. While collecting audio footage, I mostly concentrated on three different households for the specific aural elements they offered. Two of them were in north Kolkata and the third was in the south. Despite studying film, I decided to develop these ambience recordings into a sound-only compositional mix-down, using 'creative sound design'. A composition made from the recorded, everyday sounds of urban households could powerfully evoke the intimate details of domestic auditory settings as living, urban microcosms. The work revealed a precarious interaction between indoor and outdoor sounds due to the intrusion of public sounds into the domestic setting.

Kolkata's continuous urban expansion over the last 300 years has resulted in a diverse, cosmopolitan settlement full of distinctive Bengali domestic life. The northern part of the city is older than its southern part, which has developed into a metropolis within the last 200 years. Throughout this process, sounds have transformed within and outside of household interiors – the aural characteristics of domestic life have shifted and new sounds have emerged such as those from televisions and mobile phones within a backdrop of increasingly less prominent sounds such as those from the radio and gramophone. However, a typical Kolkata household still retains memories of these lost sounds while accommodating newer sounds in its cumulative ambience. In Satyajit Ray's *Charulata* (The Lonely Wife, 1964) the elaborate use of ambient sounds from street-sellers and their aural antics intrude into the drawing room of the lonely wife waiting for the days to pass by lazily. They inform their audience of the secluded and idle interior of an elite 1870s Calcutta neighbourhood. As a period piece, the film captures a number of indoor sonic details, including the archaic grandfather clock, and sounds from the palanquin bearers.

In the last sequence of *Seemabaddha* (1971), another of Ray's late masterworks, the sound of children playing in the small playground outside slowly disappears as the protagonist Shyamal paces up the stairs. His footsteps increase until they dominate the auditory setting. When finally at the door of his tenth-floor flat, we hear only his filtered breathing reflected in the setting's enclosed space. There are other sequences in the film where ambient sound has a crucial role in suggesting alienation and miscommunication between the inhabitants of modern, nuclear family households, and the discontents these engender. Scholars argue that Ray's later films are relatively verbose, relying on dialogue between characters to form the narrative (Sengupta 2007). Indeed, these films lack the realistic treatment of sound that invoked a sense of site or situatedness in his earlier films. Ray's self-imposed limitations due to failing health resulted in his auditory settings becoming increasingly domestic with few outdoor locations. Ray's last film, *Agantuk* (The Stranger, 1991), is a delicate domestic drama, which revolves around the unsolicited visit to a middle-class family in Kolkata from an old anthropologist and world traveller who claims to be their relative. His visit disrupts the household's safeguarded auditory setting with new sounds, utterances, perspectives and a global tone, which call for the interior room tone's reconfiguration. In one pertinent indoor scene, a heated debate takes place between the visitor and a harsh neighbour, a lawyer. The discourse illustrates the differences and intersections between Eastern and Western cultures – traditional, tribal life and modern, technological society, respectively – through its questioning tone aimed at revealing the stranger's intention for visiting. As the debate grows in intensity, the domestic space's harmony – the room tone mixed in monaural with small details, voices and their hollow reflections – is disturbed. The claustrophobia of an otherwise engaging conversation transcends the room as the stranger leaves the next morning for a tribal village for the film's finale. The outside world's entry into the close confines of this interior space, which triggers the curiosity of an otherwise narrow-minded middle-class family, is a profound experience. Providing a setting for unfolding a nomadic life's realisation expanding the site of home is an apt swansong.

This sense of curiosity for the outside world from within the environs of an interior space leads the protagonist in Alfred Hitchcock's *Rear Window* (1954) to discover a murder in an apartment opposite his. The elaborate and complex setting of a housing complex as viewed from the window was constructed inside Paramount Studios. A wide range of ambient sounds bleed into the room. Their continuous intermingling, reflections and residue effects configure the room tone of the indoor setting, where the protagonist, a photojournalist, is confined after breaking his leg. The indoor reflections of outdoor ambience include nearby street sounds, music from record players and the piano, cats and dogs, and rain. They all interact with private conversations and indoor telephone and radio sounds. This coalescence of the private and private locations via the medium of sound, driven by curiosity, places the listener directly in the environment and encourages engagement with the mystery as its narrative unfolds. The cumulative auditory setting sounds verisimilitudinous – as clear and perceptible as lived experience.

Some indoor auditory settings are relatively more contained by the intense proximity of a few characters and their interpersonal dynamics. *The Bitter Tears of Petra von Kant* (Rainer Werner Fassbinder 1972) focuses on a narcissistic fashion designer's bedroom and her obsessive and co-dependent relationship with her assistant; they are the only two characters in the film. This persistent focus on one indoor setting augments the dramatic tension and provides an insular backdrop that reveals the female character's own entrapment within the props of her failed relationship. The stuck sounds become increasingly repetitive and emptier.

As in *Charulata* (Ray 1964), Bengali filmmaker Rituparno Ghosh develops an intimate yet segregated sound world in *Subho Muharat* (2003). The film follows an elderly Bengali woman's acute sensitivity and curiosity for events taking place outside her home. Her world is accompanied by a vibrant, local neighbourhood, a few pet cats, the antics of her outgoing niece and her itinerant phone calls. The cosy details of the interior auditory setting are a mix of street-seller calls entering the room, sounds of the clock on the wall, the cats purring and other sonic oddities, which were all recorded and layered with care in a monaural re-recording and mix based on guide tracks from location recordings – a standard practice in Indian cinema.

In the early days of digital sync sound and Dolby systems, this standard practice was slowly dismantled. *Dil Chahta Hai* (The Heart Desires, Farhan Akhtar 2001) was among the first films to use sync sound. This Hindi film now enjoys cult status due to its refreshing approach, which embraced a sense of the here and now largely provided by the practice of shooting on location with sync recording, followed by surround sound design. Right from the beginning of the film, which is set in contemporary Mumbai, the accurate sound portrayal of traffic is in such contrast to audience expectations and experiences of studio-recorded sound that it places the audience immediately 'on the streets'. A major portion of the sounds used in the film's indoor sequences consists of room tone, a noise-like 'hum' (Holman 2002), which comes from different electrical and other indoor devices. The incorporation of such low-frequency room tones in the ambience was a novel approach at the time, and was made possible by emerging digital technologies. Each indoor sequence, therefore, affords the right perspective and placement of the characters within the mise-en-sonore, which is heard through the reflection of the voices on the walls as well as through the room tone surrounding the audience. In the last major sequence of the film,[2] the synchronised sound perspective manifests in the diegetic use of wedding songs. This sequence is noteworthy for its novel use of diegetic music, sans studio processing, unlike earlier Indian films. By using sync sound at the location of the story-world, the sequence offers ample information to the audience about the site's specificity, which is so well-reconstructed sonically that viewers feel situated within the embodied experience even though it is mediated.[3] Such a renewed sense of realism in the narration of fictional sites has driven the production of several subsequent Indian films such as *Asha Jaoar Majhe* (Labour of Love, Aditya Vikram Sengupta 2014). The auditory settings of these films were produced through the careful spatial organisation of recorded on-site ambient sounds. Set in the crumbling environs of a Kolkata household, *Asha Jaoar Majhe* is a deeply lyrical and sublime unfolding of ordinary lives trying to survive economic recession. The film sensitively observes and carefully listens to the domestic setting of a working couple, estranged from each other due to their different work shifts. The auditory setting was developed by recording rich layers of ambient sounds variously present indoors: the hum of machinery, electrical buzz, singing lessons from neighboring houses, car horns, tram bells from the adjacent street, political demonstrations on the move, crows cawing and the voices of street-sellers bleed into the home's stasis interspersed with cats meowing, radio news announcements and diegetic music on TV diffused through indoor walls, staircases and balconies, and other recognisable ambience present in everyday domestic environments. The careful inclusion and elaborate spatial organisation of these arrays of ambient sounds give this film and others like it a 'gritty documentary feel' marked by an immersive, immediate realism that contrasts with the typical song and dance films from conventional Bollywood. As this film didn't require any dialogue to communicate its content and context it could focus on the ambient sounds that surround the characters, which anchor them to the indoor setting that they live by. *Asha Jaoar Majhe*, like other independent Indian films, represents a renewed sense of situatedness in everyday life through the meticulous portrayal of ordinary sites in contemporary India. Due to their inclusive auditory settings, these sites become substantial characters in the narrative, contributing to a strong sense of verisimilitude within the filmic space.

This sonic spatial shift is inspired by the new wave Asian cinema. Tsai Ming-liang's films, for example, are far from verbal-centric; the voice, which is seldom used, comes across as a mundane layer that does not add much to the cinematic narrative within the overall sonic environment. Ming-liang's *Vive L'amour* (1994) is set in a disused apartment where three characters negotiate their urban alienation in mutual separation. The film begins with a long, indoor sequence without any dialogue, where one of the characters sneaks into an apartment and unsuccessfully tries to commit suicide. His loneliness is exacerbated by loud traffic sounds that enter the closed room. His heavy breathing is ungrounded, floating in thin air, reflected from the walls, suspended like his own existence. The female character speaks to her clients on the phone. Her voice and high-heeled footsteps reverberate inside the room and the corridor of the apartment. The hollow auditory setting of the indoor locations suggests the characters' lack of belonging to these spaces. The film communicates urban alienation, loneliness and ennui through its empty and echoing ambient indoor sounds. *The Wayward Cloud* (2005) also starts with a sequence that lasts around half an hour without one spoken word yet includes a varied layer of ambient sounds. Although verbal silence is not a central aspect of these films, dialogue is not required in their design. They are eye-openers or rather ear-openers to the fact that cinema, through its entire narrative history, has overemphasised dialogue. Importantly, these films allow environmental and site-specific ambience to provide an augmented and potent narrative above dialogue in the auditory setting.

This new trend in film sound practice was intermittently practised by a few earlier filmmakers. Jean-Jacques Annaud's *The Lover* (1992), based on Marguerite Duras's novel, is an early example which creatively used ambience to evoke the emotional complexity of an indoor setting. Set in Saigon, the film explores the love and loss of a doomed romance in Asia's colonial era. In a moment of domestic intimacy, the protagonist listens to the continuous urban clamour outside – people moving carts, murmuring, selling and stockpiling – just beyond the room's silent auditory setting. In a voice-over, she informs the audience that she feels exposed in the private room invaded by public sounds while searching for proximate quiet and the closeness of breathing to express her tenderness. The predicament makes her memorise the room.

Rooftops, balconies and courtyards are transitional locations – sites of meeting between the indoors and outdoors that are relatively more public. Going out onto a balcony leaves a room's interior comfort behind for the chance to meet the outdoors. In my final talk at the American University of Beirut as a Mellon Postdoctoral Fellow, I began the presentation with a recording from my balcony.[4] I wanted to sensitise the audience to the many splendours of everyday sounds that are present on the threshold of home environments and raise awareness of the daily events, which we are indirectly part of. The Mediterranean Sea was a short distance from the balcony and could be heard through the array of buildings. The day was so clear that I could see individual waves. A far ship passed by; I could almost read its name. Sounds appeared as if part of the sunshine. Every voice reflected off the city's many surfaces and arrived with clarity. Traffic, a drilling machine, an electrical hum and a surveillance helicopter all sounded crisp and discreet as I recorded them.

How many film sequences shot on a balcony or rooftop care to capture such exhaustive sonic presence? A select few filmmakers like Ray go beyond obvious sounds to capture and include manifold ambience in their sound design. Take, for example, the rich layers of sound from Calcutta that intrude on the silence of two lovers meandering on the terrace of a house in *Pratidwandi* (1970). The sounds of a dehumanising city overwhelm the lovers' intimate moment on the terrace, and yet they resist immersion through their personal silence, with only their breathing evident. Author Amit Chaudhuri points to Ray's capacity for in-depth listening, 'not just to what his characters are saying but also to the unfolding of life in the next house and street, to the negligible ramifications that the camera can't record but the soundtrack can'. He suggests that it's 'something he learnt from Renoir's *The River*, an underrated film that captures the simultaneity of Indian existence through its extraordinary soundtrack, which is constantly alive to the interrupted flow of what's happening elsewhere'.[5] Ray was present when *The River* (1951) was made in Kolkata during his formative years, where he learnt how to listen to the context of an auditory setting rather than allowing sound to be lost to visual images.

In a similar vein, *L'assedio* (Besieged, Bernardo Bertolucci 1998) captures the indoor setting of a crumbling household in Rome with its two inhabitants, a young, African migrant woman, Shandurai, studying medicine but working as a housemaid, and a British expatriate composer and pianist, Jason Kinsky. The non-verbal connection between these two individuals eventually and incorrigibly blossoms into love inside the cosy yet emptying[6] confines of the composer's apartment. In one sequence, which occurs in the drawing room, their subtle communication through sound takes an ethereal note. Kinsky is working on a new composition and the sound of his piano playing is suspended inside the room full of ambient sounds from a very lively neighbourhood. He is distracted and not in the mood to work. Shandurai is cleaning the room with a noisy vacuum cleaner. As they share glances, full of unexpressed affection for each other, Kinsky starts to respond to the sound of the vacuum cleaner in his next notes, which take more adventurous and rhythmic form. The new work is also influenced by the African songs he overhears played on the radio in Shandurai's room. Shandurai stops cleaning and responds to the composition through restrained body movements, which show that she likes the tune. Theirs is a collaboration via non-verbal dialogue based on intimate listening to affective presence, desire and racial boundaries within the socio-politically loaded context of a demanding outside world, where migrants gather to find work, a place to live and survive in Italy and elsewhere to escape war, famine, military coups and poverty.

For a collaborative media art project, *San Lorenzo* (2008),[7] I worked with Matteo Marangoni to record ambient sound from a historic area in downtown Florence, Italy, for an installation with still images made by the students and teachers from a local school of photography. The project was about personalised approaches to looking at and listening to certain local, urban sites. The images were looped on nine large wall-mounted monitors and the sound reproduced the essential atmosphere in a multi-speaker set-up. Recording sound (or taking images) in a vibrant site demands more than mere documentation when information is personalised. Every ambient sound present at a site has a narrative, which goes beyond the materiality of its presence; this unfolding narrative should be carefully captured to reveal the depths of its occurrence. When I started to record in the area, I realised my listening could be lost to the surface of the auditory settings that had a complex, multiple and intertwined narrative. To record at the site, I needed to get closer to it, experientially as well as conceptually. I simply allowed myself to fall in love with the auditory setting I encountered. The photographers had already dismantled their tripods and heavy analogue cameras. The entire location was left for me to record those sounds that reflected on my senses. However, the act of recording sound (or image) can kill the moment of their perception. Photography and phonography are equally perverse processes of anthropogenic registering and quantifying an alive and ephemeral reality on fixed media – they deal with dead moments. Recording is also the art of reconstructing meaning from the moment. A handy digital camera can reproduce a live moment into a static image. Jonathan Sterne would argue that analogue recording has more advantages than the digital to record a space with micro-detail, in terms of grains, which reflect emotional involvement in further depth. However, sound practitioners commonly consider that digital technology's high resolution enables a greater registration of reality. In the case of sound recording, space becomes time on a recorded track. That's why sound is a time-based medium. Sound can transcend the temporal plane when it is installed/reproduced in another setting if the recording is artistically rendered to reconstitute depth of field and perspectives. Careful and context-aware listening can be an appropriate process for translating a sonic environment into augmented perception. It is much more complicated to achieve the same on recording media, especially when avoiding mere surface capture to maintain the sonic flux. While working on this project, I tried to practise context-aware listening, which not only involved spending time in the area and capturing sound on a digital recorder but also concentrating while trying to 'feel' the microcosmic world of sounding details that the site offered. In downtown Florence, a few enormous buildings were abandoned within the confusion of urban development. One of them had been proposed as a space for art installations. A few local artists/curators visited the building, which had not been opened in twenty years; I went to record the setting for them as a reference. It was a multistorey building with four aboveground and three basement levels. The site's total area measured almost half a football pitch. Inside, there were only remainders of construction material – quite an interesting place for an ethnographic, site-specific recording. Before I arrived, a few photographers had already started working with their medium and large format cameras. I also began engaging with the site, listening intently to the sounding space. Soon enough I realised that the setting was quite scattered in different atmospheric areas and to record them I would have to be within the zone and forget my own presence. A few months earlier, while recording inside the Dalí Theatre-Museum in Figueres, Catalonia, Spain, I also felt that the auditory setting combined a number of interconnected areas separated by specific sound envelopes. A painting can communicate beyond the visual in sound, due to the acoustic space and ambience it covers. For example, *Self-portrait with Grilled Bacon* (1941) sounded quite bizarrely of air-conditioners, cheap digital camera shutters and verbal hisses from people. In the Florentine building, I soon disappeared into darker corners. While exploring the underground levels, I found an area of incredible beauty in the deepest basement– a large foreground of silence was interrupted by water dripping in the background and the floor was covered with ancient fungus that had been drowned in a semi-flood of water. The floor emanated a low frequency. I attuned my ear to its base tones. The entire setting sounded of water dripping onto water. As a sound practitioner, I believe that my religion is listening, and I belong to the sounding space that I can hear – that is my personal geography. I slowly lay down on the floor to be able to hear more and absorb the sound into my body. I started to hear sounds from the water that were radiating towards the wall before being reflected back to form an endless row of gentle, mellow reverberations. It was then that I remembered to use my binaural microphones to keep a registry of this unique setting. When I later listened to the recordings,[8] I missed much of the embodied experience I had had at that enclosed, indoor basement site in Florence.

In films, the indoor sites like basements are usually rendered and reduced to represent primal human emotions, such as fear and degradation. In the South Korean film *Parasite* (Bong Joon-ho 2019), two indoor settings, socially and economically distant from one another, meet through a convoluted narrative, as the characters from the former come to work at and slowly occupy the latter. The first setting is the semi-basement home of an impoverished family living on the edge of town and the other is that of an affluent household situated in a wealthy neighbourhood. The outcome of this meeting is disastrous, resulting in the murder and the physical and psychological damage of several characters.

While the basement apartment, from which its inhabitants constantly dream of escaping, sounds messy and claustrophobic (the room tone includes the ambience from busy streets), the other household sounds clean and sanitised (from the crisp texture of voices and smaller audible sounds), appearing almost lifeless. However, the basement of the second indoor site hides the narrative's underbelly, a disguised and subconscious setting in which the parasitical seeds of the film's climax develop into a full-blown violent conclusion. The film is mixed in Dolby Atmos, which helps to spatially demarcate and underline the diverse ambiences established for the narrative's different settings. However, an abundant musical score eats much of these details.

Notes

1. Founded by an artist network of the Rijksakademie, Amsterdam, and supported by the Mondriaan Fund. See: https://internationalactivities.mondriaanfonds.nl/artist_in_residencies/calcutta_art_research_foundation_14/
2. The film is available online: http://www.dailymotion.com/video/x2j637i
3. See: interview with Nakul Kamte, Sound Designer of *Dil Chahta Hai*, in Chattopadhyay (2021).
4. The talk is available on YouTube: https://www.youtube.com/watch?v=URenKhc41dQ (last accessed 9 April 2020).
5. See: https://www.ft.com/content/d4b1d302-fb82-11e2-8650-00144feabdc0
6. The composer was selling his furniture piece by piece, and finally the piano, to secretly fund the release of Shandurai's husband, a political prisoner in Africa.
7. An abridged version of the work was released by the Phonophon compilation: http://compilation.phonophon.de/kuenstler_tracks.htm
8. The recordings were used in a composition, available for listening here: https://cyland.bandcamp.com/track/watersong

12 RIVERBANK, BEACH, ISLAND

Where land meets water such as at a city's riverbanks or on a seashore, a dynamic encounter between stillness and motion is enacted. Relentless waves crashing on a shore invite land to break away and delve into an unknown realm, a wild nature of abandon. However, the land cannot always move. It is often bound by girders and fences, culture and civilisation. The subtle drama that emerges from this tension (sound-)marks most water sites: riverbank, beach or island. This is a collection of interrelated sites; all of these, however, are situated around water. There are degrees of human involvement in these sites. Some of them could be natural as such. On the whole, I refer to the cityscapes, as in the river by a city, whose banks have been constructed. Island would perhaps be the least humanly constructed. When these sites are recorded on media, the constructed auditory settings provide a glimpse of the conflict between water and human habitat, mobility and stasis, nature and culture.

In 2005 I spent a few weeks in Varanasi (Benares), an ancient city in north India built around the legendary River Ganges. Approximately eighty jetties (*ghats* in Sanskrit) extend the city into the river, providing vibrant meeting places between the built environment and water where fishing boats can rest and people can bathe in the holy water. Crematorium sites are located between some jetties to perform the Hindu ritual of lighting funeral pyres. The most well-known and well-frequented jetty is Dashashwamedh Ghat, crowded with worshippers, bathers, widows, street-sellers, yogis, tourists and fishermen. I compulsively made recordings at this ancient meeting place of the river and the city, and its resultant aural dynamics. The recordings were shaped into my first published work *Benaras* (2006).[1] As one reviewer states, the work comprises 'relatively "pure" field recordings (...) which build arrangements from "real" sounds (water ripples, birds, chanting voices, boat creaks, wind)'.[2] It was a location study with a subjective approach focused on Varanasi's history as one of the oldest cities in the world. I wanted to represent an evocative auditory setting that relates a historical trajectory from elements that have survived over time and those that emanate from the city's development into a quasi-modern environment. I relied on different media to record these elements in mono and stereo, from digital recording to cassette and MD recorders. These multiple levels of mediation are reflected in the texture generated, evoking a sense of decay and survival, retention and loss.

Satyajit Ray's *Aparajito* (The Unvanquished, 1956), the second film of his *Apu Trilogy*, was shot in and around the same Dashashwamedh jetty over fifty years ago. The film opens with a long shot at the jetty. Harihar, Apu's father, offers prayers and religious knowledge. Later, the camera follows Apu as we distinctly hear different areas of Varanasi, where most of the story takes place. As Apu's exploration of the city guides us through intriguing environments, we listen to the riverbank, the water of the Ganges interacting with the city and the social formation around the river. The respective cinematic passages were mostly built with direct location recordings of ambient sounds that provide detailed site-specific sonic information from the depth of field and perspective that was available on location. However, the auditory setting is informative rather than evocative: the sounds are concentrated in the centre of the screen due to monaural mixing; and the film is faithful to the mise-en-scène and visual narrative.

In the hope of overcoming this limitation, Ray used off-screen environmental sounds to expand the sound palette for other films from his *Apu Trilogy* and later works. The final sequences of *Apur Sansar* (The World of Apu, Ray 1959) are situated in and around the house of Apu's in-laws, a dilapidated building on another riverbank, this time in Khulna. Here, Apu once met his wife and love, lost her, and later rediscovers his son, Kajal, there. The off-screen sound of songs sung by boatmen enter the house and merge with the river and the wind's elemental and eternal presence. These sounds set the backdrop for Apu to confront life's mysteries, from love to loss and from death to rebirth through suffering. He comes to terms with his fatherly responsibility in the last scene accompanied by the river's dramatic sounds, wind and the same birdsong from the other films of the *Apu Trilogy*, a rhythmic staccato that sets the tone for the undeniable encounter between times and generations, being and the presence of lives lived and their interconnectedness. The riverbank witnesses this circularity of time as the wind, bird and splashing water coalesce with a momentous musical passage.

Ray revisited Varanasi and Dashashwamedh jetty in his later work *The Elephant God* (1979), made for children. As recording technology advanced to tape-based magnetic medium, a wider palette of ambient sounds is captured from the same site. In expanding and creating diegetic, real-world presence, Ray's use and treatment of ambience respects and recognises the pro-filmic site, giving it prominence within the narration, revealing beauty in the everyday. Béla Balázs's aforementioned proclamation (1985) that sound's role is 'to reveal for us our acoustic environment, the acoustic landscape in which we live' – a statement at the core of this book project – is exemplified in Ray's works, which delineate the possibilities of narrating and revealing intricate details of lived sonic environments and natural auditory settings for future generations of Indian filmmakers and media practitioners. Ray emerged from the synchronised sound tradition of Indian filmmaking after sound first appeared in cinemas in the 1930s with very few followers at the time. However, his sonic sensibility is enjoying an influential revival in contemporary, digital Indian cinema production, reflected in now standardised location sync sound recording. Digital practices facilitate realistic auditory production informed by spatial awareness. Varanasi has become the auditory setting for many other films made during this digital era such as *Masaan* (Fly Away Solo, Ghaywan 2015) and *Mukti Bhawan* (Hotel Salvation, Bhutiani 2016). Both film narratives are enriched by their picturesque riverbank setting, where many sonic shades of life enter as characters – the sounds of cremation fires, constant and primordial water.

However, media artwork recordings of rivers and other water sites go beyond the mere soundmarking of water splashing against built spaces. These works attend to a multitude of other environmental sounds that are present in such sites without eliminating them in the production process. The aforementioned commission I undertook from 2007 to 2008 for the Calcutta Art Research Foundation included recordings of the city's west Ganges riverbanks.[3] The River Bhagirathi, a branch of the Ganges, runs between Kolkata and the older township of Howrah. Kolkata's urban periphery has developed around Bhagirathi and the city's association with the river is legendary. According to Kolkata historian Radharaman Mitra, most of the Bhagirathi ghats were built by rich, feudal landowners (*jamindars*) to create bathing spaces for their own people and room for holy rituals. Ghats were respectively named after the feudal lords who built them. Sobharam Basak Ghat, named after a rich landowner and British East India Company cotton merchant, is clearly visible from Howrah railway station. It is commonly known as Jagannath Ghat after the shrine to the deity made by Sobharam Basak himself. This ghat is marked by many religious activities throughout the day and bathing in the early mornings and late evenings. Nearby Babu Ghat, named after Babu Rajchandra Das from Janbazar, central Kolkata, and built by his wife Rani Rashmoni, is situated at the crossing of Dharmatala Street and Strand Road, and is one of the most active transportation hubs in this part of the city, with frequent shuttle steamers between Howrah and Kolkata used by daily commuters. The jetty is large enough to provide mooring for ferries. It has a small bathing space and a nearby Kali temple. A ghat is more than a mere meeting point of people, water and ferries. It is an organic exchange: the body of water close to a ghat appears caught within a static frame but, from afar, is always on the move. Ferryboats pass by as morning bathers take to the river. A ghat's open space becomes a playground for street children and a holy shrine for religious practitioners. The Ganges consecrates the lives of those who collect its assumedly sacred water. A metropolis can survive urban claustrophobia if water touches the body; a city by a river or sea is habitable when water absorbs the sweat and neurosis of modern, urban life. The Ganges is Kolkata's source of sustenance and the city breathes through the auditory opening of its ancient ghats.

A ghat's ambience is unique yet aurally connected with the city through its vibrant sonic corpus. A wide depth of sonic variety can be perceived on an alert sound walk. The constant sound of water splashing on the age-old city steps merge with innumerable other sounds: the circular railway; boat and steamers that carry people and goods; construction sites; discreet street-sellers; hand-drawn rickshaws; radio melodies from forgotten film soundtracks; and sounds from the other bank in the distance. Sounds from moving trains cross-fade with steamer sirens and merge with Kali temple chimes. Frequent unexpected aural juxtapositions and silences are observed within this complex and multi-layered sonic environment.

In the media art project, these sounds were carefully observed, collected on recording media and reproduced in the studio to provide an aural anthropology of the river setting as a transformative site with manifold acoustic terrains. While collecting audio material, I mostly concentrated on three jetties for the specific aural elements they offer, namely the Babu, Armenian and Jagannath ghats. In order to shape up the ambient recordings of each ghat's setting in a compositional mix-down, I followed a form of creative sound design unlike the strict prescriptions of film sound production. Creative sound design is characterised by the presence of recognisable environmental sounds that invoke the listener's associations, memories and imagination related to the setting. It is an exercise in 'framing' environmental sounds, taking them out of context and directing the listener's attention to it as a representation. The design technique tends to be minimal, involving mostly selection, transparent editing, unobtrusive cross-fading and optimal processing of recorded ambient sounds.

When dealing with transformative sites such as a riverbank or seashore, cinema is more oriented towards a fictional representation than the autonomous media artwork. Even self-proclaimed realists like Ray eliminated directly recorded ambient sounds from his sonic palette. Asynchronously produced sounds are more frequent as exampled by Ritwik Ghatak's film oeuvre. Ghatak's position in Indian cinema is antithetical to that of Ray and his followers. His is a cinema of transcendence to counteract the pain and horror of partition and mass migration. The auditory settings in his films are rather supernatural, melodramatic and not anchored to the dry actuality of the here and now. They often avoid surface realism, seeking many layers of reality instead, including historical, mythical and timeless references. Ghatak's *Titas Ekti Nadir Naam* (A River Called Titas, 1973) is set on the bank of the Titas River in Bangladesh. The view of the river and the languidly moving boats on the horizon form the epic film's mise-en-scène. Nevertheless, the Foley sound of water splashing on the boats and jetty doesn't seem to add to the construction, as it reflects its synthetic studio effect, including room reverb, rather than ambient sounds recorded by the river itself. Ghatak often relied on music's melodramatic effect to propose subjective and malleable diegetic spaces, and in *Titas* he evokes a sense of nostalgia through the use of folk music from the local fishing community. As a reviewer notes, 'Ghatak looks at human relationships alone, as his individuals and the larger social forces run parallel, they remain dissociated within the diegetic space'.[4] He places less emphasis on the representational authority of ambient sound and more on sound effects and music to transport his audience to an affective plane and share his sufferings and despair.

Many cinematic narratives revolve around a boat or ship crossing a river or sea. The moving boat or ship is considered an enclosed but socially alienated site where human encounters can be questioned and probed in relation to a quintessential relationship with water and, therefore, nature. In a symbolically loaded sequence from *Knife in the Water* (Roman Polanski 1962), two male figures engage in a heated and psychologically tense encounter over a woman's amorous attention. A knife has generally little to do with water. Indeed, during the encounter, the weapon plays a fetishistic role as the men fight to gain control over one another, and the sound of water splashing against the boat remains an inert sonic backdrop indifferent to the human obsession about ownership, power and social hierarchy.

Michelangelo Antonioni's *L'Avventura* (The Adventure, 1960) dwells on a similar theme of human relationships on a boat and island in the Mediterranean Sea. Unlike Polanski, who prefers to narrate the psychological states of his characters, Antonioni studies the human condition from a deeply philosophical position and explores the environmental contexts within which his characters operate. Antonioni's use of ambience is more alive and powerful with an impact on his characters and their actions. The sound of the Mediterranean drowns out unspoken words, the telling silences that the characters cultivate. They are often aware of the sea as a natural force and its dehumanising capacities. Within the sea's strong auditory setting and its tumultuous relationship with the land, the complexity of human relationships unfolds for acute observation.

While films by Ray, Ghatak, Polanski and Antonioni integrate environmental riverbank, beach or island sounds into evocative narratives they build, populist and less thoughtful, commercially minded works tend to use such environmental sounds less dynamically and less interestingly. Often, ambient sounds have little to say on their own and their qualities drown under the pressure of a 'nicely told story'. The islands and beaches in films such as *The Blue Lagoon* (Randal Kleiser 1980) and *Castaway* (Robert Zemeckis 2000) are not made into fertile situations for in-depth listening. The Tom Hanks blockbuster was primarily filmed on Monuriki, a remote Fijian island. Touted as a story of survival, the film's environmental sounds, which would have been abundantly present on the island, are scant and hardly adventurous.

On the other hand, some popular films are occasionally mindful of the creative potential that the environment's sounds can offer storytelling's interwoven threads. In *The Beach* (Danny Boyle 2000), Richard, the protagonist, asks his companions, 'Hear that?', and the beach's spectacle is introduced to the audience through the sounds of unseen sea creatures, though throttled by beach party music. In *Dear Zindagi* (Gauri Shinde 2016), the auditory setting of sunny, mellow beaches in Goa becomes a playground for the characters, finding solace and sanity away from their hyper-modern world.

In situations that involve the sea and sounds of water around a boat or ship, the auditory setting is prominent, wild and immersive. However, this sense of being sonically surrounded is rarely experienced in film, be it an artistically oriented or more commercially driven work. Cinema's primary focus often remains with human characters and the anthropogenic realm. The intricate, site-specific impact of water as a natural force over humans remains largely withheld from the cinematic experience. I write 'largely' because a degree of presence is reproduced, as explained in the introduction. Many of the previous examples of films by Ray, Ghatak, Polanski and Antonioni are mixed and experienced in a monaural optical mix. When Dolby introduced magnetic tape-based mixing, which enabled noise reduction and a more dynamic range, as a precursor to Dolby Stereo, even popular films such as *Jaws* (Spielberg 1975) sounded more perceptually engaging and plausible. As one reviewer writes, '[John] Williams' music makes a huge difference in Jaws. But so does the sound of water lapping against a clanging buoy. In that first scene, all the noises – musical and atmospheric – create a sense of isolation well before the low pulse of strings creep in'.[5] In surround sound mixing, the sonic presence of surrounding water and its powerful force is amplified, multiplied and intensified, as exemplified by *Life of Pi* (Ang Lee 2012) made in Dolby Atmos and *All is Lost* (Chandor 2013) made in Dolby Digital. In both cases, digital technology enhances the sense of reality from a simulated auditory wild sea setting: the storm scene in *All is Lost* was shot in a large studio tank – similar to that used for *Titanic* (Cameron 1997) – and later made to appear real. However powerful these films are in terms of immersive storytelling that engages audiences and, therefore, makes a profit, their artistry is still under review in relation to the thoughtful, philosophical and poetic positions they can take in terms of ambient sound.

Notes

1. Audio Art Compilation 03, Gruenrekorder. See: https://www.gruenrekorder.de/?page_id=105
2. Ron Schepper reviewed the work in textura in January 2007, available on the label page: https://www.gruenrekorder.de/?page_id=105
3. Commissioned by Praneet Soi at the Calcutta Art Research Foundation, which is run by the Rijksakademie's artists' network, Amsterdam, and supported by the Mondriaan Fund.
4. See: http://sensesofcinema.com/2017/cteq/a-river-called-titas/
5. Noel Murray writes in *DISSOLVE* magazine: https://thedissolve.com/features/movie-of-the-week/649-jaws-and-the-sound-of-dread-and-wonder/

13 STREET, PUBLIC SQUARES, URBAN NEIGHBOURHOOD

On a hectic morning in a busy street, pedestrians are walking by without looking at one another. They may listen to the footsteps of others, but such listening implies recognition of the social other's existence and encourages public confrontation through eye contact. Such private contact within public spaces, whether streets, squares, parks or public gardens, counteracts the rhythm that city life demands. Many people are absorbed by the acute socio-political aura that urban sites underscore. Sounds of heavy traffic, electrical machinery and electronic devices, directly human-made sounds such as rustling clothes, a cough, discernible footsteps, a car horn being used, a shout carved out from the background – all of these sounds will eventually dissolve into the city's monotone, leaving no trace. Little memory of their occurrence will remain. Everyday urban sounds are indifferent; they alienate by absorbing everything into one great cacophony. City inhabitants may endeavour to survive this sonic onslaught by existing on its margins, immersing themselves in their mediated mobile phone world. A personalised city is an augmented environment of soliloquy that outlines selfhood.

As I listen to the city and its urban sites, my attention is transfixed by a wall of sound. What if I am part of the people passing by? My ears avoid listening to engulfing sounds, except for my own footsteps. I wonder what my fellow city inhabitants might think of me. Do they look at the microphone and see me as its shadow? But my thoughts are not at all sustained. They quickly dissolve into the crescendo of sounds emanating from hand-drilling machines that merge with those of an escalator, just at the edge of interaction. Could the act of attentive listening in a public space be considered madness? If it is madness, why do those with their ears containing silicon plugs observe other passersby? In essence, everyone wants to connect with someone else, to express their empathy, to reach out to someone nearby. How difficult would it be to translate the feelings of that seemingly spiritless girl slowly walking by. She's afraid of the city's clamour, isn't she? Look at that man standing at the crossroads, reluctant to step out into the frenzied street. His steps are suspended as if the air were full of uncertainty today. His remorseful eyes don't know where to rest their perfect glance. Within all the people and objects moving in the street, he remains static and doesn't care to move forwards. Could he be listening to his inner flow of sound and silence? Is the frantic world around him discouraging him from making a mindful navigational decision? His mind is somewhere else. He seems lost by the roadside. His steps hover over the minor chords of the sounding city. Positioned on the boundaries of urban tone, his inwardness reflects the margin of listening experienced every now and then that separates him from the flow and affects how he engages with the city.

Urban sites often alienate sensitive, itinerant listeners. This state of alienation and desire to reconnect are points of entry into my urban field recordings. The media art project *Exile and Other Syndromes* (2016–2019) responds to contemporary discourse around migration, hyper-mobility, placelessness and nomadism (Braidotti 2012; Deleuze and Guattari 1986). The work assumes that these conditions manifest when the perceptual sonic boundaries between the local and global, the digital and corporeal, private and public, and intimate and dehumanising spaces blur, instilling a sense of semantic fatigue (Demers 2009). Based on these assumptions, this project's interactive and generative artwork develops a fluid, sculptural form of sound in closely mediated interaction with sound-generated live visuals. The visuals are derived from scribbles and notes made at various urban sites[1] such as squares and busy streets in densely populated neighbourhoods within a number of European, Asian and US cities. These notes serve as artefacts that make visible the intangible and ineffable contemplations of a nomadic listener. The artwork combines a multichannel projection of digitised visuals generated live on multiple screens with a multi-channel sound installation played through a four or eight channel Ambisonics system or configured for a set of wireless headphones. This specific method of artistic intervention examines how the memory, imagination and subjectivity of an itinerant listener become sensitised to everyday city sounds found within the context of intense urban interaction and navigation. The work relies on the intuitive capacities of listening rather than ontological and epistemological reasoning, evaluations and deduction, which are often used to decipher the immediate meanings of sound. As such, the poetic suggestion allows for an inclusive interpretation of the intersecting sonic environments in contemporary cities. This belief in the inward contemplation and subjectivity available to wandering urban listeners enables the work to reconnect with places, people and environments ordinarily estranged from the immediate here and now and counters the neurosis of contemporary urban living. Particular emphasis centres on the ineffable yet poetic attributes of an expanded mode of listening, which provides a context for exploring the unexpected splendour of everyday urban sounds and their transcendental potential. The emergence of contingent moments in the urban listening experience expands the Cageian idea of a chance composition that creates certain fertile conditions, which facilitate a fluid and nomadic interaction with urban sounds. In exploring these elements, the work approaches the introspective capacity of mindful listening to transcend the barrier of immediate meaning and touch upon poetic sensibilities that create a sense of well-being in the midst of a volatile milieu in contemporary cities. The work responds to the current flux of urban migration and estrangement through an exploration of sound's poetic capacities to relate and reconnect with urban sites. The installation employs field recordings and on-site writings as acts of poetic contemplation that encourage the artist/listener to journey from self-alienation towards self-understanding. The project's methodology reflects the migration, hyper-mobility, placelessness and nomadism experienced in my own urban navigations. Such a self-critical approach manifests in the analytical revisiting of select texts within the piece. This sense of estrangement offers a contemplative distance, which is articulated through both the recording processes and their layers of conceptualisation. Such an approach to thinking through media and mobility may help connect ideas of sound and listening in sites like streets, public squares, and urban neighbourhoods with experiences of everyday mobility and social estrangement.

How are urban sites, which can alienate their listener, captured and presented in cinema? The last sequence of *Of Human Bondage* (John Cromwell 1934) takes place in the middle of a busy street. After the death of a sick and destitute Mildred, the protagonist Philip is finally freed from his youthful crush when he meets Sally, who he wants to marry. As they cross a street, their intimate conversation of being able to devote themselves to one another at last and have a family is completely overwhelmed by ambient traffic sounds. Although nothing of their conversation is heard, their expressions show that their affection is mutual; their intimacy is rendered private in a very public auditory setting. It is only at this very moment that Philip simultaneously becomes part of the public and ordinary life that he was estranged from while living in his head, due to his compulsion for femme fatale Mildred. As they cross the street holding hands, looking into one another's eyes, a matured Philip confesses his love while the directly recorded and unfiltered sounds of a roaring city embrace them.

In *Aparajito* (The Unvanquished, Satyajit Ray 1956), Apu gains a college scholarship that takes him to Kolkata. After leaving the village where his mother lives, he arrives in the city, steps off the train at Sealdah station and walks through busy, central Harrison Road. The auditory setting of downtown Kolkata with its loud symphony of blaring car horns and tram sounds drowns out his presence and the faint sound of the call of one migratory bird. Both of these are insignificant aliens in the city; the birdsong is symbolic of the struggle that Apu will soon face. As he approaches Patuatola Lane, a quieter street marked by the cries of street children, a number of cars drive past quickly, as if reiterating his marginality in this urban environment. From thereon in, Apu prepares himself to confront the alienating auditory setting of a city where everyone goes to try and make a living and some disappear. Will Apu also disappear or will he embrace a harsh life and succeed? His predicament is reflected in the continuous mechanical sounds of the printing press in the workplace where he gets his first job. The sound forms the ambience of his urban life. He writes his first letter to his mother after arriving in the city, 'Dear Mother, I arrived safely! Calcutta is a very big city. I found Akhil Babu's place and he has given me a room. It has electric light. Instead of paying rent, I am going to work on his press.' Later, he spends time by the Ganges, where the sounds of a distant ship signify his longing for further journeys ahead.

When I went to study in Kolkata in 2002, like Apu and many other migrants I arrived by train at Sealdah station. I left the small town where I was born and grew up with high hopes of studying and finding my place in the city. I heard overwhelming traffic, machines, heavy construction site vibrations and the oppressed conversations of migrant workers who arrived from the suburbs in search of work every day. I missed my hometown the most during the relative silence of early afternoons, gently interrupted by the sound of water pumps from nearby houses. I was staying in a small room, just like Apu, and sent long letters home. I felt alienated from my environment; the sounds of machinery could not replace the natural sounds of morning birds and evening crickets from my small town. Much later, when I started to find the ground beneath my feet, I began exploring the urban sonic environment and my individual position within it. The results were the sound and media artworks *Eye Contact with the City*, *The Well-tempered City* and *Elegy for Bangalore*, which examine the trajectories of urban auditory settings in India.

The majority of Indians move from the countryside to settle in cities like Kolkata, Chennai and Bengaluru that are re-emerging from their post-colonial rubble to become megalopolises. The potentially hyper-modernising effects of urban life opens debate about the status of the Indian city's atmosphere, ambiance and general appearance. In particular, spatial dynamics contribute to a broad set of concerns about India's urban planning since its much-deserved independence in 1947 from colonial misrule. But burgeoning urban landscapes overwhelm their rural hinterland by prioritising growth and expansion over aesthetics. Simultaneously, these cities are severely affected by globalisation, hybridisation, digital convergence and, most significantly, decolonisation, in which the old and new are shifting contexts and meanings through constant interpenetration.

Within the present scenario of rampant and sporadic urban development, the active and intense interplay between tradition's complex trajectory and current trends fuelled by economic growth result in the typical perception of Indian cities being untidy and frenzied. As well as being experientially overwhelming, urban planners and theorists associate these contemporary urban atmospheres with words and expressions such as 'unintended', 'continuously thwarted', 'hopelessly inadequate' and 'chaotic' (Bhan 2013: 58). According to veteran urban planners, the disparity between the conceived scheme and the perceived appearance is largely due to urban design being relegated to the margins. Urban planners have come to rely heavily on rapid development and growth while ignoring the fundamental well-being of citizens. The basic tenets of urban design prescribe that spaces nurture a reciprocal relationship between people and the city via creative processes that emerge from a subjective understanding of the urban environment as settings (Waterman and Wall 2010).

This disparity explains the generally syncretic, chaotic and inchoate structure of Indian cities. The effect is evident in the general disposition of urban atmosphere, especially in the composite character of everyday ambience: multiple layers of sound from pre-industrial and pre-colonial eras coalesce with sounds in the post-colonial or, more precisely, contemporary decolonial era. Drawing on the writings of Althusser (1976) and Gayatri Chakraborty Spivak (1988), it can be argued that the historical evolution of a place, its social fabric and atmosphere may not necessarily be linear but a multi-layered, multi-linear or plural process, which is open to multiple influences and peripheral interventions. From this perspective, the idea of social formation emerges, which refers to a society, a social structure at any level such as in an Indian city with all its historical and contemporary complexities. Against a static or nationalistic idea of 'society', the flexible term 'social formation' includes all of the internal contradictions that exist within a city, all of the emerging and disappearing tendencies in social relationships that comprise its ever-evolving atmosphere. Indian cities survived approximately 200 years of largely oppressive, exploitative and deeply damaging colonisation marked by the astounding atrocities wrought by British Empire officers and troops, including economic plunder and genocide such as the 1877 and 1943 Bengal famines and the notorious Amritsar massacre. During and after the painful partition in 1947, cities like Kolkata were covered with screaming refugees suffering from hunger, homelessness and dying – a stark contrast to the serene descriptions of sylvan Bengalese landscapes from pre-colonial literature. Such dichotomies hint at the processes of auditory social formation in many Indian cities.

It is no wonder that a typical Indian city's sound environment is a spatiotemporal cacophony that overwhelms and potentially disorientates the listener. It could be argued that grasping the complex nature of a sound environment by listening to its immediately immersive everyday sounds could be considered a phenomenologically reductive exercise (Cogan 2006). In following this argument, the investigation of a sound art practice approach capable of providing a comprehensive understanding of the historical dynamics in an urban sonic atmosphere appears appropriate. The media artwork *Eye Contact with the City* (2010–2011) and composition *Elegy for Bangalore* (2013), which were produced through extensive fieldwork, provide such examples.

The sensory experience of a city such as Bangalore is dominated by the interaction between urban 'noise', layered in tone, texture and depth, and a broad spectrum of other frequencies, including traffic, machinery, household sounds, architectural vibrations, speech and media devices. A multitude of different sounding objects are scattered over various sites within an urban landscape. According to traditional sound theorists such as R. Murray Schafer, sound abatement is necessary for a balanced soundscape (Schafer 1994). I have argued in my doctoral thesis (2017a)[2] as well as in the introduction of this book – in line with many other sound scholars – that Schafer's approach is non-inclusive in nature and unnecessarily burdened with the ethical ideas of urban pollution and sanitisation (Kelman 2010; Thompson 2004). I maintain here that it is important for the listener to recognise a fuller spectrum of sounds and incorporate it into subjective experiences via 'adaptive perception', a term I use to describe an approach that suggests that sound pollution or an imbalance in the acoustic ecology of any given city reflects a lack of reciprocity. This deficiency encourages playful design and aesthetic mediation between sound sources and the human ear, where the listener's individuality and selfhood are considered important. I further argue that a necessary prerequisite for a comprehensive and inclusive understanding of urban atmosphere is the listener's contemplative detachment from their urban setting. Through this detachment, the listener can gather knowledge about historically constitutive sonic character and atmosphere. Given the specifically chaotic and disorganised nature of Indian cities, it is a challenge for city dwellers to envisage the city in order to mentally speculate on 'hard ambiances' such as architectural outlines. It is therefore necessary firstly to adapt to, in the light of 'psychogeography', the 'soft ambiance' (Sadler 1999: 70), such as the sound environment. The city can be thought of as a circular urban constellation with inner and outer peripheries. Contemplative and mindful listening would then involve a deterritorialised sound-walking from the inner to the outer, delving into spatiotemporal experiences and conjuring up emergent sonic imagery by interacting with and reflecting upon specific ambience and 'auditory situations'.

By listening and drifting through an unfamiliar site in this way, the listener indulges in a mental journey, a psychogeographic exploration in 'an attempt to transform the urban experience for aesthetic purposes' (Coverley 2010: 10). The 'nomadic listener'[3] can excavate a part of the acoustic geography more thoroughly than an everyday city inhabitant/'insider'. This deterritorialised and unsocial position of the listener helps to transform the perspectives of the unfamiliar city into something creatively fruitful and imaginative, which, according to Guy Debord, entails 'playful-constructive behavior' (Sadler 1999: 77). In this media art project, I intended to find an urban imaginary, speculating not only the 'hard ambiance' but also the historical constituents of the (soft) ambiances through listening to the ambient sounds and field recording. Locating ambient sounds was achieved by employing a mode of contemplative listening and exploring the specific artistic potential of psychogeography – where the listening subject can be detached like an onlooker – outside of the social margin – in other words, like an alien or a stranger. Otherwise, in the mode of usually immersive listening in the city, the situated listener will lose the critical faculty of observation, failing to construe the historically constitutive atmospheres. In *The Savage Mind* (1962), anthropologist Claude Lévi-Strauss perceived artists as savages or aliens within society. Such a position can enable the sound artist to access critical ears removed from the everyday, urban grind.

Psychogeography was a primary methodology for the Bangalore project. I playfully engaged with the environment as a nomadic listener. This experimental approach resulted in field recordings from these itinerant encounters that were composed through studio sound production techniques. This trajectory of artistic processes followed my 'lived experience', a personal sonic interaction with the city's shifting atmosphere, which I could not have approached in a cartographic sense. Instead of mapping the immediately unfathomable and indiscernible city to demarcate its acoustic terrain, I acted as what I like to call a 'sonic drifter' – the auditory equivalent of dérive in psychogeographic practice (Debord 1956).

The project culminated in an electroacoustic composition *Elegy for Bangalore*[4] and the audiovisual installation *Eye Contact with the City*.[5] The work's central compositional methodology explores spatial and temporal disjunctures imbued with a keen sense of history. Sounds restored from records and tapes found at a flea market provide insights into the city's auditory history. Field recordings from industrial and construction sites, meanwhile, preserve the contemplation and the poetically detached musings from an urban present, much like other comparable works such as *Sarajevo* (2004) and *Helgoland* (2013) by German sound artist Lasse-Marc Riek – both these works by Riek are developed through urban drifting and recording on site. Likewise, *Elegy for Bangalore* was created from a fluid and malleable process where recognisable, contemporary sounds and historical recordings could collide with one another and find transcendence through interaction. The project evokes the listener's spatial and historical associations. It charts the re-emerging city as it sublimates unsettling and gloomy colonial memories in its contemporary decolonial moment.

The use of urban ambient sounds in film is more straightforward. As Satyajit Ray explains in an interview,[6] realistic urban sounds in his films often replace non-diegetic music embedded with their emotive-escapist overtones, and serve to anchor the spectator in the real world of the contemporary city through these monaural ambiences. In *Mahanagar* (1963), set in Kolkata, the middle-class neighbourhood is brought to life by a rich depth of ambient sounds, including children shouting on the street, temple bells, bicycle and rickshaw bells, and the sound of a radio – all of these sounds exist off screen, creating an expanded diegetic space around the household, which makes the audience feel both situated in the filmic space and aware of an expanded universe at play beyond the frame.

In *Kanchenjungha* (Ray 1962) different areas of Darjeeling are represented with certain recurring, observational sonic details. When ensemble characters from a wealthy family from Kolkata move in and out of one area into another, the 'realistic' ambient sounds, as Ray explains above, change accordingly. For instance, the characters' meeting place in the middle of the town is complemented by layers of multiple, man-made ambient sounds such as murmurs of speech, footsteps, rickshaw and bicycle bells. While the characters are moving towards or away from town, up or down the hill, some sounds stand out, such as a birdcall while the uncle continues his dialogue with Ashoke, the young man. Likewise, the sound of crickets stands out as protagonists Bannerjee and Manisha, a would-be couple, take their afternoon stroll along the hills. As they move from the countryside to the centre of town, the sound of a barking dog fades in, replacing the then distant bird and cricket sounds. These ambient sound motifs are heard across multiple places, overlapping with one another and, in the process, connect different places into a whole, helping to envelop the narrative encounters and evolving relationships among characters. Several location-specific sonic details add particular narrative aspects: the sound of typical Darjeeling horses passing the characters; the bells from cattle as they also pass the protagonists, punctuating their conversation as well as providing a site-specific context that they are in a hill station; and the prominent church bell suggesting a reconciliation between Anima, the family's eldest daughter, and her husband, Sankar. These sounds intersect as the myriad characters perpetually meander through areas, integrating the multiplicity of narratives within different places, all held together by the sense of site provided by Kanchenjungha, the picturesque Himalayan mountain.

The above examples were largely made with direct sound. Concurrent film production in Italy, which extended from the 1960s into the 1980s, was often dubbed. For example, two of Federico Fellini's well-known works, *La Strada* (1954) and *La Dolce Vita* (1960), were shot in urban locations but, as with all of his films, were dubbed in the studio afterwards. Location recording and accurate dialogue lip sync were not that interesting to Fellini and many other Italian filmmakers from this period. The poor synchronisation of film dialogue with its visuals was standard during this era of Italian cinema. Ambient sound was also freed from the burden of being synchronised with the on-screen setting. Fellini scholar Thomas Van Order comments on Fellini's freedom in how he treated ambient sound, preferring to cultivate 'a subjective sense of point of audition' (Chion 1994) in which what is heard on screen represents a character's subjective perceptions and thought stream as opposed to the setting's visible, mimetic reality. However, Fellini was also uninterested in developing parallel narratives with sound through careful design. He seemed to follow a totally asynchronous audiovisual relationship where ambient sounds are deterritorialised and unhinged from their site-specificity, even when depicting real locations such as streets, large public spaces and parks; most of his characters display escapist tendencies. As film scholar Maurizio Corbella notes,

> One of the most important features of Fellini's cinema since the 1960s is precisely its ability to take advantage of this awareness to realize its extraordinary underlying representational power. Fellini used the breaking of the synchronization rule in order to reconfigure the cinema as a new sensorial experience that would suit his dreamlike approach. As a result, asynchronous dubbing of actors, as well as surreal soundscapes, assume a binding role in his dramaturgy. (Corbella 2011: 14)

Urban ambient sound from films produced during the Indian dubbing era (1960–1990s) were also treated with little care and attention. In *Maine Pyar Kiya* (Sooraj Barjatya 1989), Suman leaves her village for a big city. Apart from the sound transition of a train, no ambient sound layer testifies to the noisy Indian city's presence. Sound designer Pramod Thomas sheds light on the prescriptive practices for creating stereo sound mixes in Indian films during the dubbing era that were avidly followed by sound practitioners. Convention dictated that the voice occupied the centre of the screen while sound effects and music were placed in the side speakers on a stereo soundtrack. No place remained for ambient sound layers in this standard approach.

Digital sync and surround sound design transformed the use of multidimensional ambient sound from the late 1990s onwards. It reached a significant high point in *Slumdog Millionaire* (Danny Boyle 2008), which is essentially an Indian production due to the number of actors, writers, locations and technicians the film employed from the Indian film industry. Production sound mixer and location sound recordist Resul Pookutty won an academy award for his work on the sound. He later became a campaigner for the use of sync sound in Indian cinema. In this film, several sequences[7] are shot on location in a Mumbai slum area using multi-track digital sync recording.[8] These sequences portray the complex acoustical environment that Indian urban sites offer. Right from the film's opening sequence in a police station, with its rich, multi-layered rendering of environmental sound in Mumbai coming from the surround channels – front, rear and centre – the audience is provided with a bodily sense of the site's spatial presence (Skalski and Whitbred 2010). For example, the sync recordings of the actor's voice carry the room's dense ambience and detailed reflections on the site. External sequences are brought to life through the immersive quality of ambient sound recorded at the busy street locations within the film.

'Independent' Indian filmmakers, who prefer to stand apart from the mainstream and establish their auteurism, have picked up sync sound as a stylistic feature. Dibakar Banerjee is one of several from this new breed of Indian filmmakers who has used location sync sound to its fullest potential. In *Shanghai* (2012), the raw, rustic soundscape[9] of an Indian city and its familiar phenomenal world is represented 'true to life'[10] through sync sound and surround design.[11] In one film review, Raja Sen highlights the sense of familiarity evoked by the sound strategy: 'The time is now, the location pointedly fictional and decidedly familiar.'[12] Saibal Chatterjee, meanwhile, stresses the sense of place provided by the sound: 'Lensed with great sense of place and occasion [...] *Shanghai* projects the dark, dank, redolent-with-danger innards of small-town India to absolute perfection [. . .] The most striking aspect of *Shanghai* is its marvellous use of sound, both ambient and otherwise, to build up dramatic tension.'[13] In another review, Chatterjee emphasises the atmospheric and convincing use of ambience: 'They embrace the ambience of *Shanghai* with complete conviction, aiding and abetting the build-up of tension and atmosphere.'[14] The sound practitioner's experiential accounts reaffirm these claims. When commenting on the film's sound design, *Shanghai*'s re-recordist, Hitendra Ghosh, says that the surround sound has been used to create 'a very real experience and immers[e] the audience into the director's narrative'.[15] He points to the film's novel approach and a potential shift in contemporary Indian cinema: '[. . .] for the first time you will notice throughout the film that we have not used much of the Foley [sic] sounds recorded in the studio. We have tried to use sound from the location. That's why the feature sounds very real and authentic.'[16] These contemporary approaches in the digital era resonate with Ray and his ethos of real ambient sounds as a primary source of building urban auditory settings.

As with busy Indian cities, other Asian urban locations provide a wealth of ambient sound material for contemporary films. Tokyo is the setting for *Lost in Translation* (Sofia Coppola 2003), which creates fertile ground for the interaction and exchanges between protagonists Charlotte and Bob. Film scholar Maria San Filippo notes that Tokyo is 'an audiovisual metaphor for Bob and

Charlotte's world views'. She explains that 'the calm ambience of the city's hotel represents Bob's desire to be secure and undisturbed, while the energetic atmosphere of the city streets represents Charlotte's willingness to engage with the world'.[17] Their encounter is enlivened as these two sound worlds coalesce. Charlotte invites Bob to accompany her to a private Karaoke party at a friend's place. As they cross the city, Bob's curiosity and involvement with the outside world beyond his hotel's bar increases. However, after their outing, they go back to the safe and sanitised room tone of the hotel, where they have an intimate conversation about life, relationships and the future. The dance across these settings intensifies as their relationship deepens. In the film's final sequence, they meet and embrace in the middle of a busy street as the city immerses them in its sounds – Bob finally breaks away from his reserved nature and expresses his feelings for Charlotte.

An even more detailed handling of urban ambient sound is heard in the Dolby Atmos surround sound environment of Alfonso Cuarón's *Roma* (2018). Set in 1970s Mexico City, the film explores autobiographical content and the city's recent history through the sublime narrative of a dysfunctional family and a housemaid. The auditory setting is the Mexico City neighbourhood known as Roma, where affluent families live in large houses with adjoining garages. Cuarón's cinematic ear closely observes the household at 22 Tepeji Street, Colonia Roma, just opposite the house where Cuarón grew up. The excruciatingly detailed observation of daily street sounds and the internal household spaces slowly exposes an intimate world on a panoramic scale. Why did such a mundane plot and characters need the epic scale of Dolby Atmos? Cuarón wanted to capture the beauty and grace of the everyday. As the author of the script, his ears were attuned to the 1970s urban environment in which he grew up. His approach of such sensitive listening helps to acknowledge the unsung heroes whose voices are usually suppressed due to their indigenous background and language.

Notes

1. The errant listeners interact with various intersecting places during their everyday navigation, often considering and/or perceiving them as spatiotemporally evolving but gradually disorienting 'auditory situations' (Chattopadhyay 2013a, 2015a). The listener may relate to these situations by thought processes (Barwise and Perry 1999; Wollscheid 1996) generated by means of cognitive associations in the context of psychogeographic (Coverley 2010) navigation through the situated sonic phenomena. Essentially subjective, private and contemplative, the itinerant sonic interaction between listeners and these constantly emerging situations as cognitive processes of listening may arguably transcend the ontological and epistemological constraints of sound towards including the poetic contemplations of the listener.
2. Chattopadhyay (2017a): 'Audible absence: Searching for the site in sound production'.

3. My own term used in my article: 'Auditory situations: Notes from nowhere'. *Journal of Sonic Studies* 4.
4. The work was released on German sound art label Gruenrekorder.
5. See: http://budhaditya.org/projects/eye-contact-with-the-city/
6. The interview is available in transcription in my article, Chattopadhyay (2018b).
7. Excerpt from *Slumdog Millionaire*: https://www.youtube.com/watch?v=QII_TAJ 2BBY
8. See interview with Resul Pookutty (2020) in Chattopadhyay (2021).
9. The notion of soundscape (Drever 2002; Schafer 1994) is a point of departure for studying the evocation of site in the sound of Indian cinema as a shift away from the linear film 'soundtrack'.
10. Theatrical trailer of the film: https://www.youtube.com/watch?v=ozitAKOrJVU
11. See the interview with the film's sound designer Pritam Das (2020) in Chattopadhyay (2021).
12. Rediff.com, 8 June 2012: http://www.rediff.com/movies/review/review-shanghai-a-frighteningly-finefilm/20120608.htm
13. NDTV Movies.com, 7 June 2012: http://movies.ndtv.com/movie-reviews/movie-review-shanghai-715
14. *The Sunday Indian*, 8 June 2012: http://www.thesundayindian.com/en/story/movie-review-shanghai/112/36105/
15. Hitendra Ghosh's notes on the use of sound in *Shanghai* on FutureWork's page: https://m.facebook.com/note.php?note_id=382123985181336&_ft_
16. Ibid.
17. San Filippo, Maria (2003). 'Lost in translation'. *Cineaste* 29/1: 28.

14 PUBLIC TRANSPORT

The seat next to me is unoccupied. Someone drops her glance after momentary eye contact. The subtle vibration of the moving train progresses rhythmically; the city's trace slips backwards beyond the partly soundproofed window. Dark, heavy clouds are gloomy in the sky, but I can't hear any incoming thunderstorm. I drop a hint in the hope of opening a conversation with the person sitting opposite to me. In response, the face turns opaque. The look of most co-passengers is fixed on nowhere as if they are waiting for a catastrophe to happen. The shared space in the compartment is speechless. The absence of any preconceived dialogue in the faces around me renders our environment one of soliloquy. Sporadic announcements cause everyone to focus intensely on the disembodied voice, but it disappears, leaving some information about the direction of the train and the name of the next stop in an automated voice to evaporate. What do the boy and woman sitting in opposing seats think about one another? Their numb glances say that they are completely oblivious to one another's presence. As if separated by a pane of glass and joined by loneliness, the young woman moves her glance from the child to concentrate on the open book lying in her lap instead. Interaction is at a standstill. The air doesn't carry any odour of adjacent bodies. Someone turns a page in one moment and another moment enters the gap. The proximate faces look isolated and dead, reflecting only the recurring and rhythmic vibration of the train compartment.

Whereas the ambience within a moving train is defined and always enveloped by the railway line, accommodating many stories, events, faces and anecdotes, an aeroplane's environment is more sterile and there is often little to look at or listen to outside. There is also even less chance of having real contact with fellow passengers who might reveal new stories, as there are very few face-to-face encounters. Moreover, the aeroplane's continuous drone when in flight is heavily overwhelming to the ears, blocking out subtle conversations that might otherwise take place. Inside a moving car, similar engine sounds might occasionally overpower human presence if there is a degree of interaction between the inside and outside through its windows. However, inside a car there is a relative sense of intimacy due to its spatial structure. All of these enclosed spaces of public transport in movement, namely train compartments, aeroplanes and cars, tend to restrict the auditory setting from interacting with outside environments, thereby providing an alternate, mechanical spatiotemporality. The listener, who is inside, may look outside, but external ambient sounds are largely barred from entering and internal sounds are self-contained. Add to this the recurrent vibrations of a vehicle in motion and the setting remains dynamic.

In film, such enclosed, moving spaces of public transport are often settings for narrative development and character building, but in sound and media arts they are settings for textural exploration of sound, such as *TransMongolian* (Roland Etzin 2012) and *Swiss Mountain Transport Systems* (Ernst Karel 2011). However, as I will discuss, most of these auditory settings in films do not portray the claustrophobic environments these spaces suggest. Rather they are concerned with the human encounter and focus on the quality of the dialogue unhindered by engine sounds. Very few filmmakers make use of the sonic textures and rhythm of a train and the drone of aeroplanes or cars as backdrops for revealing the complexity of these internal situations, where mechanical ambient sounds are the palette and tones that delineate the human interaction.

In the early Hollywood sound film *Twentieth Century* (Howard Hawks 1934), all the story's characters are travelling on a long train journey. The entire film is set within a few adjacent compartments. The constant sound of the train travelling along its rail is present throughout, punctuated only occasionally by the sounds of intermittent station platforms. The train's movement works as an omnipresent rhythm within a static auditory setting produced in the early days of direct sound and monaural mixing. But such specific ambience does not add to the ensuing love drama and reconciliation, which is presented as a slapstick comedy. Only towards the end of the film, when the love and legal conflict between the main protagonists is at a climactic point, does the train's frequent signal horn becomes a secondary layer of connotation in the narrative.

The rhythmic sound from a train interior is used more creatively in Indian film *Nayak* (The Hero, Satyajit Ray 1966). It is one of Ray's most remarkable stylistic experiments, which demonstrates his ability to create narrative development from the ambient depth of animated atmospheres. This he does by depicting the specific zones inside a train, within which most of the story takes place. Direct sound method is incorporated despite the sonically limited monaural mix. Each of the train compartments – the berth where the hero sleeps, the dining car, the toilet cubicle and the corridor, where various, intermingling narratives threads unfold – is represented by thorough, specific and consistent vibrations distinct to their setting, whose specific texture accentuate the characters' situations and their mental states. For example, the toilet cubicle's vibration appears more intense, claustrophobic and alienating for the film's heroic character after a nightmare. The auditory settings defined by the moving train's rhythm help to differentiate the spatial identities of sites through their ambiences that are synchronised with the image, emanating from behind the screen or off screen, to realistically establish as well as expand the diegetic space. As Brandon LaBelle describes, sound has the potential to demarcate sites 'toward a greater understanding of the interconnectedness of space' (LaBelle and Martinho 2011: viii). Ray adds to atmospheres in the film space's auditory setting by attentively listening to the pro-filmic space for exploring sound's creative potential.

Richard Linklater's poignant and thoughtful *Before Sunrise* (1995) proposes a train journey as an icebreaker for two strangers. A boy and girl meet inside the dynamic yet secure confinement of a train to Paris via Vienna. The usually alienating auditory setting of a train becomes tender as their impromptu conversation develops an exchange of minds, hearts and intimacy. The train's rhythm helps organise their thoughts of sharing and connecting. This connection becomes serious in the film's sequel *Before Sunset* (2004). Inside a taxi with closed windows, sitting side by side, physically close but still distant due to the nine years that have passed since they first met, the characters reveal the dissatisfaction they feel with their lives. Their projections intertwine with their true presence and exchange, encouraged by the car's intimate setting.

A number of long sequences from Abbas Kiarostami's films are shot inside moving cars. In *Taste of Cherry* (1997), Kiarostami sets his discursive existential narrative, if such a thing exists, inside a car. The very sensitive and subtle narrative transforms as the car's windowpane changes from semi-closed to half-open. Through interactions with the outside world and people, voices change from the private to the public, from reverberantly stuck within the car's spatial structure to diffused within the outdoor environment. The film reveals a man named Badii, who is deeply immersed in his personal grief – the audience does not 'know' the reason but 'feels' his melancholic mood. His sense of alienation from others is mirrored by the tension and recurrent change between the interior voice texture and the outdoor auditory setting of a lively industrial site. In the final scene, the film's cinematic devices are exposed when the pro-filmic space and film space merge in a radical and rapturous interplay between diegesis and mimesis, 'suddenly liberating us from the oppressive solitude and darkness of Badii alone in his grave' as Jonathan Rosenbaum notes.[1] *The Wind Will Carry Us* (Kiarostami 1999) also has sequences in which a car interior is presented as the contained auditory setting where the discursive conversational elements within a complex and unresolved narrative unfold. *Ten* (Kiarostami 2002) is remarkable for its simple yet profound and relatively unmediated access to the complex lives and manifold thoughts of modern Iranian women and their actual, lived sonic environments. Shot almost entirely inside a moving car, the interior space's intimate auditory setting encourages the expression of private, otherwise unheard voices.

Note

1. See: http://www.jonathanrosenbaum.net/2017/06/fill-in-the-blanks/

15 AIRPORT

The airport is a site of perpetual movement, punctuated by awkward periods of waiting, inclined towards an insular private way of being in an essentially public space. Such a public site is usually built with large metallic pillars and transparent glass panels on which the empty face of a nomadic passenger may fall and be distorted. Voices slip away and are rendered redundant. A gentrified lounge has no odour. Rows of metallic doors open and shut silently. Elevators go up and down carrying tired travellers keen to rest for a little while. Instructions appear on large LED screens. The lack of curiosity on the faces of itinerant travellers breeds social alienation. Moments of interest in an unknown other evaporate as the gentle automated announcement makes people aware that the time to leave is approaching. The sounds of escalators echo aimlessly along grey walls and ceiling skylights. Reclining figures and their organised belongings keep changing places. A vacant seat doesn't remain empty for long – someone soon appears with an expressionless face and occupies the void. The felt vibrations of digital devices are mutually enticing. They converse, create intimacy and merge orgiastically to render the networked resonance a machine vision. This is the generic sonic environment of a typical airport. There are many similarities between the world's largest airports, irrespective of dissimilarities between the languages used for announcements, built structures, background muzak, etc. A sonic environment of similar aural perspectives makes them uniform – all sounds, including human and automated voices, machinery, footsteps and baggage trolleys, coalesce with one another in an amalgamated futuristic atmosphere, within which individual voices and sounds are dehumanised and made part of an inert auditory setting.

In the American film *Singapore* (John Brahm 1947), pearl smuggler Matt Gordon lands in a Singapore airport and is greeted by a departures' announcement. The reverberant ambient sound of the Southeast Asian airport is dominated by voices speaking English. It is no surprise that the announcement is in English too and the flights leaving the airport are destined for the colonial cities of the time such as Calcutta. The figures moving within the mise-en-scène are mostly Westerners, with little to no local presence. The conversation of an elderly couple is clearly heard. Gordon's co-passengers are obviously American tourists organising their itinerary with the help of a tour guide. Announcements and footsteps are the primary ambient constituents. They are high-pitched and exclude any of the low-frequency rumbles commonly heard in modern airports; early sound film recordings had a certain quality that couldn't capture low frequencies (Kerins 2011). As discussed in the introduction and Part 2 of this book, monaural mixing positions ambient sound centrally behind the screen with a limited frequency response, while voices are usually given centrality. *Singapore* was no exception to this rule – a vibrant Asian airport's ambience remains flat throughout as the sequence's story quickly focuses on Gordon's lost love.

Playtime (Jacques Tati 1967) is a sarcastic and humour-driven observation of contemporary life in Europe immersed in technology-obsessed modernity. The film's semi-futuristic sites of the city consist primarily of steel and glass office blocks and aquarium-like shops constructed specifically for the set. Post-sync dialogue and amplified sound effects modify the sonic environments and dominate the sound palette. They add to the engaging confusion and release/relief of inhabitants as the urban locations appear less grounded in reality and more akin to comic, futuristic fantasy. As part of this mediated construction of architectural space, the airport site is presented as a sanitised and gentrified auditory setting, which is repeatedly interrupted by cleaning personnel and sporadic announcements asking for 'silence'. Travellers become the props to this mediated atmosphere as they listen to their own voices reflected throughout the space. A film reviewer comments on the film space's sonic environments (i.e., the airport):

> Playtime is as inexhaustible to the ear as to the eye, given Tati's singular use of post-synched sound, with silence as integral to his comic arsenal as any plink, boing or buzz. One Tati trademark is to use speech not as dialogue proper, but as sound effect: Playtime is a lot funnier without subtitles, as the pleasure lies in getting the gist of what people are saying, and how, rather than catching their literal meaning.[1]

A sequence from the radiant and uplifting film *Alice in the Cities* (Wim Wenders 1974) is set in New York's JFK airport. Journalist Philip Winter meets a young girl called Alice quite by accident. Her mother leaves Alice in his care and eventually they fly together to Europe. Throughout this journey, they begin to develop an unlikely friendship, which is therapeutic for Philip who is emerging from a crisis of inspiration and identity. While sitting in the airport, where their journey begins, Alice asks Philip if he likes flying and he nods reluctantly. In the background we hear a busy airport lounge with an aeroplane getting ready for take-off just outside the glass panel, breathing heavily through its engine. The bodily sounds of the aeroplane filter through the window and overpower the other ambient sounds present in the airport – footsteps, luggage trolleys and even the TV that tends to drown out voices. While Alice is sitting in front of an airport lounge TV screen, waiting and fidgeting, the popular Italian song 'Volare' bursts into the ambience of perpetual movement, flying ungrounded, deterritorialised. Alice then takes a stroll down the airport and introduces the viewer/listener to the many sounding zones dominated by duty-free products and easy entertainment that lack any organic, humane connection – these are the typical dehumanising zones of homogenising airports where individuals find themselves to be insignificant and tiny entities recognised only as buyers and consumers.

Two of Steven Spielberg's underrated works *Catch Me If You Can* (2002) and *The Terminal* (2004) were partly shot in elaborate sets constructed and designed based on New York's JFK airport. Indeed, the latter's setting was influenced by Tati's design of the airport in *Playtime* (1967). In *The Terminal*, the protagonist traveller, a fictional character named Viktor Navorski, is stranded in the airport after his passport is deemed invalid due to a military coup in his fictional home country. Afterward, the airport terminal becomes his indefinite home, where he meets both resistance to entering America and kindred souls who help him return home. The film is a sweet and innocent tale told with impeccable craftsmanship, but the film misses the real horror of an airport's oppressive and alienating border control ambience. The film was inspired by *The Terminal Man*, the disturbing autobiography of an actual traveller from Iran named Mehran Karimi Nasseri, who spent a staggering eighteen years in Paris-Charles De Gaulle airport as an alien. Due to the bureaucratic glitches at French, British and Belgian border controls, his free movement was curtailed, forcing him to become a stateless person. In comparison, Viktor Navorski's narrative is far less traumatic. His auditory setting is relatively pleasant and comic. It sounds gentrified, clean and not as oppressive as most airports are to the ears, which prioritise architectural grandiosity over individual voices and personalised sonic elements. The film's auditory setting captures Viktor Navorski's voice in crisp and intelligible grain. His entourage in the airport communicates remarkably easily with him.

My personal experiences of many European and American airports are rather grim in comparison. At London Heathrow Airport, I recorded sound and noted the following:

> I do not belong anywhere, even if a place might ask for my fingerprints, passport photos and biometric details to allow me to stay for a stipulated period of time, after which the feeble data and evaporating information will be erased. Whose land is this? Do I have consent to step in? To whom it may concern regarding the geopolitics? I am deported, pushed further into exile as the passport photos, regulatory stamps and signatures ensure that validity of my drifting remains unambiguous. However amorphous, the opaqueness of the wall around the booth conceals documentation of my identity, immigration status and mobility, leaving me perplexed in an inexplicable fear of being watched and ignored, measured and excluded, scrutinised and removed. This small room of waiting, in which they have put me, is not silent, but the drone of the vacuum cleaner is dominated by fear and a certain kind of impermanence, which in turn define the psycholocation.[2]

This above entry in my book *The Nomadic Listener* (2020b) records the schizophrenic atmosphere at the border control of a Western airport, where racial profiling is the norm and segregating people on the basis of their name, religion and skin colour is a regular occurrence. The auditory setting of an airport is dislocating and disconcerting for a sensitive listener forced to be under constant surveillance and scrutiny. The prevailing machinery reduces ambient sound as impermanent and lost.

In the Bengali film *Mayurakshi* (Atanu Ghosh 2017) a son leaves behind his father suffering from dementia and Alzheimer's disease. As he waits at the airport, crying, the sound of his tears diffuses into the hollow ambience of the airport like a hideous, misplaced echo.

Notes

1. 2014; see: https://www.theguardian.com/film/2014/oct/24/jacques-tati-playtime-intensely-complex-life-affirming-comedy
2. Chattopadhyay (2020b): *The Nomadic Listener*. See the publication website: https://errantbodies.org/nomadic_listener.html. Distribution link (US and Canada): https://www.artbook.com/9780997874464.html. Distribution link (Europe): https://www.lespressesdureel.com/EN/ouvrage.php?id=8175

16 UNDERWATER, OUTER SPACE

Ever since I was a child, I have been afraid of water. My mother's only brother drowned in a lake while learning to swim. He was just twelve years old at the time. I have developed a deep fear of unknown depths and underwater crevasses, knowing that the only uncle I could have had from my mother's side of the family was taken away by water. In the bathroom of my childhood home shivers would run down my spine when I looked at the world under the water scattered on the floor, even though they were mere reflections upside down. I have never learnt to swim because every time I went underwater I would hear ghostly, unknowable, otherworldly sounds that were beyond my cognitive universe.

What is the 'unknown' embedded in a sonic experience? Does it operate beyond normal human perception? Why are we affected by such unknown or unknowable sounds and images, and why do we term them 'cosmic' – a word which relates to the cosmos, extraterrestrial vastness, the vast aquatic world or the universe in contrast to the Earth? The word also relates to an abstract spiritual or metaphysical realm and/or is characterised by greatness especially in terms of its extent and intensity evading human comprehension. How do humans relate to these sounds emanating from phenomena beyond the everyday, cognitive realm? Object-oriented philosophers such as Graham Harman (Kimbell 2013) have argued that the reality of anything beyond the correlation between thought and being remains unknowable. If we explore such an immediately unknowable sonic phenomenon as underwater sound it leads to a personal listening state inside the listener, who may indulge in taking the phenomenon as a premise or entry into a world that he or she did not know previously existed. This is an exploratory process through which unknown sounds can be personalised.

Current field recording practices using digital technology often involve capturing environmental sounds that vary between animal sounds from the remote wilderness to everyday urban sounds that are subliminal in volume and frequency. As a result, they tend to be complex in texture, tone and characteristics.[1] In response, artists often push the technical limits of sound recording, demanding low noise and extended frequency responses in portable, easy-to-use recording formats, ranging from high-resolution, multi-track recording devices to DIY contact microphones. The emergence of digital technology has made it possible to explore advanced, diverse recording techniques and methods. The digital era has become an ideal time for field recording-based sound art to emerge. After their advent in the late 1990s, digital sound recording devices, applications and facilities have become widely available and easy to handle, providing a variety of options for contemporary sound practitioners. As a sprawling contemporary investigation, field recording-based sound art facilitates practices that capture sound in specific locations in intricate detail: a deeper depth of field and wider dynamic range of frequencies is now available, which provides more precise and controlled documentary evidence of a site. These recording capacities allow practitioners to explore uncharted territory, including sites underwater, below ground, in Amazonian forests, in arctic landscapes and even in outer space. NASA's sound archive, for example, contains a large collection of recordings made in outer space.[2] These weird and wonderful sounds of distant stars and obscure planets include radio transmissions of the solar system and beyond. Apparently, no sound vibrates in space due to the lack of air, but there are ways of capturing frequencies using scientific tools and systems. Sound artists like Andrea Polli have sonified data retrieved from atmospheric phenomena around and beyond Earth to present sounds that were previously imperceptible.[3] One well-known recording from the anthology of sound works by US-based artist Stuart Hyatt is the sound of cosmic gravitational waves recorded at LIGO (The Laser Interferometer Gravitational-Wave Observatory).[4]

Deep underwater sounds have also been revealed by the work of scientists. In 1956, French oceanographer Jacques Cousteau made a documentary *Le Monde du Silence* (The Silent World), which won both the Palme D'or and an Oscar that year. The premise of the film, as its title suggests, was that the underwater world was a quieter world. We now know, sixty-four years later, that the underwater is anything but silent. Freight carriers, oil and gas drilling rigs, fishing trawlers, war-torn submarines and other industrial, sea-based machinery have conquered the depths. The aquatic world has been exploited as if it were human territory. Although oceanic sounds are inaudible above water, as the transmission of sound in water is different from that in the air,[5] an underwater sonic environment can be as noisy as any jungle or rainforest. Invertebrates such as snapping shrimp, fish and marine mammals all use sound to study their habitat, communicate, navigate through underwater flora and coral reefs, detect advancing predators and hunt.[6] They also use their listening faculty to know more about their sonic environment – sound is an important sense modality for sea creatures. However, the physical habitat of the sea is changing rapidly as humans explore these sites; as a result, the acoustic environment too is fluctuating. It is as if these creatures have been picked up from a quiet countryside location and dropped into a big city in the middle of rush hour. Seas and oceans are no longer quiet places. Ambient sound levels have increased greatly since the advent of motorised ships and sonar for navigation. In addition to these continuous sources of low-fi sounds, human action such as pile driving for offshore construction, seismic surveys for oil and gas exploration and underwater explosions cause high-volume, short-duration, impulsive sound bursts. Although the impacts of such man-made sounds on marine life are not yet understood nor well researched, they are likely to have adverse effects, which may range from disrupted behaviour and physiological stress to hearing loss and even death for natural inhabitants of the aquatic world. Today's underwater auditory setting is an accumulation of a constant background buzz of both natural (waves, wind, rain and even earthquakes) and man-made sounds.

I have tried to overcome my initial resistance to water by using field recording to gain knowledge about the unknown. In 2009, while in Aarhus, Denmark, as a master's student, I began recording the sea using an Aquarian hydrophone. Later, while in Beirut as a Mellon Postdoctoral Fellow, I developed a sound installation *Le Souffleur* in collaboration with composer Nadim Mishlawi and design collective District D, which was produced by The Neighborhood Initiative.[7] The work was composed with archival underwater sounds from the Mediterranean Sea mixed with those recorded at the Ain el Mreisseh fish market. The aim of the work was to bring the sea to listeners and invite them to experience its mysterious presence through past and present environmental sounds. How can the sea's relationship to the city be understood? Is its shoreline becoming experientially distanced from the city's mainland? The Mediterranean is an integral part of Beirut's history, legend and urban way of life. However, the city's accelerated urban development has recently resulted in concrete barriers being constructed between urban space and the sea. Highrises that restrict the view and sounds of the sea make city inhabitants long for its vast openness. The installation and a corresponding event *Ode to the Sea* – an evening of live sound performance[8] – endeavoured to revive the sea's presence and invite the audience to experience its otherwise distant presence through recorded ambient sounds.

Sound artist Jana Winderen's work probes deep waters, finding dark and eerie beauty in the unknown. Exposing my ears to work such as *Energy Field* (2010)[9] has helped me overcome my fear of water, replacing it with a deeper curiosity and keener appreciation of the sublime. More generally, her work with underwater sounds provides an aesthetic engagement with the natural world from which humans are increasingly estranged. According to Bruno Latour, humans need to (re-)connect with the natural world in order to cure the rupture and imbalance in human/natural environment relationships, which can 'only happen through heightened attention to sensory perception' (Latour quoted in Jørgensen 2019) such as listening to environmental sounds. Winderen's *Energy Field* is based on recordings made 'deep in crevasses of glaciers, in fjords and in the open ocean'[10] in Norway, Russia, Greenland and Norway. Her other work *Pasvikdalen* (2014) is based on recordings made 'both above and underwater close to the border between Norway and Russia'.[11] Although realised using high-end audio gear such as hydrophones, these works are examples of 'pure' experience that separate themselves from technological mediations. They provide a corporeal and sensual engagement with aquatic worlds previously unheard by human ears that are not only entertaining for concertgoers but also trigger thoughts about nature unfolding into culture. These environmental sounds 'edited and layered into a powerful descriptive soundscape'[12] provide stratified narratives.

How are underwater and outer space settings featured in commercially distributed feature films? American filmmakers have set films in underwater locations on a number of occasions: *20,000 Leagues Under the Sea* (Richard Fleischer 1954), *The Abyss* (James Cameron 1989) and *Underwater* (William Eubank 2020) are just three examples. Although these films were made in different eras of sound production, namely monaural, stereophonic (Dolby NR) and surround sound (Dolby Atmos) periods, they all present underwater sites as something external to be afraid of, conquered and colonised using man-made technologies. As a result, all of these films follow horror or sci-fi narratives, using common cinematic devices such as remote, alien settings to create terrifying sonic environments, dominated by dialogue and musical scores with very little space for creative exploration of the otherwise fascinating ambience of these sites. These films were artificially made – they were mostly shot inside expensive studio sets with large water tanks.

Numerous films have also been set in outer space. Among them, a few deserve to be critiqued for their use of – or, more precisely, lack of – environmental sound. *Solaris* (Andrei Tarkovsky 1972) is a remarkable example of a pre-composed score that uses an ambient soundscape to evoke a sense of alienation and emptiness in outer space; encountering such settings poses philosophical and psychological issues around a cognitive connection with the lived environment, which results in the film's intense foreboding for failing to return to Earth. In *Gravity* (Alfonso Cuarón 2013), this sense of emptiness, silence and a lack of ground in outer space is captured in a Dolby Atmos-powered sound design, whereby voices leave their respective bodies to roam freely and trigger thoughts about a loss of gravity. The audience can hear internal elements such as breathing and heartbeats, which are treated as ambience. Both of these films approach outer space as a site of contemplation rather than an audiovisual experience. Their strategy for producing a sonic environment is based on abstraction rather than documentation to address outer space's lack of site-specific ambience.

Notes

1. Lane and Carlyle (2013).
2. See: https://www.nasa.gov/connect/sounds/index.html
3. Polli (2004).
4. The work features in a release and in the corresponding book: Hyatt (2018).
5. Sound travels up to five times faster and sixty times further than in air. See: https://www.sciencelearn.org.nz/resources/572-sound-on-the-move
6. See: https://www.theinertia.com/environment/can-an-underwater-soundtrack-really-bring-coral-reefs-back-to-life/
7. The installation was first exhibited at Le Semaine Du Son Liban, 7–11 May 2019. See: https://www.aub.edu.lb/Neighborhood/Pages/LeSouffleur.aspx
8. See: https://www.aub.edu.lb/articles/Pages/The-Week-of-Sound-in-Beirut.aspx
9. *Energy Field* was awarded a Golden Nica at Prix Ars Electronica in 2011, while my work *Eye Contact with the City* (2010–2011) received an Honorary Mention in the same year at this prestigious festival of media arts. I also had the chance to perform live with Jana Winderen, for example at Donau Festival, Krems (2015): https://touch33.net/news/touch-live-at-donau-festival-krems-2nd-may-2015.html
10. Listen to this at: https://janawinderen.bandcamp.com/album/energy-field
11. Listen to this at: https://janawinderen.bandcamp.com/album/pasvikdalen
12. See: https://janawinderen.bandcamp.com/album/energy-field

PART 4

CRITICAL LISTENING

Above all, I feel that the sounds of this world are so beautiful in themselves that if only we could listen to them properly, cinema would have no need for music at all. (Andrei Tarkovsky, in Tarkovsky and Hunter-Blair 1989)

17 MAPPING THE AESTHETIC CHOICES IN SOUND PRODUCTION

17.1 LISTENING THROUGH FILM AND MEDIA ARTS

Sound is instrumental to our everyday navigating, place-making and situating ourselves in lived environments. We cognitively associate with the locations we occupy, traverse through or experience remotely through their sounds. For us, sound is part of the world's natural order – the way it moves and stops, turns and self-regulates. We know how sounds intimately connect us to sites and their environments when a gentle breeze murmurs in the forest and leaves vibrate, a plate or dish has a conversation with a spoon or a train engine starts up on the railway track. The immediate cognitive appeal of these sounds, if we pay the minutest attention to them, is the emergent causality of identifying a site and its situation.

However, perceptual affordances, biases, limits and specific sensibilities mean places are heard differently from how they really are – 'noisy', multi-layered, with wide depths of field and perspectives perhaps beyond ordinary human hearing capacities. More research into animal listening would shed light on how site-specific sounds are deciphered by other species, but it is most likely that humans can hear only a limited dynamic range and frequency spectrum (from 20 to 20,000 Hz). Within this framework, human hearing can only attend to a few sounds at once. Likewise, cognitive worlds that are built, shared and consumed tend to reflect these anthropogenic limitations and affordances, biases and apparitions, precincts and postulates. Human-made audiovisual environments that depict or mimic these sites in film and media

THE AUDITORY SETTING

arts mediate reality through many intersecting yet differing methodologies and varying approaches to sound production.

This book has investigated these processes of reconstructing a sonic environment through the diegesis and mimesis of a site and the setting in film and media arts. As defined, the setting is understood in narrative works as the mediated space in which a story or event takes place. Setting includes specific information about place and time and presents a backdrop for narrative action. Production of the setting within a mediated universe such as a film or media artwork requires comprehensive information about place and time that organises aural and visual elements to evoke the narrative's context. I have coined the term 'auditory setting' to study the mediated presence of place and space (re)constructed in film and media artworks by using a specific sound component known as ambience or ambient sound, which is a film and media practitioner term that denotes the environmental sounds present in a place. The book focuses on listening analytically to the production and mediation of environmental sounds in film and media arts. It examines how ambient sound is used as a site-specific element to compose the auditory setting that renders spatial awareness in film and media. A critical approach has been taken towards notions of narration, diegesis, mimesis, presence, rendering, human intervention, the transformation and representation of environments, and technological innovations. The aesthetic mediation that reduces site-specific reality into a condensed auditory setting has received much needed scholarly attention and in-depth analysis, primarily within the context of sound studies.

Sites have been variously rendered and reproduced throughout different phases of sound production. These trajectories have been divided into three primary, historical categories to locate and map sound production's foremost technological shifts. The various aesthetic choices embraced by sound practitioners have been studied to reveal how the sonic presence of sites has been reproduced in different technological eras. In other words, the impact of technological innovation on the degree of site-specific presence reproduced through the use of ambient sound components has been central to this investigation. Ambient sound's usage in film and media arts has been explored through three main technological frameworks: (1) synchronised sound recording (e.g., direct sound recorded optically on location, a.k.a sound-on-film) and monaural mixing; (2) dubbing, tape-based studio processing and stereophonic mixing; and (3) digital multi-track synchronised recording (e.g., sync sound), digital noise reduction and surround sound design (e.g., Dolby Atmos).

This study reveals that the advent of digital technology has been instrumental in enabling richer layers of ambient sound components to be incorporated into sound organisation, homogenising sound production and sonic experiences worldwide. The spatial perception of sound has changed through the use of digital technology, namely multi-track synchronised sound recording and surround sound design. Filmic space has been reconfigured by these newer environments, such as Dolby Atmos and Auro 3D, which diverge considerably from screen-centric mono and stereophonic mixing. Auditory settings are now spatially augmented. When environmental sounds are incorporated into contemporary cinema, the resultant sonic environments are spatially wider, and more elaborate and enveloping than screen-centric, monaural soundtracks or the flat surface of a stereophonic composite soundtrack. Likewise, sound practices in the digital era encourage spatial awareness.

Questions might be raised as to whether this historical overview suffers from its broad perspective. In its defence, I refer to the argument of many film and media historians, including Casper Tybjerg, who maintain that writing history demands a wide position that can accommodate historiographical accounts (Tybjerg 2013). This book, which emerges from a void of serious and sustained research on ambient sound, may generate a context for future research that could present more detailed studies of specific sound production periods. Moreover, the book has been inspired by my own professional background as a sound and media artist and researcher, which opens the topic to a range of knowledge production. As Tybjerg further argues: 'In order to connect the dots of the historical record into some sort of coherent pattern, historians must inevitably draw on their own experience and understanding of human life and behavior [... W]e must inevitably rely on our background knowledge of the world when we discuss the past' (Tybjerg 2013: n.p.). World cinema consists of diverse fields of practices, productions and experiences. This book locates the dominant tendencies and predilections from such diversity for a comparative study of auditory settings mediated in global cinema and media arts using a practice-led approach alongside critical and reflective observation methodologies.

Certain sites, identified for their actual sonic attributes, have been investigated within cinema and media art contexts. The auditory settings of selected film passages and media artworks have been analysed for their mediated ambient qualities. Sonic material has been gathered that illustrates the impact of processes that utilise a multitude of methods, e.g., on-site recordings, studio recordings and/or pre-existing sound bank recordings. Emphasis is placed on how these sites have been variously mediated in different sound production eras. Critical listening was primarily based on a phenomenological or experiential understanding of the sites firstly through personal experiences and then through the various diegetic and mimetic mediation in film and media arts evident in the chosen examples. This latter process was examined to evaluate the nature of translating the acoustic atmosphere of these sites. It has been observed that sites are more cared for and respected in media artworks than commercial films. The 'site-referenced' aspect of these works enables their listener to refer back to a more credible sense of the ambient sounds' situatedness, authenticity and verisimilitude. The book embraces sonic ethnography and the study of locations in order to shift the conventional focus in film sound from a 'sound/image' relationship to the rarely discussed 'sound/site' interconnection. In making this shift, the book advocates for spatial awareness and location-sensitivity in present and future sound production trajectories.

17.2 Locating models in sound production

A taxonomical model has been devised to shift the focus of sound production studies towards the site's presence as a vital narrative component. Although specific phases of technological innovation and transitions in sound production have been identified as points of departure, the model is not limited to the history of sound technology. On the contrary, it highlights the aesthetic characteristics of sound that have emerged from these most prominent technological phases, thereby linking film sound studies to sound in media arts. The use of environmental sounds in each of these technological phases or strategies can be broadly categorised accordingly to era and mapped as follows:

1. Synchronised sound recording and monaural mixing – ambient sounds used as direct evidence of a location (1930s and 1940s).
2. Dubbing, studio processing stereophonic mixing – a lack of ambient sounds in preference to site-unspecific spectacles, which engage the audience through emotive manipulation (1950s–1990s).
3. Digital multi-track synchronised recording, digital noise reduction and surround sound design – richer layers of ambient sounds recorded and used in surround to create spatially evocative environments (1990s–present).

This model helps to map the various technological shifts within sound production practices and categorise the types of experiences these practices have facilitated when producing an auditory setting in global cinema.

With reference to the three phases above, the following corresponding model categorises the approaches that are behind the use of ambient sound in the production of film and media auditory settings:

1. Locating the site
2. Escaping the site
3. Being sited

This tripartition shows that ambient sounds were used in phase one when analogue, monaural, synchronised sound recording and, to varying degrees, monaural mixing provided direct, observational evidence of a location. In contrast, ambient sounds were largely ignored in the dubbing, studio processing and stereophonic mixing phase to facilitate 'un-sited', fantastical spectacles. In the present era, they have been reincorporated, but this time with greater richness and wider spatialisation in order to create spatially evocative environments. Many of the production aesthetics of the 'direct sound era' are finding a revival in the digital era albeit augmented as spatialised sonic environments. Particular inspiration is being sought from Italian neorealists and French New Wave filmmakers, who strived for realistic (re)presentations of sites in their auditory settings.

I have used the nomenclature of these three corresponding categories for the simple purpose of order and taxonomy. These categories could be questioned for their historical accuracy. However, such a three-part division could be considered a heuristic, pragmatic and useful way to read the fragmentary and uneven trajectories of global film sound production processes. Other shifts have occurred in parallel or have intersected these frames to a certain degree, but these three prominent markers facilitate an understanding of the use of ambient sound within highly diverse global cinema in a more or less coherent and comprehensive manner. The divisions also reflect the discourse and vocabularies used by sound practitioners. Moreover, this categorisation is not arbitrary – the proposed model takes its inspiration from existing sound studies and new media research and theories. In her book *Sounding New Media* (2009), Frances Dyson observes some key 'rhetorical manoeuvres' that accompany the transition of sound media from its analogue phase to the digital realm, stating that:

> [T]he shift from 'looking at' to 'being in' [. . .] is reflected by the artful dropping of analogical markers: the 'it's as if you are there' of screen-based media is truncated to a 'you are there' [. . .] By 'being in', rather than 'looking at' [. . .] the viewer is said to occupy the space and time, the here and now, the virtual present of a separate but ontologically real space. (Dyson 2009: 2)

The transformation of diegetic space from a screen-centric, monaural soundtrack via ultra-screen, expanded, stereophonic space to today's spatially enveloping surround sound environment can be understood as a paradigmatic shift from 'looking at' to 'being in' – a clear indication of the changing relationships between film space and sound as well as between site and sound as proliferated by evolving production practices. Much of this shift has been made audible through the use and spatial ordering of ambient sounds to create an immersive environment that facilitates an embodied experience of a site's presence. I have shown how the direct evidence of synchronised ambient sound through screen-centric, monaural recording and mixing 'traced the site'. The deliberate lack of ambient sound in dubbing and ultra-screen stereophonic mixing 'escaped the site' and created an unsited auditory setting as spectacle instead. I have also demonstrated that the contemporary digital era is more generous than former eras at including ambience in sound organisation. As a consequence, the site becomes more bodily 'present'. I have analysed significant passages from relevant films post-2000, showing how many embraced digital multi-track sync sound recording before it became standard practice worldwide by around 2010. The novel experience of listening to the filmic space in the digital era is marked by low-frequency room tones and atmospheric content recorded from the location more in synchronisation with the site of the pro-filmic space. The mise-en-sonore is carefully rendered when the spatialisation of these ambient sound recordings is elaborate and provides ample evidence of the site in an enveloping surround sound environment. These new methods and approaches produce a sense of 'being sited' as an embodied experience of the site's convincingly realistic presence.

It is widely acknowledged that film was 'the first medium to efficiently accommodate sound' (d'Escriván 2009: 65); my interest in this book has been to study how creativity in film sound has developed historically and where this intersects or differs from sound art or sounding media art practice. As demonstrated in Part 3, the sonic mediation of dynamic sites in films is far more fictionally oriented than independent media artwork. Even self-proclaimed realist filmmakers remove and eliminate directly recorded ambient sounds from their sonic palette; asynchronously produced sounds are frequent occurrences in film. In sound-oriented media arts, on the other hand, the practice of field recording captures more nuanced accounts of sites.

17.3 Sonic mediation and expanding the notion of rendering

As elaborated in the introduction, sonic mediation is based on rendering. To briefly recapitulate: rendering is an important concept in film and audiovisual media production that denotes a production process whereby a medial device or system (e.g., recording media, microphone, a digital audio workstation or sound recording gear) produces and presents a simulated and augmented experience. The process can be compared to a maker reproducing a scene from a realistic source, for example, within a photographic composition. In film, it can be understood as the making of the filmic space from a given pro-filmic space. In sound recording and reproduction for film, rendering connotes the use of sounds to communicate an emotive sensation related to the depiction on screen, which provides, as Michel Chion suggests, 'the illusion of a natural narrativity of sounds' (Chion 1994: 111). This often happens in opposition to the faithful reproduction of sounds that can be heard in real situations in order to translate one order of sensation into another via some sort of narrative manipulation (Chion 1994). Audio rendering aims to convey a feeling associated with the sound source. Rendered sounds translate tactile sensations into auditory sensations. The sounds suggest a narrative associated with composite sensations rather than an event's auditory reality; the filmmaker or media practitioner modulates the sound according to the narrative. For example, a car chase is often accompanied by a shrill screech of tyres, conveying tension. The filmmaker intends to render the scene through studio processing, which systematically modulates the sound's contrast and intensity. This cinematic and medial device is a narrative trope for keeping attention and emotive engagement at the expense of sonic realism. The audience recognises these sounds to be truthful, effective and fitting not so much because they are reproduced the way they would be heard in reality; instead, the sounds are rendered to convey or express the feelings, moods and emotions associated with the situation, thus making the setting perceptually consistent. As Chion points out: 'cinema systematically exaggerates the contrast of intensity. This device of exaggerating contrast is a kind of white lie committed even in films that use direct sound' (1994: 113). In other words, rendering in filmmaking is used to exaggerate and underscore a sensation for the purpose of narrative attention. With the increasing sophistication of film and media production, rendering has become a distinct technical process of editing and reproducing. Part 3 shows how a site rendered in film generally pays little attention to the intricate details the profilmic space has to offer. It also explores how the auditory setting concerned is reduced to catering for pre-scripted narrative entertainment intended to please its audience. Drawing on the critical reflections made in Part 3, the idea of rendering can be expanded to denote a phenomenological reduction of site-specific environmental sounds that mediates and condenses reality. In media arts, rendering is a more careful process of augmenting site-specificity through the artist's subjective intervention and creative autonomy.

Rendering and the phenomenological reduction of lived sensorial environments are under-theorised in media studies. This book has investigated broader aspects of environmental and locative sounds rendered in film and media arts as a narrative component. The focus has been on examining processes that reconstruct an auditory setting by mediating and reducing a site and its acoustic environment through technological means. Questions have been raised regarding the extent to which site-specific presence is reduced in sound practice and whether the site remains elusive within the rendered experience. This study has identified the specific methods and creative strategies that are used to construct or evoke the relatively convincing presence of a site within the mediated and rendered environment in varied degrees by means of various forms and formats of sound recording and the spatial organisation of these recorded environmental sounds. Drawing on contemporary philosopher Timothy Morton's distinct manner in unpacking the term, rendering appears to be not only an immensely important tool for the sound practitioner but also a significant concept in the study of phenomenological reduction. It is the principle means of reducing, mediating and manipulating sound to produce a sensation that is 'material and physical, though somewhat intangible' (Morton 2009), to surround audiences with a make-believe atmosphere that is 'more or less palpable yet ethereal and subtle' (Morton 2009) in generating engagement. Within sound studies, an enquiry into rendering's concept and its functions illuminates an anthropogenic perception and interpretation of the environment.

18 AUDITORY PRESENCE AND BETTER PRACTICE

18.1 COMPARATIVE ANALYSIS: FILM SOUND/SOUND IN MEDIA ARTS

In Michel Chion's book, *Film, a Sound Art* (2009), he argues that watching movies is more than just a visual exercise, describing it also as a process of 'audio-viewing'. The audiovisual makes use of a wealth of tropes, devices, techniques and effects that convert multiple sensations into image and sound, therefore rendering, instead of reproducing, the world through cinema as a 'truly audiovisual language'. Chion's formulation adheres to the image-centric reading of sound in cinema and, therefore, fails to make a clear distinction between approaches towards the auditory and visual setting as two distinct production practices. This book aspires to make this distinction clear not only by using the coinage 'sound art' and 'media arts' as a metaphor but, unlike Chion, to also cite real works of sound-centric media artwork to show how the creative possibilities and potentials of sound in film are delimited and often suppressed to cater to the industrial needs of storytelling, diegesis and narration with an overwhelming desire to juxtapose sound events with visual cues (Chion 1994). The discussion on sound in media arts offered here opens comparative analysis of the similarities and differences between the use of ambient sound to construct and narrate the site within the interior world of film and the use of field recordings in certain site-driven, sound-based media artworks.

I have shown that field recording practices emerged in response to the advent of digital sound recording technology. Whereas location recording with analogue recorders was, firstly, cumbersome and, secondly, almost always financially unfeasible, lightweight and accessible digital equipment has made recording more democratic and widespread. Therefore, this is an appropriate time to comment on the differences and similarities between film sound and sound/media arts that are informed, influenced and enhanced by digital technology. It has been demonstrated that environmental sounds in field recording-based media artworks are used not as a means to construct immersive environments for audiences by creating a feeling of 'being sited', but as material to develop a more nuanced impression of the site ingrained with many complex social, cultural, political and ethical issues.

In the works cited, the tension between site-specific evidence and artistic abstraction engages the audience's attention in inclusive and often playful ways. The sound work *Elegy for Bangalore* is just one example. As described earlier in detail, an extensive repository of field recordings and other audio materials, such as retrieved audio from old reel-to-reel tapes found at a city's flea market, eventually took the form of an elegiac composition, infused with random recordings gathered through sonic drifting and reflecting on them. The work creates a conceptual, practical and methodological premise for in-depth listening to the passage of time, and offers a psychogeographic reflection on re-emergent urban sites in India, with their chaotic, noisy and hybridised sonic environments, many of which are often absent in Indian films. Like many comparable works such as *Sarajevo* (2004) and *Helgoland* (2013) by German sound artist Lasse-Marc Riek, *Elegy for Bangalore* suggests a kind of apt ethnographic methodology that emphasises subjective and adaptive auditory perception (1) for listening to the sonic environment of a place by engaging with multi-layered auditory contexts and aural histories and (2) for composing a truthful and nuanced sonic portrayal in a new auditory setting through the research.

As a comparison, let's take, for example, the commercial Indian film *Gori Tere Pyaar Mein* (In Your Love O Lady, Punit Malhotra 2013) shot in various locations in Bangalore during the same period that recordings were made for *Elegy for Bangalore*. The street corners, restaurants and airports as settings in the story-world present fewer sonic details than are necessary for an inclusive and thorough understanding of these urban sites and their auditory characters. Although shot during the digital sync era of sound production, the sonic quality of Bangalore has been practically erased within the filmic space.

Both film sound and field recording-based sound and media artworks record specific sites with similar equipment. However, there are fundamental differences in how these ambient sound recordings are utilised. The distinction stems from sound being deployed as a narrative component within functional storytelling structures in cinema. On many occasions, the dense and noisy parts of ambient sound recordings are sanitised through editing and advanced noise reduction to provide 'cleaner' sonic textures, which provide 'aestheticised' and rather sterilised accounts of the sites. This compulsion for achieving clarity in the cinematic soundscape often leads the sound practitioner to employ easy and obvious 'soundmarks' instead of accurately capturing and rendering the sites' complete ambience. This tendency towards highlighting a stereotypical sound, often at the expense of the many other ambient sounds emanating from a specific site, is intended to reduce the need for post-production noise reduction and editing of the pilot recording or the guide track. These industrial norms, practical rules and creative regulations embedded in the essentially 'functional' aspects of film sound production often hinder the sound practitioner's artistic potential and fail to enrich a film's spatial features. Here, knowledge concerning the ways sound and media artworks are conceived and developed using attentive field recording methods may influence and inspire, if not radically alter, film sound practices.

18.2 Constraints of the Sonic Environment in Film

Stereo soundtrack conventions dictate that the voice occupies the centre of the screen while sound effects and background music are placed in the side speakers. In this standardised scheme, ambient sound layers have no place.[1] In referring to Béla Balázs's statement that film sound's role is 'to reveal for us our acoustic environment, the acoustic landscape in which we live' (1985: 116), this book notes that the relative absence of ambient sound in most films from the pre-digital era denies the very revelation of the rich acoustic environments in which these stories take place. Throughout the trajectory of film sound production, the sonic environment or ambience has been associated with an inert backdrop, which has little role to play in the story rather than an important yet ignored layer of extra-visual evidence. However, as Timothy Morton suggests, 'Ambience denotes a sense of a circumambient, or surrounding, world. It suggests something material and physical, though somewhat intangible, as if space itself had a material aspect' (Morton 2009: 33). It is mostly in social realism films, art-house cinema and media artistic productions rather than popular commercial films that this material aspect of ambience and an environmental sensibility is taken into consideration to form a convincing auditory setting. To convey this sense of a dynamic sonic atmosphere taking an active role in enlivening mediated or filmic space, artists, media producers and makers are required to give thorough attention to the environmental or ambient sound presence in the sites under consideration for cinematic and artistic engagement.

As discussed in the introduction, environmental or ambient sounds provide depth by establishing an association between the viewer and the site, reinforcing 'the impression of reality' (Percheron 1980: 17) in the diegesis. This is achieved by providing a testimony of the site in sound perception and localisation of sound as discussed in Part 2, whereby the spectator can relate to the sonic environment or the auditory situation of the pro-filmic space. Sound scholar Mark Grimshaw has shown that adding ambient sounds to narration 'can create an immediate experience of presence and reality' (2011: 32) in media productions. If included, ambient sounds could supply layers of realistic depth to replace the one-dimensional, flat surface of soundtracks associated with the dubbing era in Indian, Italian, Hong Kong and other dubbing-dominated world cinema. It was no surprise that voice and processed sound effects ruled sound mixing during the dubbing era and merely served the visual authority of the narrative instead of a multi-modal sensorial experience. In other words, dubbing offered what film scholar Giorgio Biancorosso articulates as:

> [. . .] the illusion of a sumptuous, perceptually vivid impression of a causal relation which is known to be purely imaginary – one that is forced down our throats, in fact. As such, dubbing stands in spectacular contrast to our everyday experience of a great many causal relations that, though known to be scientifically true, cannot be grasped through our senses.[2]

Alternatively, according to theories of presence (Lombard and Ditton 1997; Skalski and Whitbred 2010), ambient sounds can affect spatial presence by instigating a sense of 'being there' in the embodied auditory setting experience. This is achieved by presenting vivid and elaborate information about a site that places the audience within the filmic space and contributes to the narrative diegesis with a sense of reality (Skalski and Whitbred 2010). The absence of ambience, therefore, renders the cinematic site imaginary – audiences cannot relate bodily to the site they encounter in the story. Pre-digital cinema, particularly those films made during the dubbing era, provides such an experience. As discussed in Part 3, by keeping ambience at bay, commercial films of this period and later created a remote and imaginary cinematic landscape, a spectacular experience of a momentary escape from the burden of locative presence.

18.3 Challenging Best Practice in Film Sound Production

A primary concern of this book has been to uncover the similarities and differences between the treatment and incorporation of environmental sounds in commercially oriented films and sound-driven media art productions to generate novel and relevant insights for producing a specific set of new knowledge that could challenge and redefine the notion of 'best practice'[3] in film sound production.

Little official documentation and no comprehensive manual related to best practice in creative sound production exists for the global film industry. Many of the film sound practitioners I have interviewed[4] have received awards such as Best Sound Editor, Location Sound Recordist, Sound Designer and Re-recordist of the Final Mixed Track from national and international film bodies based on the industry's evaluation of the highest level of craftsmanship in sound production. But what do their 'best' works sound like? Do they indeed represent and exemplify exceptional works of film sound production, those that demonstrate sensitive artistry? In my opinion, sound-based creative endeavours are often characterised by a refusal to be standardised, destabilising existing systems of industrial norms and protocols. Interviews and in-depth conversations with various sound practitioners[5] have revealed that the idea of producing persistently 'better' sound based on personal standards of quality and efficacy set within the film industry's significant constraints is more important.

Ambient sound is categorically singled out by these established practitioners as film sound's primary artistic exploration. However, sound production in mainstream cinema is still dominated by pervasive film industry norms and rules despite the digital realm opening up possibilities for creative intervention, shaking up the hierarchical and feudal chains of industrial and studio-centric production. Sync sound's requirement of the esteemed actor's commitment on set, for example, is on a par with the location sound technician, who has long held lower status in the film crew's hierarchy. In this book, the lens provided by sound and media art has been presented as a useful cue for how film sound could be more playful, exuberantly creative, rational, thoughtful and location-sensitive, and more site-aware, as well as more nuanced in its application. Here, I intend to distance myself from the norm in search of more freedom, hacking the technology and subverting industrial standards. I am critical of the standardised idea of 'best practice' when it comes to individual artistry and send out a call for greater inclusiveness and sensitivity to the site-specificity of sound. 'Better practice', as I apply the concept here, envisions a future of film sound where these creative sensibilities can be explored artistically, using industry-dependent ideas of 'best sound' in film only as a point of departure to continually reinterpret and re-contextualise conventional notions of 'best practice'.

It is in independent, so-called 'art-house' cinema rather than commercial cinema made for mass entertainment where the possibilities for artistic exploration and developing exceptional examples of creativity in sound are most present. Take, for example, a review of the independent Indian film *Anhey Ghorhey Da Daan* (Alms for a Blind Horse, Gurvinder Singh 2011): 'Even a still scene can create its own sound and tell [you] what's going on.'[6] The director was present when the film was shown at the Rotterdam International Film Festival in 2012 and spoke about his ideas of sound in Indian cinema.

The statement clearly emphasises the deeply evocative effectiveness of ambience to establish a landscape's poetic presence within a static frame. Sound, in a handful – yet growing number – of independent art-house films, takes its own course by creating multiple sonic impressions within, around and beyond the visual narrative and overarching story. Here, both the film director's and sound practitioner's subjective interpretations of filmic sites are paramount and crucial when developing an evocative auditory setting.

Subjectivity is similarly central to sound and media artworks developed from field recordings. I have shown how the artist's personality, idiosyncratic state of being, playfulness and sense of abundant freedom makes an artwork more engaging and evocative than it would be if produced with a merely functional approach. While many film sound works tend to be inflexibly culture specific and controlled, sound artworks seem to strive for a subtler sense of subjective truth and contingent universality. As Brandon LaBelle argues, sound art 'attempts to tell the truth, to locate origin, capturing, harnessing, finding, and researching the environment, its inhabitants, and delivering up its [. . .] reality' (2006: 220). Hence, film sound can learn from how sound art is developed. Throughout the history of motion pictures, we have witnessed a complex discourse concerning the reciprocal relationship film establishes with other art forms, mostly defined by creative efforts and experimental gestures in mutual domains, permeated by dialogic enquiries into how those other art forms express themselves in film and how the latter transmutes into the former. In this respect, this book is aligned with existing discourse and opens up space for further stimulating dialogue. Film music scholar Julio d'Escriván notes in his article 'Sound art (?) on/in film' (2009) that: 'a fair evaluation of the work of sound artists in film is still largely virgin territory [. . .] film has gradually brought into focus the practice of sound art as something distinct from music yet existing at the end of a unified continuum between abstraction and representation' (2009: 65 and 72).[7] From d'Escriván's statements it is possible to speculate about potential dialogues and how such dialogues can contribute to the enrichment of film sound and inform sound art in its many modes of expression. This book makes a conscious and deliberate effort to step into this 'virgin territory', intervene and develop relevant new knowledge in both fields.

18.4 Tracing an Emergent Spatiality

The emerging spatial sensibility in digital sound production is apparent in the way contemporary cinema has incorporated a proliferation of ambient sounds to develop a believable topography close to that of lived experience for the audience. The use of ambient sound via intricate digital surround spatialisation[8] produces an enhanced sited experience. It is no surprise that the current breed of films made with digital technologies compel audiences to utilise their sensorial and ambient or environmental faculties of listening. This new realm of sound production supports an embodied experience of the site.

Don Ihde articulates embodied experience in this way: 'Sound permeates and penetrates my bodily being. [...] Its bodily involvement comprises the range from soothing pleasure to the point of insanity in the continuum of possible sound in music and noise. Listening begins by being bodily global in its effects' (2007: 45). The pleasure derived from relating bodily to constructed film and media environments is based on how convincing and realistic they sound to the ear. Likewise, the realistic portrayal of fictional sites in digital films leads to popular appreciation and a sense of euphoria. In user reviews of the Indian mainstream film *Jab We Met* (When We Met, Imtiaz Ali 2007), one of the earliest Indian films shot with digital sync sound, two film buffs underscore the distinct experience of recognising the site:

> The scenes have been mostly shot at outdoor spots like Chandigarh, Kulu, Manali and Shimla, and this entertains us as if we are experiencing a real tour ourselves. Again and again, seeing daily studio scenes made the eyes wounded and fed up the mind [sic].[9]
>
> [...] the execution is so [...] realistic that no situation in the movie looks out of place [...] absolute[ly] real, natural and believable.[10]

This euphoria reflects new developments in cinematic experience, acknowledging a renewed sense of realism in the narration of fictional sites created by a spatial ordering of ambient sounds to 'produce a space for the film to exist in' (Holman 1997: 177). A number of recent films made in India such as *Asha Jaoar Majhe* (Labour of Love, Aditya Vikram Sengupta 2014), *Court* (Chaitanya Tamhane 2014), *Masaan* (Fly Away Solo, Neeraj Ghaywan 2015), and *Killa* (The Fort, Avinash Arun 2015) do not rely on the musical score. Instead, they practically do away with it, using a reduced amount of dialogue (or no dialogue, as with films like *Asha Jaoar Majhe*). These films are packed with rich ambient sounds – recognisable, ordinary ambiences that permeate everyday Indian life. I have discussed several of these films at length (e.g., *Asha Jaoar Majhe*) and have shown that they have a gritty, documentary feel, marked by an immersive, immediate realism due to the careful inclusion and elaborate spatial organisation of ambient sounds that stands in stark contrast to conventional Bollywood song and dance films. These independent films represent a renewed sense of situatedness, meticulously portraying ordinary sites as those inhabited and traversed in everyday life. In Hollywood, Gianluca Sergi (2004) and Mark Kerins (2011) located such expanding spatiality after the digital revolution spearheaded by the introduction of Dolby Digital systems. Due to the narrative strategies of careful listening in newer films, sites may become characters within narrative development, contributing a more concrete spatial presence to the filmic space.

However, even in the conducive creative environment of digital sound production, it is of course a question as to whether all the subtler aspects of the phenomenal worlds from the multitude of cinematically exposed sites are narrated truthfully and faithfully. For example, the typically syncretic, chaotic and inchoate structure of contemporary global cities reflected in the general manifestation of the urban environment, particularly in the complex character of everyday urban ambience – with multiple layers of sounds from pre-industrial, industrial and post-industrial eras – are simultaneously active in juxtapositions or contrapuntal relationships with one another (Chattopadhyay 2014b). The urban sound environment is thus sonically overwhelming and potentially disorienting for the listener. The complex and multi-layered ambience of urban and rural sites does not always completely appear in the augmented auditory settings of digitally produced films; sometimes more 'aestheticised' accounts of these sites are delivered in their surround sound environment. However, this spatial atmosphere can no longer be understood as a linear and one-dimensional 'soundtrack' and, therefore, is termed 'cinematic soundscape' in this book. The compulsion to achieve clarity in the cinematic soundscape leads the practitioner to use selected 'soundmarks' instead of faithfully capturing the complete ambience of sites, as discussed in the introduction. In the popular Indian road-movie *Highway* (Imtiaz Ali 2014),[11] the two protagonists, an abducted girl and her fugitive captor, travel through North India in a truck, staying in hidden places for a few days before running away. Every place is established with a certain 'soundmark' specific to the site. A location in the state of Rajasthan, northern India, for example, is narrated through the distant and proximate calls of peacocks, since Rajasthan is well known for its variety of peafowl. This tendency to underline a particular sound, often at the expense of many other ambient sounds emanating from specific sites, serves as a kind of sonic 'compensation' for the noise reduction and editing of digital multi-track sync sounds in post-production.[12] These 'industrial' norms, rules and regulations embedded in the film industry's sound production hinder the sound practitioner in applying a more artistic approach that might further enrich the spatial experience offered by the film.

Despite these apparent drawbacks, pervasive digital technologies endow contemporary films with an impressive amount of site-specific environmental sounds in recording and design methodology. Contemporary sound production narrates the site far more believable than previous production eras with an enhanced and intensified sense of the site's spatial presence and the illusion of non-mediation in the film's augmented auditory settings, crafted with digital multi-track sync recording and surround sound design. In the introduction, the 'spatial turn' in film sound and sound practice is discussed in general terms of 'the increasing recognition of the intimate links between sound and space' (Eisenberg 2015: 195). In the digital realm, films incorporate six discreet channels (5.1 surround sound) and more channels in other advanced multi-channel formats, such as Dolby Atmos, wider panning for sound spatialisation, including multiple rear, overhead and below, and full-frequency channels (20–20,000 Hz) with a flatter response, including previously elusive ambient sound layers, such as low-frequency rumbles and room tone. Sync sound offers a wider sound palette when recording, including previously ignored ambient sounds. This expansive material can be creatively layered within numerous surround sound tracks to design a spatially rich mise-en-sonore. Reference has been made to a number of sound scholar perspectives that predict the future of technological innovations in sound production, enabling more mimetically realistic, spatially credible and cogent representations of places and their sonic environments in the sensorium.[13] Such emerging spatiality is underlined as an important development in film sound as the ground where more artistically oriented audiovisual media artworks may intersect.

18.5 Rethinking the concept of auditory presence in film and media arts

Taking account of relatively recent historical developments in sound production and looking forward, this book reconsiders 'presence' as a concept in the (re)presentation of sound in film and media arts. It discusses how presence was perceived within an analogue sound recording context and how it is gaining currency in contemporary media that negotiate and establish place in digitally mediated experiences (introduction and Part 2). In reading the trajectories of presence's conceptualisation, one primary theme emerges – namely, a contribution to the sense of embodied experience through a perceived notion of realism. This sense of embodiment elicited through perceived realism is a literal translation of stepping into a site's manifestation through its acoustic elements; 'thus, presence may be the key to understanding the processes of embodied experiences' (Ahn 2011: 25). If the goal of media is to reproduce the illusion of non-mediated communication, the degree of vividness or realism that users experience during their perception of a media environment is crucial to the production of presence. In this context presence is 'the psychological state of feeling that the mediated experience reproduced by virtual environments is "real"' (Ahn 2011: 22). Here, I refer to the first-ever phone call made in 1876 by Alexander Graham Bell to his assistant, Thomas Watson, saying: 'Mr. Watson, come here. I want to see you.'[14] Perhaps it is no surprise, therefore, that presence is always desired in media, which it can only achieve by overcoming its inherent limitations. If the goal of media is to present the illusion of non-mediated communication, the degree of realism through truthfulness and vividness that users experience during their perception of the media environment is crucial to the production of presence. Likewise, in film sound, presence is produced by creating the illusion of the audience 'being there', which intensifies as filmmakers employ digital technology that is inherently capable of providing the means to simulate reality in a more perceptually lifelike fashion. Cinema's use of digital sync sound recording and surround sound design, similar to any other augmented digital media environment, creates a spatial presence to the point at which an audience 'feels that the mediated environment and the objects within the environment that surrounds him or her is real to the extent that the environment responds realistically' (Ahn 2011: 25; see also Grimshaw 2011; Lombard and Ditton 1997; Skalski and Whitbred 2010). On the other hand, more artistically oriented works using audiovisual media handle presence in more complex ways. The possibility of multiple interpretations of these works with a subjective approach opens poetic possibilities.

Contemporary media's mobility and portability contributes to the so-called 'spatial turn'[15] referred to in media and communication studies, the social sciences and humanities. On the issue of 'spatial presence' within a broader context, philosopher Hans Ulrich Gumbrecht states that 'the (spatial) tangibility effect coming from the communication media is subjected, in space, to movements of greater or lesser proximity' (2004: 17), indicating the importance of contemporary media to include increasingly spatial features. This development may explain the intensified sense of a site's presence in the digital realm. As discussed, such views are shared by not only digital media scholars but also sound scholars. For the latter, sound strengthens the condition of the 'preconceptual sensory experience, for immediacy, bodily presence, or states of immersion' (Gess 2015: n.p.). In her recent article 'Ideologies of sound: Longing for presence from the eighteenth century until today', sound scholar Nicola Gess notes how in contemporary discourse on sound: '[...] the key concepts of the aesthetics of presence promise an experience beyond symbolic orders, that is, an experience of immediate contact with "materiality", "phenomenal being", or the "real"'.[16]

However, she further explains that this promise often establishes an 'ideology of presence' rather than an actual, 'historically informed, critical and concrete examination of sound' in contemporary theories. Through an engaged review of literature, she shows how this promise is often 'accompanied by an appeal to a past era when these essences are thought to have been central, or at least when the experience of sensory presence is thought to have been more central' (2015: n.p.). For her, the essence and appeal of this promise are marked by a romanticised view of the past, longing for its lost glory of immediacy, and sensory and corporeal presence of the genuine and truthful.

Whereas my principal findings may resonate with this promise of the unmediated merging with reality in the digital era, this book also demands a close, critical look at presence. In looking through the lens of sound art, the presence of a site in film emerges through a functional approach that mimetically (re)presents sound's inherent site-specificity. Presence is, therefore, often 'manufactured', technically crafted and/or constructed, rather than being an immediate, sensitive and direct exploration of the many layered, nebulous yet wonderful sonic environments of 'real' sites. The site's truthfulness withdraws or slips away under the pressure of cinematic devices of storytelling. In my opinion, the habitually elusive veracity of sites in films is first of all an outcome of the film industry's and market's pervasive control at the expense of the practitioner's greater artistic freedom, which is often not indulged. Sincere artistic efforts have historically met with resistance[17] arising from film industry norms such as time and money constraints and/or a lack of appreciation. This has led to inaccurate and untruthful (re)presentations of reality in favour of manufactured presence. Film scholar Stephen Prince calls this 'perceptual realism', meaning that unreal images and sounds appear 'referentially fictional but perceptually realistic' (1996: 32). In earlier chapters, I mapped out and reflected upon the formidable absence of subtler site actualities in dubbed films. Here, I would like to point out once again that the apparent intensification of presence in digital cinema is largely artificial and constructed – with the help of market-driven digital technology with its readily available tools, presets, formats and systems – rather than tapping or hacking into the contemporary post-digital[18] realm's open-source playing field with its immensely creative applications.

Conversely, in sound art and compositions, the artist can intervene more intimately and render a rather subjective account of a site. When writing about the works of Canadian sound artist Hildegard Westerkamp, including *Kits Beach Soundwalk* (1989), Brandon LaBelle speaks of the artist's own 'interference' that helps to embrace 'a counternarrative [. . .] against mimesis and toward alterity [. . .] while accentuating the real [. . .] and chart[ing] the dynamism of acoustic spaces inhabited by both real and mythological beings' (2006: 213). However, despite this openly interventionist and performative process, sound artists may remain 'sensitive to the acoustic environment' (2006: 215) by becoming mindful of the deeper intricacies of a site and its complex sound world. Unlike film, the performativity (Gallagher 2015) of field recording-based media artworks is embedded in the independent quality of their sounds often presented without a dominant visual cue. Therefore, the possibility of multiple, open-ended interpretations leads to 'poetic presence'. With such an evocative sense of presence, sound operates beyond the confines of immediate meaning-making and readily available signification. This is the condition where a site's 'realness' may intermingle with LaBelle's imaginary 'mythological beings', thereby transcending a state of mere spatial presence towards eliciting an 'associative' or poetic-contemplative state in the listener's mind. In an article for the *Journal of Sonic Studies*[19] and, subsequently, in other writings, I have articulated this state in terms of the 'fertile auditory situation' (Chattopadhyay 2013, 2014a, 2015a), suggesting the associative capacities of contemplative listening the way LaBelle reads 'listening that wanders across thresholds of presence and absence, the immediate and the remembered to create all sorts of associations' (LaBelle 2015: 319). LaBelle cites the article in the new edition of *Background Noise* and interprets it this way (2015: 319):

> The artist and writer Budhaditya Chattopadhyay investigates the question of presence, and how sound suggests another understanding of perceptual experience. For him, sound and listening are intensely 'associative', never singular but always already superimposed across multiple levels of presence and that easily stitch together present and past, now and then. As he suggests, 'Knowledge about the locative source of sound becomes blurry in its juxtaposition with memory, contemplation, imagination and mood', which creates a rather 'disorienting experience'.

As with many other field recording artists such as Lasse-Marc Riek, David Velez and Francisco Lopez, capturing the real or constructing a presence of the real is not my primary aim. Rather, as Christoph Cox notes in general on post-Cageian sound art, field recording 'offers [...] an aural opening onto a region of this sound' (Cox 2009: 23). The works foreground the 'background' by framing, accentuating (LaBelle 2006) or amplifying (Cox 2009) the 'real' to trigger fertile imagination and a ground for the listener to participate. By coalescing presence and the imaginary, the real and the virtual, these works tend to obscure site-derived information 'through a superimposition of sound that interpenetrates preexisting spaces, effecting a layering or doubling, which can produce hybrid spaces' (Gallagher 2015: 574) to create the fertile premise for an evocative and more profound reconnection with the site.

Going back to LaBelle's analysis of Westerkamp's work, he appears to be concerned that the artist presented an unmediated account of the Kits Beach site despite it being clear that significant manipulation was employed during the sound's recording. Although *Kits Beach Soundwalk* was constructed by the recordist, the recording device, the post-production, the playback and so on, in my opinion, this critique does not hold much ground. Field recording-based sound artists do not record reality as it is, nor do they intend to compose presence. They aspire to open up multiple realities by creating an interplay between presence and poetic imagination. As Cox (2009) suggests, field recording does not so much capture as transduce, amplify and reiterate a site. LaBelle also recognises this:

> place paradoxically comes to life by being somewhat alien, other, and separate, removed and dislocated, rather than being thoroughly

mimetically real [. . .] [A]s a listener I hear just as much displacement as placement, just as much placelessness as place, for the extraction of sound from its environment partially wields its power by being boundless, uprooted and distinct. (2006: 211)

These sensitive readings suggest that listeners are asked to engage more creatively with these works. They are encouraged to participate by unfolding the many potential interpretations and imaginings inherent in such works.

Questions can be raised as to whether it is possible to present reality as thoroughly mimetically real at all, because reality always needs some sort of representation to appear. Philosophers would argue that presence or reality is always mediated and endlessly deferred within any form of representation. As sound studies scholar Marcel Cobussen writes (2002: n.p.):

> The real is always already permeated with a deficit, a shortage. However, if the real cannot exist without its representation, if the latter is established as the precondition for the presence of the real, then representation should become the point of departure. On the other hand, representation also prevents the real from appearing; it defers the real.

This book, with its inherent limitations, has humbly redrawn attention to this triangular relationship between reality, its representation and presence within the context of sound production, arguing that different approaches enact this relationship through various forms of sonic media. Reality is perceived and constructed in the mind of the listener with ardent and helpful contributions from sound practitioners and artists, depending on the extent to which expressiveness and creative freedom – as well as care and sensitivity – are used in building the delicate bridge between the listener and the creator of media artworks.

Notes

1. Sound mixer Pramod Thomas stresses that in mono and stereo track-laying, the adequate space is not there for fuller inclusion of ambient material. See personal interview with Thomas in Chattopadhyay (2021).
2. Biancorosso (2009: 260–267).
3. As explained earlier, 'best practice' is a method, technique or approach that is generally considered better than its alternatives either because it produces results that are deemed superior to those achieved by other means of production or because it has become a standard way of doing things in compliance with certain aesthetic references. As a result, best practice becomes widely accepted as better than any alternatives that traditionally have been embraced in the production process.
4. See: Chattopadhyay (2021).
5. See: Chattopadhyay (2021).

6. See the film review by JvH48 (28 October 2012): http://www.imdb.com/title/tt2085746/reviews?ref_=tt_urv
7. What d'Escriván broadly refers to as 'sound artists in film', I call 'sound practitioners', with a specific focus on the creativity they have introduced to film sound.
8. In multi-channel, experimental soundscape composition and electroacoustic music creation, production and performance, the term 'spatialisation' is increasingly used to denote diffusion of sound in space. The origin of the term can be found in the English translation of the French term 'l'espace' introduced by Henri Lefebvre (1974) with reference to sociocultural perception and cognition of geographical space.
9. See: user reviews on IMDB: http://www.imdb.com/title/tt1093370/reviews
10. See: user reviews on IMDB: http://www.imdb.com/title/tt1093370/reviews
11. For an excerpt from the film, see: https://www.youtube.com/watch?v=mIiGry20tiI
12. Production work done on a film (or recording) after filming or recording has taken place.
13. In Part 2, Chapter 7, 'Digital Surround Sound and the Mimetic Site'.
14. See: http://www.americaslibrary.gov/jb/recon/jb_recon_telephone_1.html
15. The term 'spatial turn' is described in the introduction's subchapter 'Sound studies' as 'the increasing recognition of the intimate links between sound and space' (Eisenberg 2015: 195).
16. Gess (2015: n.p.).
17. In some of the interviews to be published in Chattopadhyay (2021), sound practitioners have expressed their frustration with not being able to contribute their creative best by responding with sarcasm, irritation, withdrawal or hostility to the suggestion of instigating change or voicing their opinion. While their defence of their profession and their own positions in the system is understandable, it is also imperative to pay attention to what they truly aspire to, revealed through the intermittent flashes of inspiration with which they describe their work.
18. The term 'post-digital' will be elaborated in Chapter 20, 'Emerging Trends and Future Directions'.
19. See Chattopadhyay (2013a).

19 THE GOD OF SMALL SOUNDS

19.1 ANTHROPOCENIC LISTENING

Jacob Bronowski argued that humans are always ingrained in natural landscapes and habitual sites, whether knowingly or unknowingly (1973). And yet, as Timothy Morton suggests, humans endeavour to distance themselves from nature as separate entities (2009). Location-driven film and media arts perhaps function as a mirror or lens through which we can see the sites we occupy and ourselves as we occupy them, perceive them, abandon them or personalise them through the agency of humanistic/artistic intervention and mediation. Through technological advancements, the world has entered the Anthropocene – a new geologic era defined by unprecedented human disturbances over earth's environment and ecosystems. In this era, the ecological integrity of natural sites is being endangered. Land is being intensely developed, especially in the Global South, to facilitate rapid urbanisation and industrial growth. As a result of this speedy development, many natural and rural locations are becoming SEZs (special economic zones), which deeply affect the environment. Consequently, as these areas become homogenised, industrial sites, they are decaying into bucolic landscapes. This transition is complex to grasp, especially when considering their traditionally rich auditory culture and history.

I have used this book premise as an occasion to assess the portrayal of these environmentally troubled sites in film and media arts and assess how sensitive they are in handling their sonic environments. I have pointed out how the intricate layers of environmental sounds from these sites can be lost through technological mediation when recorded, turning natural environments into sites of spectacle, consumption and entertainment, much like the human colonisation of natural landscapes. Questioning the cultural appropriation of nature, the environment and its audiovisual resources into man-made film, media and cultural production environs is a motivation for this book. I was moved by the fact that natural sounds are being engulfed by human-made sounds, fulfilling human needs to the detriment of other organisms. Humans inhabit, transform, misuse and manipulate to consume both remote and immediate physical surroundings. Not only natural but also built environments such as rural, urban and suburban sites, whether indoors or outdoors, are the habitual environments that humans live by. They are often perceived as the setting that provides specific atmosphere or ambience when describing, depicting, narrating, producing and reproducing increasingly mediatised worlds in films and media arts. The sonic environment, as indicated in this book through other scholarly works, has rapidly changed in the last 100 years through accelerated industrialisation and urbanisation. Such interventions have also been made for entertainment and tourism – sonic environments are still constantly consumed, (re)produced and mediated through film and audiovisual media. An investigation of these processes that mediate environments for their aesthetic consumption – in other words, human agency in expending the environment – has been undertaken to indicate the complex relationship between humans and the environment. Although not separate from the natural world, humans can be seen as strangers, aliens and savages within this context. This book facilitates the study of the (re)production and mediation of environmental sounds from several exemplary natural and man-made sites to produce auditory settings for films and audiovisual media arts that are consumed for both entertainment and aesthetic engagement. The impact that humans have had on the environment is measured in relation to the current environmental and ecological crises, and the prevailing Anthropocene triggered this research interest in relation to sound studies and media art history.

19.2 Environmental sounds lost

How do environmental sounds affect human hearing? Perhaps the idea of the 'Sharawadji effect' answers this question, which composer Claude Schryer defined as 'a sensation of plenitude sometimes created by the contemplation of a complex soundscape whose beauty is inexplicable' (Waterman and Harley 1999: n.p.). Like the God of small but subliminal sounds, the Sharawadji effect is the illumination when a sudden and unexpected everyday environmental sound appears to give immense pleasure to sensitive ears, harmonising the emergent auditory situation without any human intervention such as recording and re-composing. Is it satisfying because of the capacity to momentarily reconnect with nature on a subconscious level from which humans have become estranged? In their book *Sonic Experience: A Guide to Everyday Sounds*, Jean-François Augoyard and Henri Torgue define the Sharawadji effect this way:

> Unbridled and unintentional structures disrupt the nature-culture binary and reveal new forms of life beyond their disorder, which paradoxically can be completed fabricated. Thus technological and industrial sounds can become more natural than any imitation of nature. It is this blurring of the edges of aesthetics, this shifting at the frontier of art itself, that defines sharawadji. (2006: 118)

Composer David Rothenberg suggests that: 'All of us are searching for that enveloping soundscape that takes us beyond to indescribable realms of beauty, what the Persian philosophers once called the Sharawadji effect' (2013: 193).[1]

Even so, environmental sounds are generally taken for granted in film. As sound designer Walter Murch suggests,[2] 'We begin to hear before we are born, four and a half months after conception' (1994: vii–viii), but, after birth, our sight and the visual sense become dominant over sound; aural realisation surfaces only when the visual is absent in perception. This is somewhat like a blind person feeling insecure when objects around him or her are moved. But film is a mediated construction, not a replica or lived splice of our perceived world. In the value system of filmmaking, environmental sounds are mostly perceived as noise – as discussed, a film soundtrack includes or excludes particular sound elements depending on the story. If its use is diegetic, then the soundtrack will not disturb the audience's attention from the camera focused on the characters. In the case of non-diegetic usage, the soundtrack will highlight sounds that may not actually exist but add colour in post-production. With this approach, some environmental sounds are used as refrains comparable to musical motifs in films when made by authors with sensitive ears, as shown in Part 3.

Environmental sounds, when present within the auditory setting, like the Sharawadji effect, can supply moments of subdued and sublime pleasure that we usually do not acknowledge. They inject hues of vibrant aural colours to replace a one-dimensional, dialogue/background score/sound effects scheme of film soundtrack production, which merely serves the visual dominance of the film's narrative.

Popular films generally seem hostile to ambient sounds being an integral part of the soundtrack even when a film is shot on location. Sounds from the direct environment are usually controlled on location to minimise what enters the filmic space. On a film set, sound tends to be limited to mere voices and sync effects, making the construction of a soundtrack predominantly dependent on asynchronous sound sourcing often from stock sounds. Through this process, instead of representing the established locality, film sound drifts away from documenting the unique site. The production approaches a synthetic design made by an operator working under the spectre of mechanical craftsmanship; the sound practitioner's independent listening sensibilities find no place there.

Indeed, the sound practitioner is familiar with their material being marginalised by a film's visual aspect. Sound has long been taken for granted as a mere appendage within the world of experiences that cinema produces. It has hardly ever been conceived as having an independent, distinct identity that could acquire a separate voice. Sound has not been allowed to carry a parallel narrative but has merely played a supportive, storytelling role. Film sound rarely provides a complete aural journey that the listener could appreciate with their eyes closed in the cinema. Right from the beginning of sound films, compulsory song sequences or typical background scores take up most of the 'soundtrack' space and often limit it from becoming a 'sonic environment'. The remaining layers are given to character dialogue. Performed voices and hyper-real sound effects float on the background score and, in some cases, song sequences provide relief or punctuation to a narrative – this has been the usual soundtrack structure since talkies began.

Recently, despite sync sound's revival, location sound technicians, with immense power to capture even micro-sounds, still depend on the choices of decision-makers in the film crew's hierarchy. From location recording to post-production stages, sound technicians have maintained the film industry's overarching scheme with utmost loyalty. A creative use of environmental sound could easily provide new authenticity in surround sound mixing and reproduction systems. Different channels of sound can now be directed to different speakers when reproduced in cinema houses. This is made possible by the encoding and subsequent decoding of channels routed through a surround sound system. Dialogue, effects and background music – leaving songs aside – use separate channels. A sound technician's job is to send these channels to different speakers according to the head of production's wishes. For example, industry norms are bent on sending dialogue to the central speakers whereas music is positioned in the surround speakers. Reputed American sound designer David Randall Thom comments on the artistic scope of multi-channel sound use in Sound-Article-List:

> A [...] mono track is always better than a mediocre 5.1 track (if the channels don't hold significance) no matter what kind of movie (film) it is; [...] some of the filmmakers are using 5.1 channels because they think there is something magic about the technology itself [...] More channels don't always equal better art (if they don't have anything to say). If the sound is artfully done, and if the structure of the movie is friendly to sound, then the number of channels almost doesn't matter in the success of the track. Some of the directors I have worked with understand the

relationship between images and sound very profoundly, much more deeply than I do. On the other hand, most of the directors with lots of films to their credit are approximately as naive about the use of sound in film as the average person on the street.[3]

If ambience or environmental location sound found its due place within these expanded channels, a specific locale could be represented with auditory depth, detail and clarity in the filmic space. In this range of sound design, environmental sound can take on importance, and its depth, spectral colours and contexts can emerge as signifiers, representing an audible world. Film's auditory setting, done this way, will no more ignore the ambience of the pro-filmic space of a site, whether an actual location or plastic film set. In the case of shooting on location, the microphone would pick up and register distant-sounding objects outside of the hearing range of scripts. In the case of shooting on set, layers of ambience would be added to the sound environment while reconstructing the site in the auditory setting; separate ambient recordings associated with the site would be incorporated in place of stock sounds.

But these as yet are mere speculations. The history of film sound is a history of lost sounds.

Part 3 describes how oppressive sounds of the jungle in *Apocalypse Now* and *Antichrist*, the sounds of vendors and palanquin bearers on the streets in *Charulata*, and those of a busy street that push at the privacy of a room in *The Lover* establish their presence in our memory of films. They transcend the status of being mere sounding objects to become sonic images and they play vital roles in structuring our mental topography of localities and our associations with them that leave indelible marks on our memory. I have watched and listened to *Ashani Sanket* many times, but what remains unchanged from the very first experience is the expectation of the village's ambience provided by the rice husking *Dheki*. Every time I watch and listen to *Pather Panchali*, I anticipate the sound of tree branches rubbing against one another in Indir Thakrun's death sequence. Memorised sounds – such as the tree movement in *Pather Panchali* and the wind blowing in Alexander Sokurov's *Mother and Son* – are environmental sounds that strike our hearing as uncanny, because they rebel against an otherwise flat and plastic film soundtrack.

They rebel and then die. The sound of the *Dheki* is almost lost from Bengali villages. The Oraon community is beginning to forget their own songs that can be heard in Ritwik Ghatak's *Ajantrik* (1958); they are now consigned to the status of an endangered oral tradition. Street-sellers from North Kolkata no longer sound like they do in *Charulata*'s auditory setting; the palanquin has gone. New multistorey complexes are being built at *Pather Panchali*'s location; forest sounds have been exiled from suburban Kolkata's sonic environments. These are sounds lost forever that no longer sound in the evaporating present.

How did these sounds die? Did the objects that made the sounds simply stop producing them? Isn't it an inevitable aural gesture that sounds die and fall into oblivion? The sounds of hand rickshaws no longer sound the proletariat's bell and those of the heavy DC fan hanging from India's colonial walls have faded away. AM radio receiver sounds have been replaced by the evening soap operas transmitted to FM handsets. Sounds change. They keep track with the inevitable transformations that occur in a location. Any sound that dies also signifies the loss of its cultural content, which can be perceived even as a loss of historical value (Chattopadhyay 2007). Sounds should be preserved somewhere, perhaps in a forgotten archive. Some are probably still alive in the living collective called cinema because film has long provided the scope to record sound. In fact, there has been no other medium that could record sound from a landscape so extensively. In *Pather Panchali*, when the sweetmeat vendor Srinivas enters the village, the sound of his archaic chime is heard and thus preserved on film. *Titas Ekti Nadir Naam* (A River Called Titas) preserves the sound of a dying riverbank and *Roma* archives the ignored indigenous voices. However, unfortunately, there are very few examples of this quality of recording. Thousands of films made since the world's first talkie could have documented the changing sound of our environment but, by design, they have lost much more than they captured. Sounds have been forgotten due to our failure to record them during the intensified technological developments of the Anthropocene that have consumed nature.

Film sound could become archival if it paid more attention to sound as an independent aspect on locations and in the environments that humans continue to colonise. Film cannot serve as a documentation of a changing society without recording its sonic states. Filmmaking, with its compulsion to marginalise sound's scope over the last 100 years, has by and large missed out on registering an aural society. Our sound memory does not represent the repository of lost sounds resonating in our collective unconscious. They strive to be heard within a shadowy area of our memory. Forgotten sounds should be excavated and re-read as cultural history (Chattopadhyay 2007). Lost sounds should appear to us as entities eager to be rescued from an unheard consciousness. They demand the recognition of the eternal return of the ambient.

Notes

1. Rothenberg (2013).
2. In his wonderful introduction to Michel Chion's *Audio-Vision: Sound on Screen* (1994).
3. David Randall Thom (popularly known as Randy Thom) in online forum Sound-Articles-List, 13 May 2004; available on www.filmsound.org (accessed May 2017).

20 EMERGING TRENDS AND FUTURE DIRECTIONS

20.1 POST-DIGITAL SOUND AND FUTURE LISTENING

From the outset, this book has focused on a comparative analysis of the auditory setting's formation in film and audiovisual media artworks using ambient sounds gathered from actual sites and their sonic environments. However, the findings of the book can also be considered more broadly to inform the potential future of global sound production in which various forms and formats of expression coalesce. Film sound and media art practices may intersect through intensive technological convergence, aesthetic inclusivity, a sense of democratisation and artistic freedom. A sense of inclusivity and creative freedom could trigger the production of new, hybrid artistic forms enriched with experimentation, which could subvert former and current industrial norms and their limitations.

Although I am only able to briefly speculate on these future conditions, my predictions are more than mere flights of fancy. They resonate well with so-called 'post-digital aesthetics'[1] of contemporary film and media practices (Bosma 2014; Cox 2014; Cramer 2014). When digital sound production has reached saturation point, contemporary media theories suggest that a critical juncture will occur that includes the shifts this project has discussed, analysed and hypothesised. Such a 'post-digital' context would direct researchers to explore potentially new fields of enquiry regarding sound practices.[2]

When considering the potential of post-digital aesthetics, the question of a-temporal convergences becomes pivotal. For example, the emergence of a so-called precarious aesthetic is exemplified by hybrid film and media productions, from GIF[3] artworks based on archival materials to silent films like *The Artist* (Michel Hazanavicius 2011). In foreseeing the digital revolution's demise, Kim Cascone has argued that, 'the medium of digital technology holds less fascination for composers in and of itself' (2002: n.p.). In relation to sound art and new music, Cascone advocates paying attention to digital technology's alleged failures that trigger subversive and alternative events through glitches, clipping, aliasing, distortion and so on. His formulation of the 'post-digital' thus accommodates 'digital essentialism' breaking down into fragments of digital sonic artefacts that can be reused and repurposed as artistic material in a new spatial ordering of fluid, malleable, flexible and inclusive soundworks. In riding these waves, artists may push the technical limits of sound recording by further exploring the lo-fi recording possibilities of smartphones in addition to demanding extended frequency response in portable, easy-to-use recording formats, ranging from high-resolution multi-track recording devices to DIY contact microphones. This book has shown that the emergence of field recording as a means of assembling novel materials to artistically (re)engage with sites and develop a more nuanced reproductive impression is indebted to these developments.

Such use of sound is also accentuated in the post-digital context of cinematic experience, especially in spatially fluid digital environments such as Dolby Atmos or Auro 3D. In 'A theory of digital objects', Jannis Kallinikos, Aleksi Aaltonen and Attila Marton claim that 'digital objects are marked by a limited set of variable yet generic attributes such as editability, interactivity, openness and distributedness that confer them a distinct functional profile' (2010: n.p.). This leads to a profound sense of 'object instability', with digital material being experienced as evasive and fleeting in contrast to the more solid and self-evident nature of traditional film sound media such as the optical strip, the magnetic tape and a soundtrack released on CD or DVD. The dispersed and mutating nature of digital sound objects and their diffusion across itinerant and mobile three-dimensional space makes them difficult to authenticate when compared with the fixed screen and its two-dimensional visual narrative. Sounds that are disembodied from screens cause multiple layers of mediation potentially leading to many interpretations beyond the screen – most importantly in the listener's mind.

Post-digital discourse essentially relates to the perpetual transience of these amorphous but fertile 'auditory situations' (Chattopadhyay 2013, 2014a, 2015a) that need to be navigated spatially, just as in real life. In this milieu, sound's access to greater spatiality, mobility, interaction and sensorial presence than in the cinema evidently leads to an extension of its presence beyond the visual, image-based object, which was the structure that defined Chion's classic terminology of the 'illusion of redundancy', 'added value', 'audiovisiogenic effects' and 'syncresis' in earlier sound organisation (i.e., monaural and stereophonic eras of sound production). In digital sound's reorganised space, these notions are challenged and questioned. Contemporary sound practices and their emergences contribute to the formulation of speculative, 'post-digital' concepts not only regarding sound recordings as relocated and transformed sonic artefacts in spatial reordered systems such as Dolby Atmos and Auro 3D, but also by facilitating multi-level, spatiotemporal reinterpretations of older sonic experiences in an era of rapidly converging and intensely hybridising fluid environments. I hope that this book opens up such issues for further discussion and provides fertile points of departure for future research of sound in cinema, sound art and other media arts.

Ambient sonic states in contemporary film and media art are less attached to the screen and visual image, thereby acquiring independent identities. Such states are articulated in Steven Shaviro's book *Post Cinematic Affect* (2010), which claims that

> digital technologies, together with neoliberal economic relations, have given birth to radically new ways of manufacturing and articulating lived experience [. . .] Recent film and video works are expressive: that is to say, in the ways that they give voice (or better, give sounds and images) to a kind of ambient, free-floating sensibility that permeates our society today. (2010: 2)

Such a 'free-floating sensibility' in terms of ambience loosens up cinematic structures into new forms of artistic expression, inviting and incorporating new media art practices and giving birth to forms akin to the previously ignored *Expanded Cinema* (Youngblood 1970). In the late 1960s, Expanded Cinema was considered an unfixed mode of film presentation encompassing multiple projections, live sound performances and spatial film environments. Similar to new media art installations, each individual projection in Expanded Cinema was a unique and finite durational experience where audiovisual works were structured to incorporate temporal drifts and spatial variations. Performances often depended on the artists' active participation. The form deconstructed the standard conditions of traditional, screen-centric cinema and broke down the relationship between film and viewer as well as the inherent dependence between film and two-dimensional visual images. As a result, cinema was liberated from the hidden, single projection booth mechanism and dispersed among the audience – a condition that has also become possible through the development of digital cinematic sound technology. Such freedom may lead to further experiments with spatialisation in cinema, bringing it closer to sound art, interactive media, video installations and VR and AR artworks.

Whether there will be a future condition in which these two approaches can enjoy a fruitful dialogue and bridge the creative divide remains to be seen. However, as a discursive remark, I would like to underscore the advantage of prevailing practices that employ artistically inventive means to produce new sonic experiences, which I consider are more dedicated to the nature of sites and their ambient particularities. The primary significance of this book is to substantially contribute to this evolving vision and associated discourses on sonic spatial practices, site-inherent potentialities of ambient sounds and the human agency of sound and media art while producing and mediating the lived environment.

20.2 Post-immersion

Whether we pay adequate heed or not to the facts and figures around us, climate change is a clear and present danger. Perhaps we are still unmindful of this reality. Perhaps our fear and anxiety are creating avoidance of the matter even if we cannot truly disengage from the onslaught of information about climate breakdown and the unavoidable and devastating consequences to our lives.[4] Other pressing issues such as the insensitive handling of people migrating to the West, the war-destitute from across borders, also need more public discourse.

Despite such avoidance, climate change seems to be slowly casting its long shadow over artistic production. Indeed, a handful of recent film and media artworks directly respond to environmental issues, and an unprecedented number of artists gathered in Paris for the Conference of Creative Parties, ArtCOP21, at the last climate change summit. Nevertheless, the most recent climate summit in Madrid did not result in a consensus among nations.[5] Now students are protesting on the streets all over the world, from Beirut to Delhi, from Hong Kong to Santiago, questioning the political status quo and its inadequacy in responding to climate breakdown as well as the rising conservative-protectionist, regressive forces across the globe. Artists and scholars are also joining forces. Through such collective participation, a network of global cultural engagement with climate breakdown and other crises has been created. This network of engagement sheds light on how artists and practitioners may contribute to current social and political discourse, and what their contribution may mean to local and global communities, and humankind in general. There is a growing sense of disenfranchisement with stagnant institutions, and a need to further involve issues such as climate change, global warming and mass migration in the arts to affectively engage the public. We cannot afford lazy and numb inaction in the face of grave and urgent catastrophes.

This fervent need to trigger greater public engagement, awareness, mobilisation and action through art also opens up debate about appropriate artistic practice methodologies that might appeal to those as yet unaware of burning global issues. What can filmmakers, media artists and other practitioners do within this context? How can they make committed contributions to the world's crises? Media arts often seem to possess less potential to instigate societal change due to their relative lack of actual presence in public art venues and institutions. This issue is accentuated by the generally immersive and pleasantly enveloping qualities of contemporary film, and audiovisual and interactive media arts experiences, which often fail to evoke discursive responses from their audiences (Chattopadhyay 2020a, 2019b). In the light of this problem, we should critically examine the medial experience of immersion, particularly within the context of the discourse generated in this book, in order to speculate whether more environmentally, socially and politically aware works can be produced in future.

Immersion is a fetishised term in contemporary film, experimental music, sound, and audiovisual and interactive media arts (e.g., VR). It is often specifically used to engage the audience, especially pieces that involve multi-channel sound, visuals and spatial practices. The rapid emergence of multi-channel sound in film and media arts has made it possible for the medial measure of immersion to surround the audience sonically. In these works, immersion operates as a strategy to realise the production of, as discussed earlier, an 'illusion of non-mediation' (Lombard and Ditton 1997: 590) where the presence of technology and medial devices is made to appear as unobtrusive as possible to sustain smooth and engaging entertainment. Seth Kim-Cohen terms such an immersive space as a 'soft space of light' (2013: 151) with a 'disarming tendency to lull' (Schrimshaw 2018: n.p.) producing a 'circle of interiority and immersion within which sound envelopes and centres us' (Schrimshaw 2018: n.p.).

Etymologically, the word 'immersion' suggests plunging or dipping into something or being absorbed in some interest or situation and, when applied to a human-made auditory setting, offers the idea that a person who enters such a space will be transformed. Immersion presents the idea that a space through its multitude of architectural, material, performative and technological mediation may envelop an audience (Chattopadhyay 2020a, 2019b). The ability to immerse an individual who opens their ears to such environs is related to the multi-sensorial modes of constructed narratives often involved in the suppression of a conscious, subjective formation. For the spectator's/listener's subjectivity to emerge, an opening or rupture in the experience must exist, through which a plurality of personal thoughts can be encouraged to burst forth. However, as film and media scholar Whittington notes, an immersive effect is established 'through an imaginary emplacement of the spectator in the world of the film achieved through textual strategies such as the placement of the camera in the literal position of the character' (Whittington (cf. Constance Balides) 2013: 67). Such fixed positioning and defacing of the spectator in favour of the film's characters and narrative experience closes down the spectator's intervention and ability to interpret multiple meanings, keeping a critical distance.

If I examine immersive spaces that inherently involve contexts of a consumeristic nature – such as sound diffusion in a live, multi-channel performance in a lavishly funded festival, a commissioned interactive media art experience or sound design for a commercial film or VR work – a dangerous power relationship exists between the producer and the consumer of such immersive works that are mediated and purposefully designed to overwhelm and overpower the audience while conveying direct, consumeristic information and knowledge. This is a fundamental problem because the analytical faculty of audiences should be more aware of contemporary issues given the times in which we live. If we approach immersion by emphasising the often-glorified design and experiential dimension of the space and disregard the analytical capacity of an individual experiencing it, we might err on the side of open thinking and discourse. Instead, we should critically ask why immersion is viewed as a positive entity in a philosophical and conceptual sense. Otherwise, in focusing on pleasurable entertainment, this make-belief world always hides the real. This book is concerned with how audiences tend to become passive and inactive within immersive spaces often constructed by an authoritarian, technocratic, corporate, consumer-orientated film and media industry. In this inactive mode, the audience may lose the motivation to question the work's content and context by falling into a sensual and indulgent experience, therefore rendering consumeristic, corporate powers to assume the audience's free will (Lukas 2016). As a result, the audience may succumb to the enveloping and engulfing power of a fantasy world created by a creative industry with economic, political or other hegemonic intentions. As a socially and environmentally conscious sound and media artist, I argue for producing a more discursive rather than immersive environment. Here, the term 'discursive' underlines the contemplative processes triggered by an artwork that connects the artistic object and the listener's cognition within an auditory setting. In such a discursive mode, a film or media artwork can become more socially committed, responsible, responsive and respectful towards audience awareness within a mindful context that helps form the medial experience. As most film and media artworks glorify immersion, I fervently suggest a discursive space in future works where the individuality and questioning faculty of the audience is carefully considered and encouraged as a parameter for the works' successful dissemination.

A recent popular film example shows how commercially rendered immersive experiences conceal historical truths in favour of hegemonic narratives. The British-American film *Dunkirk* (Christopher Nolan 2017) claims to be a referenced work and a benchmark in creating immersive sound experiences. The film's sound designer, Richard King, further professes that the film uses 'historical sounds as a reference' to produce 'historical truth'.[6] Indeed, the film has garnered critical acclaim for its 'stunning and immersive soundtrack'. However, a number of mostly non-European critics have pointed out how, inside this pleasantly entertaining, immersive experience, a major historical fact has been manipulated: 'Two and a half million soldiers drawn from Britain's empire in South Asia fought in World War II'[7] and helped Britain survive the war,[8] but none of these non-white soldiers is audible or visible in this supposedly historically accurate film. The entire gamut of the cordon was whitewashed to project a white supremacist image where the contribution of the Other was silenced. Meanwhile, the film's box-office takings have swollen due to the market value of its immersive experience.

Such examples of a less thoughtful and more indulgent sonic experience are more than ample not only in commercial films and popular media arts but also in the contemporary sound art scene. Take, for example, the audiovisual performances and installations made by popular sound artists such as Ryoji Ikeda and Alva Noto. Among numerous other artists working similarly, both produce pure sensorial experiences via large-scale, multi-channel sound projections alongside live or pre-programmed visuals. Their notoriously abstract and spectacular immersive sound works often drown the potent subjective contemplation of a sensitive listener to foreground the entertaining spectacle. Many noise artists, who perform regularly on the festival circuits and club scene, promote popular, immediately immersive sound works that are made to move the body and chill out.

What might a better, future medial experience sound like? Can we imagine a media artwork advocating discursivity and dissent? As *Cities and Memory*[9] informs, field recording artists 'have been recording protests around the world to create a sound map that reflects today's political environment'.[10] What these recordings mostly contain are the shouting and screaming of protesters on the street. Given the current state of inaction, a loud, earth-shaking scream might be what the future sounds like. This would occur when the pleasant mode of immersion is broken down, allowing other sounds to enter, creating a fertile premise for a condition I term 'post-immersion' (Chattopadhyay 2020a, 2019b).

To understand the term 'post-immersion', I underscore the disjunction in a medial experience when the alert subjectivity of an audience is encouraged to take form. Here, I refer to the philosopher Vilém Flusser's notion of 'homeland' and 'homelessness', which is central to his thinking. Flusser suggests that only when a person is removed from their home does he or she become aware of the ties that reveal themselves as unconscious judgements. The idea of homelessness is useful for my argument. The non-immersive/discursive situation I would like to explore is based on the spectator's awareness of potentially loosening the ties between the sited experience and its subjective formation. Sound scholar Joanna Demers notes, 'Discursive accent, then, exists in a state of ambivalence [...] discursive accent resituates the phenomenal qualities of voice (or sound, taken broadly) into an artwork, and divests sound of its signifying properties so that it can conceal, rather than reveal meaning' (2013: 149). In drawing on her perspective, a discursive situation in an artistic experience of a sonic environment may occur when the spectator/listener is free to detach themselves from the experience to open it up to a multitude of possible interpretations rather than being fixed in an ontological relationship with the experience that takes over the spectator/listener's phenomenological freedom.

This disjuncture is crucial for locating future film and media arts practice directions that can personalise an immersive experience and allow the emergence of a critical, self-aware faculty. Inspired by Flusser's and Demers's idea of discursive accent, I propose four primary approaches to disrupt immersion, which can be briefly delineated as:

1. The presence of environmental sounds as an alarm mechanism for site-awareness.
2. Asynchronism – a divorce of sound and image in the audiovisual experience (analogous to the asynchronous mode of cinema proposed by V. Pudovkin).[11]
3. Poetic intervention.
4. Audience participation to 'activate' the artwork.

Each of these four approaches facilitates a momentary split from immersion via a specific methodology: in the first approach, ambient sounds provide a cognitive connection and association with the work's sites; in the second, an abruptly out of sync sound in film or audiovisual media arts disentangles the sound from visual images, giving it autonomous agency; in the third, narrative flow is disrupted by discursive elements such as poetic utterances in textual intertitles or subtitles, or commentaries for contemplative moments; and, in the fourth, the audience is given agency to activate the artwork. Such disjunctures in narrative flow create a sense of what Gilles Deleuze and Félix Guattari term 'deterritorialisation' (1972), a notion that resonates with Flusser's 'homelessness'. Deleuze and Guattari use deterritorialisation to describe the condition of disembedding and re-embedding social relations from various objects and sites. It characterises the process that decontextualises a set of relations, rendering them remote and virtual beyond any constraint of the enveloping here and now, preparing them for more actualisations outside of a fixed, local territory. Anthropologists use the term to refer to a 'weakening of ties' between culture and place, site and self, with reference to the removal of cultural objects from a certain location in space and time for new subjectivities to form and more site-aware connections to be made. Within the context of a closed, immersive, medial experience, both ideas of homelessness and deterritorialisation help open up experiences to personalisation and subjective intervention. Through this rupture with the immersive space, an audience may regain their discursive faculty to re-territorialise, remake and augment a sense of home on their own terms within the sited experience.

Future films and media artworks may use different methodologies to disrupt sonic immersion in favour of engaging contexts and content. As Joanna Demers states, these discursive elements would move artworks 'into the realm of poetry, of poiesis, where sound can be free to exist without being grounded in a particular meaning or image' (2013: 151). These socially, environmentally and politically sensate media productions may intend to make their audiences alert by encouraging subjectivity, sensitising their listener to urgent, contemporary crises, including climate breakdown, environmental disintegration through human exploitation, emergent machine and surveillance societies, ecological catastrophe and mass migration. These future works may suggest that constructed media environments are not tied to mere enjoyment and mindless entertainment through an immersive, consumeristic approach. Instead, they could generate socio-politically aware and committed spaces that invite critical discourse within an open-ended, post-immersive experience, leading to debate and action.

20.3 Remoteness

As I finish writing this book, we are living in the strange and surreal times affected by the spectre of a pandemic. An aggravated sense of social alienation is exacerbated by thriving social media with its non-stop bombardment of information. Often this vociferous onslaught of vibrating data seems confusing and misleading to one looking for presence of mind. On the one hand, a serious physical and psychic disconnection exists between people and different segments of society; on the other, there is a globally felt need for more social exchange and solidarity. As a result of this conflict, the pandemic is revealing various issues that require serious and urgent rethinking and assessment, namely rising social inequality, the profit-based development model that is unnecessarily accelerating the Earth towards climate catastrophe, and the lack of equal opportunities, including access to health and education, especially for the poor, displaced and dispossessed.

We have received an unanticipated chance to slow down and listen more closely to the world. While this solitary and remote inner listening is practised, the idea of remoteness might arise. Solitude is always embedded with the desire to connect with oneself more contemplatively and rediscover the Other remotely – true presence becomes a central issue. If here today, Thomas Watson would not physically be able to go over to Alexander Graham Bell's place during lockdown.[12] They would fear catching or spreading the virus along the way. Practising social distancing as prescribed, however, makes us realise just how much we desire to be in the company of others, beside the bed of an ailing mother, sister, friend or other loved one for comfort and solace, for sharing worries in truest presence.

Films and media artworks generally depend on a technological component to operate. By incorporating emerging technologies into their work, makers and artists constantly redefine traditional categories of art. In contrast to older, static art forms, film and media art are created by recording sound or visual images to deliver a time-based work that changes and 'moves' not only in itself but also from one place to another more remotely. This distinction, based on the medial dispositive, underscores issues with the medium itself, whether film, sound art or video art. As demonstrated throughout this book, site-specific presence is critical to film and media arts; lived experiences tend to be mediated and abstracted through recording and production.

On the basis of these comments on emerging environments for future films and media artworks my closing remarks present a reminder to ideas of remoteness and presence as processed through media production. I would like to imagine that future developments in film and media arts may include more worldly attuned environmental concerns and may consider making more socio-political commitments, from local community building to collective action. This book reconsiders the concept of 'presence' precipitated by the process of mediation, from recording to making it heard. Future films and media artworks may bridge the emergent condition of remoteness in public life via 'poetic presence'. So how does this formulation of presence contribute to the times we are living in?

In his poem 'An Orange',[13] Indian poet Jibanananda Das writes about this longing to be present remotely even in the form of an orange by the bedside table of a dear, ailing friend or loved one in a distant land, sounding with a true presence of service, sacrifice and tending. If I can't be there, my true presence may take the form of a useful piece of fruit, carrying the deeply honest, unpretentious and truthful voice of my yearning to be there beside you. This true voice of poetic presence overcomes physical and temporal distances to arrive at the door of emancipation, where poetry is the only vehicle for a soulful meeting, merging and unification. In a recent article, historian and author Yuval Noah Harari suggests that the world may still be in extended lockdown, under intensified surveillance and more difficult to cross physically post-pandemic. The truthful voices in our societies, the artists and practitioners, need to find ways to create novel medial dispositives and more conducive media environments that facilitate and communicate the truthful presence of place to counteract remote media reception in corporal isolation. Filmmakers and media artists might be encouraged to conceive of works that empathetically, carefully and sensitively support the listener's subjective interpretation and access to situational contexts, leading to their fruitful dissemination. Future films and media works may endeavour to respond to an emergent mode of intimate, poetic and contemplative intervention in the technologically saturated and inert medial experiences in an increasingly remote, mediated, auditory setting. Through this involvement, we humans can compassionately connect with ourselves locationally apart, and with the sites we may or may not occupy and inhabit, with the environments we wish to experience and explore, in order to build what Han Lörzing calls 'respectful landscapes' (2001: 110) in film and media arts. We can interact with the non-human others present in those environments and landscapes, by breaking the hegemonic immersive space towards a socially and politically aware and responsible media.

As an article in *EcoHealth*[14] demonstrates with ample evidence, most contagious viral pandemics occur as a result of global anthropogenic colonisation, and disrespect and abuse of land. Therefore, it will suffice to say that collective resistance must grow to nurture the protection of and respect for land and the environment, and to further practise ideas of site-specificity, location and localness. If there is a future for humans, this perspective perhaps suggests a clearer direction. In line with this sentiment, I take a resounding position, advocating for films and media artworks that operate beyond a colonising approach and are respectful of land, sites, the environment and local/indigenous habitats, aiming to bridge the social divide and remoteness, and encouraging a reciprocal and egalitarian global society.

Notes

1. The 'post-digital' is a condition in contemporary creative media practice whereby applications of digital technologies do not remain an end in themselves (Cramer 2014). This tendency is exemplified by the way older mono and stereophonic practices converged with and are absorbed within the three-dimensional surround sound universe. Also, certain retro-aesthetics from the analogue sound eras have been applied to contemporary sound production, leading to an intense flexibility and hybridisation of various practices.
2. I have written about sound practices in the post-digital condition, for example see: Chattopadhyay (2014b).
3. The Graphics Interchange Format. See: http://giphy.com/artists
4. See: https://science.gu.se/digitalAssets/1671/1671867_world-scientists-warning-to-humanity_-a-second-notice_english.pdf
5. See: http://theconversation.com/the-madrid-climate-conferences-real-failure-was-not-getting-a-broad-deal-on-global-carbon-markets-129001
6. See: http://postperspective.com/richard-king-talks-dunkirks-sound-design/
7. See one of the reports among a handful reports on this historical omission: https://www.nytimes.com/2017/08/02/opinion/dunkirk-indians-world-war.html
8. See Shashi Tharoor's book *Inglorious Empire* (2017, London: Hurst Publishers). http://www.hurstpublishers.com/book/inglorious-empire/
9. A global collaborative sound project: https://citiesandmemory.com/
10. See: http://www.wired.co.uk/article/sounds-of-protest-trump-brexit-sound-map

11. See: http://pzacad.pitzer.edu/~mma/teaching/MS114/readings/EisensteinEtc.pdf
12. See: https://www.wired.com/2011/03/0310bell-invents-telephone-mr-watson-come-here/
13. The poem is translated from the original Bengali by Arunava Sinha in *The Bloomsbury Anthology of Great Indian Poems* (2020, London: Bloomsbury):

    'An Orange' – Jibanananda Das
    Once I have left this body
    Shall I not return to earth?
    Let me come back
    On a winter night
    As the doleful flesh of a chilled orange
    At the bedside of a dying friend

14. Gottdenker et al. (2014).

BIBLIOGRAPHY

Ahn, S. J. (2011). 'Embodied experiences in immersive virtual environments: Effects on pro-environmental attitude and behavior' (doctoral dissertation). Stanford, CA: Stanford University.
Allen, R. (2009). 'Pather Panchali'. In Gopalan, L. (ed.), *The Cinema of India* (pp. 86–95). 24 Frames series. London: Wallflower Press.
Allen, R. and Smith, M. (eds) (1999). *Film Theory and Philosophy*. Oxford: Oxford University Press.
Alloway, L. (1981). 'Sites/Nonsites'. In Hobbs, R. (ed.), *Robert Smithson: Sculpture* (pp. 41–46). Ithaca, NY: Cornell University Press.
Althusser, Louis (1976). *Essays in Self-Criticism*. London: New Left.
Altman, R. (2012). 'Four and a Half Film Fallacies'. In J. Sterne (ed.), *The Sound Studies Reader* (pp. 225–233). London: Routledge.
Altman, R. (2001). 'The Living Nickelodeon'. In Abel, R. and Altman, R. (eds), *The Sounds of Early Cinema* (pp. 232–240). Bloomington: Indiana University Press.
Altman, R. (1994). 'Deep-focus sound: Citizen Kane and the radio aesthetic'. *Quarterly Review of Film and Video* 15/3: 5.
Altman, R. (ed.) (1992). *Sound Theory/Sound Practice*. New York: Routledge.
Altman R. (1985). 'The Evolution of Sound Technology'. In Weis, E. and Belton, J. (eds), *Film Sound: Theory and Practice* (pp. 44–53). New York: Columbia University Press.
Altman, R. (ed.) (1980). *Yale French Studies Number 60: Cinema/Sound*. New Haven, CT: Yale University Press.
Altman, R., Jones, M. and Tratoe, S. (2000). 'Inventing the cinema soundtrack: Hollywood's multiplane sound system'. In Buhler, J., Flinn, C. and Neumeyer, D. (eds), *Music and Cinema* (pp. 339–359). Hanover, NH: University Press of New England [for] Wesleyan University Press.
Augoyard, J.-F. and Torgue, H. (eds) (2006). *Sonic Experience: A Guide to Everyday Sounds*. Montreal: McGill-Queen's Press.

BIBLIOGRAPHY

Bachelard, G. (1969). *The Poetics of Reverie: Childhood, Language, and the Cosmos*. Translated from the French by Daniel Russell. Boston: Beacon Press.

Balázs, B. (1985). 'Theory of the Film: Sound'. In Weis, E. & Belton, J. (eds), *Film Sound: Theory and Practice* (pp. 116–125). New York: Columbia University Press.

Barwise, J. and Perry, J. (1999). *Situations and Attitudes*. Stanford, CA: Center for the Study of Language and Information.

Basset, K. (2004). 'Walking as an aesthetic practice and a critical tool: Some psycho-geographic experiments'. *Journal of Geography in Higher Education* 28/3: 397–410.

Beck, J. (2013). 'Acoustic Auteurs and Transnational Cinema'. In Vernallis, C., Herzog, A. and Richardson, J. (eds), *The Oxford Handbook of Sound and Image in Digital Media*. Oxford: Oxford University Press.

Beck, J. (2008). 'The Sounds of "Silence": Dolby Stereo, Sound Design, and The Silence of the Lambs'. In Beck, J. and Grajeda, T. (eds), *Lowering the Boom: Critical Studies in Film Sound*. Urbana: University of Illinois Press.

Beck, J. and Grajeda, T. (eds) (2008). *Lowering the Boom: Critical Studies in Film Sound*. Urbana: University of Illinois Press.

Belton, J. (1992). '1950s Magnetic Sound: The Frozen Revolution'. In Altman, R. (ed.), *Sound Theory/Sound Practice* (pp. 154–167). New York: Routledge.

Bhan, G. (2013). 'Planned illegalities: Housing and the "failure" of planning in Delhi: 1947–2010'. *Economic and Political Weekly* 48: 24.

Biancorosso, G. (2009). 'Sound'. In Livingston, P. and Plantinga, C. (eds), *The Routledge Companion to Philosophy and Film* (pp. 260–267). London: Routledge.

Biggs, M. and Karlsson, H. (eds) (2011). *The Routledge Companion to Research in the Arts*. London: Routledge.

Birtwistle, A. (2010). *Cinesonica: Sounding Film and Video*. Manchester: Manchester University Press.

Blesser, B. and Salter, L. R. (2009). *Spaces Speak, Are You Listening?: Experiencing Aural Architecture*. London: The MIT Press.

Bloom, P. J. (2014). 'Sound Theory'. In Branigan, E. and Buckland, W. (eds), *The Routledge Encyclopedia of Film Theory*. London: Routledge.

Böhme, G. (1993). 'Atmosphere as the fundamental concept of a new aesthetics'. *Thesis Eleven* 36: 113–126.

Bondebjerg, I. (2005). 'The Danish way: Danish film culture in a European and global perspective'. In Nestingen, A. K. and Elkington, T. G. (eds), *Transnational Cinema in a Global North: Nordic Cinema in Transition*. Detroit, MI: Wayne State University Press.

Booth, G. D. and Shope, B. (eds) (2013). *More Than Bollywood: Studies in Indian Popular Music*. New York: Oxford University Press.

Bordwell, D. (2009). 'Cognitive Theory'. In Livingston, P. and Plantinga, C. (eds), *The Routledge Companion to Philosophy and Film* (pp. 356–365). London: Routledge.

Bordwell, D. and Thompson, K. (1997), *Film Art. An Introduction*. London and New York: McGraw-Hill Publishing Company.

Bordwell, D. and Thompson, K. (1985). 'Fundamental Aesthetics of Sound in the Cinema'. In Weis, E. and Belton, J. (eds), *Film Sound: Theory and Practice*. New York: Columbia University Press.

Borgdorff, H. (2012). *Conflict of the Faculties: Perspectives on Artistic Research and Academia*. Leiden: Leiden University Press.

Borgdorff, H. (2009). *Artistic Research within the Fields of Science*. Sensuous Knowledge 6. Bergen: Bergen National Academy of the Arts.

Borges, J. L. (1999). *The Total Library: Non-Fiction 1922–1986*. London: Penguin Publishers.

Bosma, J. (2014). 'Post-digital is post-screen: Arnheim's visual thinking applied to art in

the expanded digital media field'. *A Peer-reviewed Journal About* 3.1. https://aprja.net//article/view/116093
Braidotti, R. (2012). *Nomadic Theory: The Portable Rosi Braidotti*. New York: Columbia University Press.
Branigan, E. (1997). 'Sound, Epistemology, Film'. In Allen, R. and Smith, M. (eds), *Film Theory and Philosophy* (pp. 95–125). Oxford: Oxford University Press.
Branigan, E. (1992). *Narrative Comprehension and Film*. London: Routledge.
Branigan, E. (1989). 'Sound and epistemology in film'. *The Journal of Aesthetics and Art Criticism* 47/4: 311–324.
Bronowski, J. (1973). *The Ascent of Man*. Boston and Toronto: Little, Brown & Co.
Buhler, J., Neumeyer, D. and Deemer, R. (2010). *Hearing the Movies: Music and Sound in Film History*. New York: Oxford University Press.
Burch, N. (1985). 'On the Structural Use of Sound'. In Weis, E. and Belton, J. (eds), *Film Sound: Theory and Practice*. New York: Columbia University Press.
Burch, N. (1982). Narrative/diegesis—thresholds, limits. *Screen* 23/2: 16–33.
Cardullo, B. (2009). *The Films of Robert Bresson: A Casebook*. New York: Anthem Press.
Carrigy, M. (2009a). 'Bhuvan Shome'. In Gopalan, L. (ed.), *The Cinema of India* (pp. 138–147). 24 Frames series. London: Wallflower Press.
Carrigy, M. (2009b). 'Meghe Dhaka Tara'. In Gopalan, L. (ed.), *The Cinema of India* (pp. 126–137). 24 Frames series. London: Wallflower Press.
Cascone, K. (2002). 'The aesthetics of failure: "Post-digital" tendencies in contemporary computer music'. *Computer Music Journal* 24/4 (Winter).
Ceserani, R. (2010). 'The essayistic style of Walter Benjamin'. *Primerjalna književnost* 33/1: 83–92.
Chattopadhyay, B. (2022). *Sound Practices in the Global South: Co-listening to Resounding Plurilogues*. London: Palgrave Macmillan. (Collection of interviews with sound artists and practitioners from the Global Souths.)
Chattopadhyay, B. (2021). *Between the Headphones: Listening to the Practitioner*. Newcastle upon Tyne: Cambridge Scholars Publishing. (Collection of interviews with film sound technicians from India.)
Chattopadhyay, B. (2020a). 'Post-immersion: Towards a discursive situation in sound art'. *RUUKKU Studies in Artistic Research* 13. https://www.researchcatalogue.net/view/555994/555995
Chattopadhyay, B. (2020b). *The Nomadic Listener*. Berlin: Errant Bodies Press.
Chattopadhyay, B. (2019a). 'Listening in/to exile: Migration and media arts.' *VIS – Nordic Journal for Artistic Research* 2. https://www.en.visjournal.nu/tag/issue-2/
Chattopadhyay, B. (2019b). 'Post-immersion'. RE:SOUND, Histories of Media Art, Science and Technology, Aalborg (conference presentation).
Chattopadhyay, B. (2019c). 'Uneasy Listening: Perspectives on (Nordic) Sound Art after the Digital'. In Ag, Tanya Toft (ed.), *Digital Dynamics in Nordic Contemporary Art*. Bristol: Intellect.
Chattopadhyay, B. (2018a). 'Orphan sounds: Locating historical recordings in contemporary media'. *Organised Sound* 23/2: 181–188.
Chattopadhyay, B. (2018b). 'The world within the home: Tracing the sound in Satyajit Ray's films'. *Music, Sound, and the Moving Image* 11/2: 131–156.
Chattopadhyay, B. (2017a). 'Audible absence: Searching for the site in sound production' (doctoral dissertation). Leiden: Leiden University Press (limited edition).
Chattopadhyay, B. (2017b). 'Reconstructing atmospheres: Ambient sound in film and media production'. *Communication and the Public* 2/4: 352–364.
Chattopadhyay, B. (2016). 'Being there: Evocation of the site in contemporary Indian cinema'. *Journal of Sonic Studies* 12. Research Catalogue.

Chattopadhyay, B. (2015a). 'Auditory (con)texts: Writing on sound'. *Ear | Wave | Event* 2.
Chattopadhyay, B. (2015b), *Decomposing Landscape*. Digital download (binaural and Ambisonics B-format files). London: Touch.
Chattopadhyay, B. (2015c). 'The auditory spectacle: Designing sound for the "dubbing era" of Indian cinema'. *The New Soundtrack* 5/1: 55–68. DOI: 10.3366/sound.2015.0068
Chattopadhyay, B. (2014a). 'Object-disoriented sound: Listening in the post-digital condition'. *A Peer-reviewed Journal About* 3/1. http://www.aprja.net/?p=1839
Chattopadhyay, B. (2014b). 'Sonic drifting: Sound, city and psychogeography'. *SoundEffects* 3/3: 138–152. Special issue 'Urban Sound'.
Chattopadhyay, B. (2014c). 'The invisible sound: A study in the trajectories of sound practice in Indian films by online archival research'. *IASA Journal* 42: 89–95.
Chattopadhyay, B. (2013). 'The cinematic soundscape: Conceptualising the use of sound in Indian films'. *SoundEffects* 2/2: 66–78.
Chattopadhyay, B. (2013a). 'Auditory situations: Notes from nowhere'. *Journal of Sonic Studies* 4.
Chattopadhyay, B. (2013b). *Elegy for Bangalore*. Frankfurt am Main: Gruenrekorder.
Chattopadhyay, B. (2013c). 'Interview'. In Lane, C. and Carlyle, A. (eds), *In the Field: The Art of Field Recording*. London: Uniformbooks.
Chattopadhyay, B. (2012a). 'Sonic menageries: Composing the sound of place'. *Organised Sound* 17: 223–229.
Chattopadhyay, B. (2012b). 'Sonification of cinema: Studying the use of location sound in Indian films'. Paper presented at Music & The Moving Image Conference, New York.
Chattopadhyay, B. (2012c). 'Soundhunting in a city: Chronicles of an urban field recording expedition'. *Field Notes* 3. Frankfurt am Main: Gruenrekorder.
Chattopadhyay, B. (2008). *Landscape in Metamorphoses*. Frankfurt am Main: Gruenrekorder (Gr 057LC 09488).
Chattopadhyay, B. (2007). 'Sound memories: In search of lost sounds in Indian cinema'. *Journal of the Moving Image* 6: 102–111. Kolkata: Jadavpur University Press.
Chaudhuri, A. (2013). 'Satyajit Ray: A retrospective'. *Financial Times*, August. https://www.ft.com/content/d4b1d302-fb82-11e2-8650-00144feabdc0 (accessed on 1 May 2020).
Chaudhuri, S. (2007). 'Space, interiority and affect in Charulata and Ghare Baire'. *Journal of the Moving Image* 6.
Chion, M. (2009). *Film, A Sound Art*. New York: Columbia University Press.
Chion, M. (1994). *Audio-Vision: Sound on Screen*. Translated and edited by C. Gorbman. New York: Columbia University Press.
Clair, R. (1929/1985). 'The Art of Sound'. In Weis, E. and Belton, J. (eds), *Film Sound: Theory and Practice*. New York: Columbia University Press.
Cobussen, M. (2002). 'Deconstruction in music' (doctoral dissertation). Rotterdam: Erasmus University Rotterdam.
Cogan, J. (2006). 'The phenomenological reduction'. *Internet Encyclopedia of Philosophy*. http://www.iep.utm.edu/phen-red/
Connor, S. (2004). 'Sound and the Self'. In Smith, M. M. (ed.), *Hearing History: A Reader* (pp. 54–66). Athens: The University of Georgia Press.
Cooper, D. (2000). *The Cinema of Satyajit Ray: Between Tradition and Modernity*. New York: Cambridge University Press.
Cooper, S. (1996). 'Review of Chris Watson's *Stepping into the Dark*'. *AllMusic* magazine. https://www.allmusic.com/album/stepping-into-the-dark-mw0000189394
Corbella M. (2011). 'Notes for a dramaturgy of sound in Fellini's cinema: The

electroacoustic sound library of the 1960s'. *Music and the Moving Image* 4/3: 14–30.
Coverley, M. (2010). *Psychogeography*. Harpenden, UK: Pocket Essentials.
Cox, C. (2009). 'Sound art and the sonic unconscious'. *Organised Sound* 14/1: 19–26.
Cox, C. and Warner, D. (2004). *Audio Culture: Readings in Modern Music*. New York: Bloomsbury.
Cox, G. (2014). 'Prehistories of the post-digital: Or, some old problems with post-anything'. *A Peer-reviewed Journal About* 3.1. http://www.aprja.net/?p=1318
Cramer, F. (2014). 'What is "post-digital"?'. *A Peer-reviewed Journal About* 3/1. http://www.aprja.net/?p=1318
Cvetkovich, A. and Kellner, D. (eds) (1996). *Articulating the Global and the Local. Globalisation and Cultural Studies*. Boulder, CO: Westview Press.
Das, Jibanananda (2019). 'An Orange'. In 'Poems of Jibanananda Das', *Daily Star*. https://www.thedailystar.net/literature/news/poems-jibanananda-das-1784686 (accessed 26 March 2020)
Dasmann, Raymond F. (2002). *Called by the Wild: The Autobiography of a Conservationist*. Berkeley: University of California Press.
Dayal, G. (2013). 'Sound art'. http://theoriginalsoundtrack.com/
De, A. (ed.) (2008). *Multiple City: Writings on Bangalore*. New Delhi: Penguin Books India.
Debord, G. (1956). 'Theory of the dérive'. Translated by Ken Knabb. *Les Lèvres Nues* 9.
Deleuze, G. and Guattari, F. (1986). *Nomadology: The War Machine*. Translated by B. Massumi. Cambridge, MA: The MIT Press.
Deleuze, G. and Guattari, F. (1972/2004). *Anti-Œdipus*. Translated by Robert Hurley, Mark Seem and Helen R. Lane. London and New York: Continuum.
Demers, J. (2013). 'Discursive Accents in Some Recent Digital Media Works'. In Vernallis, C., Herzog, A. and Richardson, J. (eds), *The Oxford Handbook of Sound and Image in Digital Media*. Oxford: Oxford University Press.
Demers, J. (2010). *Listening through the Noise: The Aesthetics of Experimental Electronic Music*. New York: Oxford University Press.
Demers, J. (2009). 'Field recording, sound art and objecthood'. *Organised Sound* 14/1: 39–45.
d'Escriván, J. (2009). 'Sound art (?) on/in film'. *Organised Sound* 14/1: 65–73.
Dienstfrey, E. (2016). 'The myth of the speakers: A critical reexamination of Dolby history'. *Film History* 28/1: 167–193.
Dissanayake, W. and Sahai, M. (1992). *Sholay: A Cultural Reading*. New Delhi: Wiley Eastern Ltd.
Doane, M. A. (1985a). 'Ideology and the Practice of Sound Editing and Mixing'. In Weis, E. and Belton, J. (eds), *Film Sound: Theory and Practice*. New York: Columbia University Press.
Doane, M. A. (1985b). 'The Voice in the Cinema: The Articulation of Body and Space'. In Weis, E. and Belton, J. (eds), *Film Sound: Theory and Practice*. New York: Columbia University Press.
Donnelly, K. J. (2014). *Occult Aesthetics: Synchronization in Sound Film*. New York: Oxford University Press.
Drever, L. J. (2002). 'Soundscape composition: The convergence of ethnography and acousmatic music'. *Organised Sound* 7/1: 21–27.
Dumouchel, P. (2015). 'Mirrors of Nature: Artificial Agents in Real Life and Virtual Worlds'. In Cowdell, S., Fleming, C. and Hodge, J. (eds), *Mimesis, Movies, and Media: Violence, Desire, and the Sacred*. New York: Bloomsbury Academic.
Dunleavy, P. (2003). *Authoring a PhD: How to Plan, Draft, Write and Finish a Doctoral Thesis or Dissertation*. New York: Palgrave Macmillan.

Ďurovičová, N. (2003). 'Local ghosts: Dubbing bodies in early sound cinema'. *Moveast* 9. http://www.filmintezet.hu/uj/kiadvanyok/moveast/moveast_9/durovicova.htm

Dyson, F. (2009). *Sounding New Media: Immersion and Embodiment in the Arts and Culture*. Berkeley: University of California Press.

Eisenberg, A. J. (2015). 'Space'. In Novak, D. and Sakakeeny, M. (eds) *Keywords in Sound* (pp. 193–207). Durham, NC: Duke University Press.

English, L. (2014). 'A beginner's guide to ... field recording'. *FACT Magazine* November issue. http://www.factmag.com/2014/11/18/a-beginners-guide-to-field-recording/

Eno, Brian (1978). Liner notes from *Music for Airports*/Ambient 1, PVC 7908 (AMB 001). http://music.hyperreal.org/artists/brian_eno/MFA-txt.html

Fischer, L. (1985). 'Applause: The Visual and Acoustic Landscape'. In Weis, E. and Belton, J. (eds), *Film Sound: Theory and Practice* (pp. 233–250). New York: Columbia University Press.

Flusser, V. (2002). *Writings*. Minneapolis and London: University of Minnesota Press.

Gallagher, M. (2015). 'Field recording and the sounding of spaces'. *Environment and Planning D: Society and Space* 33: 560–576.

Ganguly, S. (2001). *Satyajit Ray: In Search of the Modern*. New Delhi: Indialog.

Gess, N. (2015). 'Ideologies of Sound: Longing for presence from the eighteenth century until today'. *Journal of Sonic Studies* 10.

Gooptu, S. (2011). *Bengali Cinema: An Other Nation*. London: Routledge.

Gopalan, L. (2002). *Cinema of Interruptions: Action Genres in Contemporary Indian Cinema*. London: British Film Institute.

Gorbman, C. (1987). *Unheard Melodies: Narrative Film Music*. Bloomington: Indiana University Press.

Gottdenker, N. L., Streicker, D. G., Faust C. L. and Carroll C. R. (2014). 'Anthropogenic land use change and infectious diseases: A review of the evidence'. *Ecohealth* 11/4: 619–632.

Grimshaw, M. (2014). *The Oxford Handbook of Virtuality*. Oxford: Oxford University Press.

Grimshaw, M. (2011). *Game Sound Technology and Player Interaction: Concepts and Developments*. Hershey, PA: Information Science Reference, IGI Global.

Gumbrecht, H. U. (2004). *Production of Presence: What Meaning Cannot Convey*. Stanford, CA: Stanford University Press.

Harari, Y. N. (2020). 'The world after coronavirus'. *Financial Times*. https://www.ft.com/content/19d90308-6858-11ea-a3c9-1fe6fedcca75 (accessed 26 March 2020).

Harper, G., Doughty, R. and Eisentraut, J. (eds) (2009). *Sound and Music in Film and Visual Media: A Critical Overview*. New York: Bloomsbury Academic.

Hayward, S. (2006). *Cinema Studies: The Key Concepts*. London: Routledge.

Helles, R. and Jensen, K. B. (2013). 'Introduction to the special issue – Making data: Big data and beyond'. *First Monday* 18/10.

Hermann, T., Hunt, A. and Neuhoff, J. G. (eds) (2011). *The Sonification Handbook*. Berlin: Logos Publishing House.

Holman, T. (1997/2002/2010). *Sound for Film and television*. Boston, MA: Focal Press.

Hyatt, S. (ed.) (2018). *Metaphonics: The Field Works Listener's Guide*. Heijningen: Jap Sam Books.

Ihde, D. (2012). 'The auditory dimension'. In Sterne, J. (ed.), *The Sound Studies Reader* (pp. 23–28). London: Routledge.

Ihde, D. (2007). *Listening and Voice: Phenomenologies of Sound*. New York: Suny Press.

Jørgensen, U. A. (2019). 'Reformulations of the "Natural" World: Jana Winderen's Sound nstallation The Wanderer'. In Ag, Tanya Toft (ed.), *Digital Dynamics in Nordic Contemporary Art*. Bristol: Intellect.

Kallinikos, J., Aaltonen, A. and Marton, A. (2010). 'A theory of digital objects'. *First Monday* 15/6.
Kania, A. (2009). 'Realism'. In Livingston, P. and Plantinga, C. (eds), *The Routledge Companion to Philosophy and Film* (pp. 237–247). London: Routledge.
Kassabian, A. (2013a). 'The End of Diegesis As We Know It?' In Richardson, J., Gorbman. C. and Vernallis, C. (eds), *The Oxford Handbook of New Audiovisual Aesthetics*. DOI: 10.1093/oxfordhb/9780199733866.013.032
Kassabian, A. (2013b). *Ubiquitous Listening: Affect, Attention, and Distributed Subjectivity*. Berkeley, CA: University of California Press.
Kastner, J. and Wallis, B. (1998). *Land and Environmental Art*. London: Phaidon Press.
Kelman, Ari Y. (2010). 'Rethinking the soundscape: A critical genealogy of a key term in sound studies'. *Senses and Society* 5/2: 212–234.
Kerins, M. (2011). *Beyond Dolby (Stereo): Cinema in the Digital Sound Age*. Bloomington: Indiana University Press.
Kerins, M. (2006). 'Narration in the cinema of digital sound'. *The Velvet Light Trap* 58 (Fall): 41–54. DOI: 10.1353/vlt.2006.0030
Kimbell, L. (2013). 'The object fights back: An interview with Graham Harman'. *Design and Culture* 5/1: 103–117.
Kim-Cohen, S. (2013). *Against Ambience*. New York: Bloomsbury Academic.
Kim-Cohen, S. (2009). *In the Blink of an Ear: Toward a Non-Cochlear Sonic Art*. New York: Bloomsbury Academic.
Kinnear, Michael S. (1994). *The Gramophone Company's First Indian Recordings, 1899–1908*. Mumbai: Popular Prakashan.
Kracauer, S. (1960). *Theory of Film*. Princeton, NJ: Princeton University Press.
Krause, B. (2012). *The Great Animal Orchestra: Finding the Origins of Music in the World's Wild Places*. New York: Little Brown.
Krause, B. (1987). 'Bioacoustics: Habitat ambience and ecological balance'. *Whole Earth Review* 57.
Kuhn, A. and Westwell, G. (2014/2015). 'A Dictionary of Film Studies'. Oxford Reference Online. http://www.oxfordreference.com/view/10.1093/acref/9780199587261.001.0001/acref-9780199587261-e-0561; http://www.oxfordreference.com/view/10.1093/acref/9780199587261.001.0001/acref-9780199587261-e-0561?rskey=5Njasa&result=555
Kuhn, A. and Westwell, G. (2012). *A Dictionary of Film Studies*. Oxford: Oxford University Press.
Kumar, A. (2020). *The Bloomsbury Anthology of Great Indian Poems*. New York: Bloomsbury Publishing.
Kwon, M. (2002). *One Place After Another: Site-Specific Art and Locational Identity*. Cambridge, MA and London: The MIT Press.
LaBelle, B. (2006/2015). *Background Noise: Perspectives on Sound Art*. New York: Bloomsbury Academic.
LaBelle, B. (2002). *Social Music*. Berlin: Errant Bodies Press.
LaBelle, B. and Martinho, C. (eds) (2011). *Site of Sound: Of Architecture and the Ear: Volume 2*. Berlin: Errant Bodies Press.
Lane, C. and Carlyle, A. (eds) (2013). *In the Field: The Art of Field Recording*. London: Uniformbooks.
Langkjær, B. (2010). 'Making fictions sound real: On film sound, perceptual realism and genre'. *MedieKultur* 48: 5–17.
Langkjær, B. (2006). 'Mediernes lyd. En multimodal analysemetode'. *MedieKultur* 40: 14–26.
Langkjær, B. (2000). *Den lyttende tilskuer*. Copenhagen: Museum Tusculanum Press.

Lastra, J. (2000). *Sound Technology and the American Cinema: Perception, Representation, Modernity*. New York: Columbia University Press.

Lawrence, A. (1992). 'Women's Voices in Third World Cinema'. In Altman, R. (ed.), *Sound Theory/Sound Practice* (pp. 178–190). New York: Routledge.

Lefebvre, H. (1974). *La production de l'espace*. Paris: Éditions Anthropos.

Lévi-Strauss, C. (1962). *The Savage Mind*. Paris: Librairie Plon.

Licht, A. (2009). 'Sound art: Origins, development and ambiguities'. *Organised Sound* 14/1: 3–10.

LoBrutto, V. (1994). *Sound-on-Film: Interviews with Creators of Film Sound*. Westport, CT: Praeger.

Lombard, M. and Ditton, T. (1997). 'At the heart of it all: The concept of presence'. *Journal of Computer-Mediated Communication* 3/2. http://onlinelibrary.wiley.com/doi/10.1111/j.1083-6101.1997.tb00072.x/full

Lörzing, H. (2001). *The Nature of Landscape: A Personal Quest*. Rotterdam: 010 Publishers.

Lovatt, P. (2013). '"Every drop of my blood sings our song. There can you hear it?": Haptic sound and embodied memory in the films of Apichatpong Weerasethakul'. *The New Soundtrack* 3/1: 61–79. https://doi.org/10.3366/sound.2013.0036

Lukas, S. A. (2016). *A Reader in Themed and Immersive Spaces*. Lulu.com

McAdams, S. and Bigand, E. (1993). *Thinking in Sound: The Cognitive Psychology of Human Audition*. New York: Oxford University Press.

McKinsey (2010). 'India's urbanization: A closer look'. *McKinsey Quarterly* July issue.

McLuhan, M. (2003). *Understanding Media: The Extensions of Man*. Berkeley, CA: Gingko Press.

Marchessault, J. and Lord, S. (eds) (2008). *Fluid Screens, Expanded Cinema (Digital Futures)*. Toronto: University of Toronto Press.

Mazumdar, R. (2009). 'Satya'. In Gopalan, L. (ed.), *The Cinema of India* (pp. 236–245). 24 Frames series. London: Wallflower Press.

Merleau-Ponty, Maurice (2005). *Phenomenology of Perception*. Translated by C Smith. London: Routledge.

Messerli, D. (2011). 'Trapped in the past'. *International Cinema Review*. http://internationalcinemareview.blogspot.de/2011/12/trapped-in-past-by-douglas-messerli.html

Metz, C. (1980). 'Aural Objects'. Translated by Georgia Gurrieri. In Altman, R. (ed.), *Yale French Studies Number 60: Cinema/Sound* (pp. 24–32). New Haven, CT: Yale University Press.

Miller, J. and Glassner B. (2011). 'The "Inside" and the "Outside": Finding Realities in Interviews'. In Silverman, D. (ed.), *Qualitative Research: Issues of Theory, Method and Practice* (pp. 125–139). London: Sage.

Miranda, M. (2013). *Unsitely Aesthetics: Uncertain Practices in Contemporary Art*. Berlin: Errant Bodies.

Mohler, B. J., Di Luca, M. and Bülthoff, H. H. (2013). 'Multisensory Contributions to Spatial Perception'. In Waller, D. A. and Nadel, L. (eds), *Handbook of Spatial Cognition* (pp. 81–97). Washington, DC: American Psychological Association.

Morris, A. K. (ed.) (1998). *Sound States: Innovative Poetics and Acoustical Technologies*. Chapel Hill: The University of North Carolina Press.

Morton, T. (2013). *Hyperobjects: Philosophy and Ecology after the End of the World*. Minneapolis: University of Minnesota Press.

Morton, T. (2009). *Ecology without Nature: Rethinking Environmental Aesthetics*. Cambridge, MA and London: Harvard University Press.

Mukherjee, M. (2007). 'Early Indian talkies: Voice, performance and aura'. *Journal of the Moving Image* 6: 39–61. Kolkata: Jadavpur University Press.

Nancy, J. L. (2007). *Listening*. Translated by Charlotte Mandell. New York: Fordham University Press.
Neale, S. (1985). *Cinema and Technology: Image, Sound, Colour*. London: BFI.
Negroponte, N. (1998). 'Beyond digital'. *Wired* 6/12.
Neumeyer, D. (1997). 'Source music, background music, fantasy and reality in early sound film'. *College Music Symposium* 37: 13–20.
Novak, D. and Sakakeeny, M. (eds) (2015). *Keywords in Sound*. Durham, NC: Duke University Press.
O'Donnell, E. (2004). '"Woman" and "Homeland" in Ritwik Ghatak's films: Constructing post-Independence Bengali cultural identity'. *Jump Cut: A Review of Contemporary Media* 47. http://www.ejumpcut.org/archive/jc47.2005/ghatak/text.html
Pemmaraju, G. (2013). 'Soundbaazi: The sound of more than music'. *ArtConnect: The IFA Magazine* 7/1: 62–82.
Percheron, D. (1980). 'Sound in cinema and its relationship to image and diegesis'. In Altman, R. (ed.), *Yale French Studies Number 60: Cinema/Sound* (pp. 16–23). New Haven, CT: Yale University Press.
Pinch, T. and Bijsterveld, K. (eds) (2012). *The Oxford Handbook of Sound Studies*. New York: Oxford University Press.
Plantinga, C. (2009). 'Emotion and Affect'. In Livingston, P. and Plantinga, C. (eds), *The Routledge Companion to Philosophy and Film* (pp. 356–365). London: Routledge.
Polli, A. (2004). 'Atmospherics/weather works: A multi-channel storm sonification project'. Proceedings of ICAD 04-Tenth Meeting of the International Conference on Auditory Display, Sydney. https://www.icad.org/Proceedings/2004/Polli2004.pdf
Prince, S. (1996). 'True lies: Perceptual realism, digital images, and film theory'. *Film Quarterly* 49/3: 27–37.
Rajadhyaksha, A. (2009). *Indian Cinema in the Time of Celluloid: From Bollywood to the Emergency*. New Delhi: Indiana University Press.
Rajadhyaksha, A. (2007). 'An aesthetic for film sound in India?' *Journal of the Moving Image*, issue 6.
Ray, B. (2015). *Amader Katha*. Calcutta: Ananda Publishers.
Ray, S. (2011). *Satyajit Ray on Cinema*. Edited by Sandip Ray. New York: Columbia University Press.
Ray, S. (1976). *Our Films their Films*. Delhi: Orient Blackswan.
Reiter, U. (2011). 'Perceived Quality in Game Audio'. In Grimshaw, M. (ed.), *Game Sound Technology and Player Interaction: Concepts and Developments*. Hershey, PA: Information Science Reference.
Ribrant, G. (1999). 'Style parameters in film sound'. FilmSound.org. http://filmsound.org/bibliography/stylepara.pdf
Richardson, J., Gorbman, C. and Vernallis, C. (eds) (2015). *The Oxford Handbook of New Audiovisual Aesthetics*. New York: Oxford University Press.
Rogers, A. (2013). *Cinematic Appeals: The Experience of New Movie Technologies*. New York: Columbia University Press.
Rothenberg, D. (2013). *Bug Music*. New York: St. Martin's Press.
Sadler, S. (1999). *The Situationist City*. Cambridge, MA: The MIT Press.
Saeed-Vafa, M. and Rosenbaum, J. (eds) (2003). *Abbas Kiarostami*. Urbana and Chicago: University of Illinois Press.
Saeed-Vafa, M. and Rosenbaum, J. (eds) (2018). *Abbas Kiarostami* (expanded second edition). Urbana and Chicago: University of Illinois Press.
Schafer, R. M. (1994). *The Soundscape: Our Sonic Environment and the Tuning of the World*. Rochester, VT: Destiny Books.

Schepper, R. (2008). 'Budhaditya Chattopadhyay: Landscape in Metamorphoses'. *Textura*, November.

Schmidt, U. (2013). *Det ambiente: Sansning, medialisering, omgivelse*. Aarhus: Aarhus Universitetsforlag.

Schmidt, U. (2012). 'Ambience and ubiquity'. In Ekman, U. (ed.), *Throughout – Art and Culture Emerging with Ubiquitous Computing* (pp. 175–188). Cambridge, MA: The MIT Press.

Schneider, S. J. (ed.) (2008). *1001 Movies You Must See Before You Die*. New York: Quintessence.

Schrimshaw, W. (2018). 'Writing Out Sound: Immersion and Inscription in Sound Art'. In Aceti, L., Bulley, J., Drever, J. and Sahin, O. (eds), *Sound Curating*. Cambridge, MA: LEA/The MIT Press.

Schulze, H. (2013). 'Adventures in sonic fiction: A heuristic for sound studies'. *Journal of Sonic Studies* 4.

Schwab, M. (ed.) (2014). *Experimental Systems: Future Knowledge in Artistic Research*. Orpheus Institute Series. Leuven: Leuven University Press.

Schwab, M. and Borgdorff, H (eds) (2014). *The Exposition of Artistic Research: Publishing Art in Academia*. Leiden: Leiden University Press.

Seel, M. (2018). *The Arts of Cinema*. Ithaca, NY: Cornell University Press.

Self, W. (2007). *Psychogeography*. London: Bloomsbury.

Sengupta, A. (2007). 'Seeing through the sound: Certain tendencies of the soundtrack in Satyajit Ray's films of the 1970s'. *Journal of the Moving Image* 6: 86–101.

Sergi, G. (2004). *The Dolby Era: Film Sound in Contemporary Hollywood*. Manchester: Manchester University Press.

Seton, M. (2003). *Portrait of a Director: Satyajit Ray*. New Delhi: Penguin Books India.

Shankar, P. (2009). 'Sholay'. In Gopalan, L. (ed.), *The Cinema of India* (pp. 160–169). 24 Frames series. London: Wallflower Press.

Shaviro, S. (2010). *Post Cinematic Affect*. Ropley, UK: John Hunt Publishing.

Sider, L., Sider, J. and Freeman, D. (eds) (2003). *Soundscape: The School of Sound Lectures 1998–2001*. London: Wallflower Press.

Skalski, P. and Whitbred, R. (2010). 'Image versus sound: A comparison of formal feature effects on presence and video game enjoyment'. *PsychNology Journal* 8/1: 67–84. http://www.psychology.org/File/PNJ8(1)/PSYCHNOLOGY_JOURNAL_8_1_SKALSKI.pdf

Sobchack, V. (2005). 'When the ear dreams: Dolby digital and the imagination of sound'. *Film Quarterly* 58/4: 2–15.

Sobchack, V. (1991). *The Address of the Eye: A Phenomenology of Film Experience*. Princeton, NJ: Princeton University Press.

Sonnenschein, D. (2001). *Sound Design: The Expressive Power of Music, Voice, and Sound Effects in Cinema*. Studio City, CA: Michael Wiese Productions.

Sorfa, D. (2014). 'A glossary of film terms'. http://www.academia.edu/1739157/A_Glossary_of_Film_Terms

Spivak, G. C. (1988). *Can the Subaltern Speak?*. Basingstoke: Macmillan.

Sterne, J. (2012a). 'Sonic Imaginations'. In Sterne, J. (ed.), *The Sound Studies Reader* (pp. 1–17). London: Routledge.

Sterne, J. (ed.) (2012b). *The Sound Studies Reader*. London: Routledge.

Sterne, J. (2006). 'The death and life of digital audio'. *Interdisciplinary Science Reviews* 31/4: 338–348.

Sterne, J. (2003). *The Audible Past: Cultural Origins of Sound Reproduction*. Durham, NC: Duke University Press.

Tan, E. S. (2011). *Emotion and the Structure of Narrative Film: Film as an Emotion Machine*. New York and London: Routledge.

Tarkovsky, A. A. and Hunter-Blair, K. (1989). *Sculpting in Time: Reflections on the Cinema*. Austin: University of Texas Press.
Thompson, E. (2004). *The Soundscape of Modernity: Architectural Acoustics and the Culture of Listening in America, 1900–1933*. London: The MIT Press.
Toop, D. (1995). *Ocean of Sound: Aether Talk, Ambient Sound and Imaginary Worlds*. London: Serpent's Tail.
Truax, B. (2007). 'Sound in context: Acoustic communication and soundscape research at Simon Fraser University'. SFU website. http://wfae.net/library/articles/truax_SFUniversity.pdf
Truax, B. (2001). *Acoustic Communication*. Westport, CT: Greenwood Publishing Group.
Tybjerg, C. (2013). 'The sown and the waste – Or, the psychedelic writing of film history'. *NECSUS_European Journal of Media Studies*, Autumn issue: 'Waste'.
Van Order, M. T. (2009). *Listening to Fellini: Music and Meaning in Black and White*. Cranbury, NJ: Fairleigh Dickinson University Press.
Vasudevan, R. (2001). 'Nationhood, authenticity and realism in Indian cinema: The double take of modernism in the work of Satyajit Ray'. *Journal of the Moving Image* 2: 52–76.
Vaughan, H. (2013). *Where Film Meets Philosophy: Godard, Resnais, and Experiments in Cinematic Thinking*. New York: Columbia University Press.
Vijayakar, R. (2009). *The History of Indian Film Music: A Showcase of the Very Best in Hindi Cinema*. New Delhi: Times Group Books.
Voegelin, S. (2010). *Listening to Noise and Silence: Towards a Philosophy of Sound Art*. New York: Continuum.
Waard, F. de (2009). 'Budhaditya Chattopadhyay: *Landscape in Metamorphoses* (CD-R by Gruenrekorder)'. *Vital Weekly* 640.
Walker, E. (2015). *Understanding Sound Tracks Through Film Theory*. Oxford, England: Oxford University Press.
Waller, D. and Nadel, L. (eds) (2013). *Handbook of Spatial Cognition*. Washington, DC: American Psychological Association.
Waterman, E. and Harley, J. (1999). 'Open Ears Festival of Music and Sound'. *Computer Music Journal* 23/1: 79–82.
Waterman, T. and Wall, E. (2010). *Basics of Landscape Architecture 01: Urban Design*. Switzerland: AVA Publishing.
Wayne, M. (1997). *Theorising Video Practice*. London: Lawrence & Wishart Limited.
Weiss, A. S. (2011). *Varieties of Audio Mimesis: Musical Evocations of Landscape*. Berlin: Errant Bodies Press.
Whittington, W. (2013). 'Lost in Sensation: Reevaluating the Role of Cinematic Sound in the Digital Age'. In Vernallis, C., Herzog, A. and Richardson, J. (eds), *The Oxford Handbook of Sound and Image in Digital Media*. Oxford: Oxford University Press.
Whittington, W. (2007). *Sound Design and Science Fiction*. Austin: University of Texas Press.
Wollscheid, A. (1996). *The Terrorized Term*. Frankfurt: Selektion.
Youngblood, G. (1970). *Expanded Cinema*. Boston, MA: E. P. Dutton.

WORKS/MEDIA CITED

Agantuk (The Stranger, 1991). [Film] India: Satyajit Ray
Ajantrik (1958). [Film] India: Ritwik Ghatak
Alice in the Cities (1974). [Film] Germany: Wim Wenders
All is Lost (2013). [Film] USA and Canada: J. C. Chandor
Anhey Ghorhey Da Daan (Alms for a Blind Horse, 2011). [Film] India: Gurvinder Singh
Antichrist (2009). [Film] Denmark: Lars von Trier
Aparajito (The Unvanquished, 1956). [Film] India: Satyajit Ray
Apocalypse Now (1979). [Film] USA: Francis Ford Coppola
Applause (1929). [Film] USA: Rouben Mamoulian
Apur Sansar (The World of Apu, 1959). [Film] India: Satyajit Ray
Aranyer Din Ratri (Days and Nights in the Forest, 1970). [Film] India: Satyajit Ray
Asha Jaoar Majhe (Labour of Love, 2014). [Film] India: Aditya Vikram Sengupta
Ashani Sanket (Distant Thunder, 1973). [Film] India: Satyajit Ray
Bali (1932). [Film] USA: Charlie Chaplin
Before Sunrise (1995). [Film] USA: Richard Linklater
Before Sunset (2004). [Film] USA: Richard Linklater
Benaras (2006). [Album] Germany: Budhaditya Chattopadhyay
Bezhin Meadow (1937). [Film] Russia: Sergei Eisenstein
Bicycle Thieves (1948). [Film] Italy: Vittorio De Sica
Blade Runner 2049 (2017). [Film] USA: Denis Villeneuve
Brave (2012). [Film] USA: Mark Andrews and Brenda Chapman
Breathless (1960). [Film] France: Jean-Luc Godard
Castaway (2000). [Film] USA: Robert Zemeckis
Catch Me If You Can (2002). [Film] USA: Steven Spielberg
Charulata (The Lonely Wife, 1964). [Film] India: Satyajit Ray
Court (2014). [Film] India: Chaitanya Tamhane
Dear Zindagi (2016). [Film] India: Gauri Shinde

Decomposing Landscape (2015). [Media Artwork] UK: Budhaditya Chattopadhyay
Deewaar (The Wall, 1975). [Film] India: Yash Chopra
Delhi-6 (2009). [Film] India: Rakeysh Omprakash Mehra
Devdas (1935–1936). [Film] India: P. C. Barua
Dharmatma (1975). [Film] India: Feroz Khan
Dhobi Ghat (Mumbai Diaries, 2011). [Film] India: Kiran Rao
Dil Chahta Hai (The Heart Desires, 2001). [Film] India: Farhan Akhtar
Disco Dancer (1982). [Film] India: Babbar Subhash
Do Bigha Zamin (Two Thirds of an Acre of Land, 1953). [Film] India: Bimal Roy
Don Juan (1926). [Film] USA: Alan Crosland
Dracula (1931). [Film] USA: Tod Browning
Dunkirk (2017). [Film] USA, UK, France: Christopher Nolan
Elegy for Bangalore (2013). [Album] Germany: Budhaditya Chattopadhyay
Energy Field (2010). [Album] UK: Jana Winderen
Entuziazm (1930). [Film] Russia: Dziga Vertov
Exile and Other Syndromes (2016–2019). [Media Artwork] Austria and Norway: Budhaditya Chattopadhyay
Eye Contact with the City (2010–2011). [Media Artwork] India: Budhaditya Chattopadhyay
F. Guyana (2017). [Album] Germany: Marc Namblard
400 Blows (1959). [Film] France: François Truffaut
Frankenstein (1931). [Film] USA: James Whale
Ghats (2007). [Media Artwork] India: Budhaditya Chattopadhyay
Gori Tere Pyaar Mein (In Your Love O Lady, 2013). [Film] India: Punit Malhotra
Gravity (2013). [Film] USA and UK: Alfonso Cuarón
Helgoland (2013). [Album] Germany: Lasse-Marc Riek
Highway (2014). [Film] India: Imtiaz Ali
Households (2008). [Media Artwork] India: Budhaditya Chattopadhyay
I am Sitting in a Room (1969). [Media Artwork] USA: Alvin Lucier
Jab We Met (When We Met, 2007). [Film] India: Imtiaz Ali
Jaws (1975). [Film] USA: Steven Spielberg
Johny Mera Naam (Johny My Name, 1970). [Film] India: Vijay Anand
Jukti Takko Aar Gappo (Reason, Debate and a Story, 1974). [Film] India: Ritwik Ghatak
Kahani (The Story, 2012). [Film] India: Sujoy Ghosh
Kanchenjungha (1962). [Film] India: Satyajit Ray
Killa (The Fort, 2015). [Film] India: Avinash Arun
King Kong (1933). [Film] USA: Merian C. Cooper and Ernest B. Schoedsack
Kits Beach Soundwalk (1989). [Album] Canada: Hildegard Westerkamp
Knife in the Water (1962). [Film] Poland: Roman Polanski
La Chienne (1931). [Film] France: Jean Renoir
La Dolce Vita (1960). [Film] Italy: Federico Fellini
Lahu Ke Do Rang (Blood Has Two Colours, 1979). [Film] India: Mahesh Bhatt
Landscape in Metamorphoses (2008). [Album] Germany: Budhaditya Chattopadhyay
L'assedio (Besieged, 1998). [Film] Italy: Bernardo Bertolucci
La Strada (1954). [Film] Italy: Federico Fellini
L'Avventura (The Adventure, 1960). [Film] Italy: Michelangelo Antonioni
Le Million (1931). [Film] France: René Clair
Le Monde du Silence (The Silent World, 1956). [Film] France: Jacques Cousteau and Louis Malle
Le Souffleur (2019). [Media Artwork] Lebanon: Budhaditya Chattopadhyay and Nadim Mishlawi

WORKS/MEDIA CITED

Life of Pi (2012). [Film] USA, UK, Canada, Taiwan: Ang Lee
Lost in Translation (2003). USA and Japan: Sofia Coppola
Love Me Tonight (1932). [Film] USA: Rouben Mamoulian
Love Sex aur Dhokha (Love Sex and Betrayal, 2010). [Film] India: Dibakar Banerjee
Mahanagar (1963). [Film] India: Satyajit Ray
Maine Pyar Kiya (1989). [Film] India: Sooraj Barjatya
Mary Had a Little Lamb (1877–1878). [Sound recording] USA: Thomas Alva Edison
Masaan (Fly Away Solo, 2015). [Film] India: Neeraj Ghaywan
Mayurakshi (2017). [Film] India: Atanu Ghosh
Metaphonics: The Complete Field Works (2018). [Album] USA: Stuart Hyatt
Modern Times (1936). [Film] USA: Charlie Chaplin
Mother and Son (1997). [Film] Russia: Alexander Sokurov
Mukti Bhawan (Hotel Salvation, 2016). [Film] India: Shubhashish Bhutiani
Music for Airports (1978). [Album] UK: Brian Eno
Nayak (The Hero, 1966). [Film] India: Satyajit Ray
Neecha Nagar (Lowly City, 1946). [Film] India: Chetan Anand
Of Human Bondage (1934). [Film] USA: John Cromwell
Oridathu (1987). [Film] India: G. Aravindan
Parasite (2019). [Film] South Korea: Bong Joon-ho
Pasvikdalen (2014). [Album] UK: Jana Winderen
Pather Panchali (1955). [Film] India: Satyajit Ray
Playtime (1967). [Film] France: Jacques Tati
Pratidwandi (1970). [Film] India: Satyajit Ray
¡Que viva México! (1932). [Film] Russia: Sergei Eisenstein
Rear Window (1954). [Film] USA: Alfred Hitchcock
Roma (2018). [Film] Mexico and USA: Alfonso Cuarón
San Lorenzo (2008). [Media Artwork] Italy: Budhaditya Chattopadhyay and Matteo Marangoni
Sarajevo (2004). [Album] Germany: Lasse-Marc Riek
Sátántangó (1994). [Film] Hungary: Béla Tarr
Seemabaddha (1971). [Film] India: Satyajit Ray
Self-portrait with Grilled Bacon (1941). [Painting] Spain and USA: Salvador Dalí
Shanghai (2012). [Film] India: Dibakar Banerjee
Sholay (1975). [Film] India: Ramesh Sippy
Singapore (1947). [Film] USA: John Brahm
Sivaji 3D (2012). [Film] India: S. Shankar
Slumdog Millionaire (2008). [Film] UK and India: Danny Boyle
Solaris (1972). [Film] Russia: Andrei Tarkovsky
Stalker (1979). [Film] Russia: Andrei Tarkovsky
Star Wars (1977). [Film] USA: George Lucas
Stepping into the Dark (1996). [Album] UK: Chris Watson
Subho Muharat (2003). [Film] India: Rituparno Ghosh
Swiss Mountain Transport Systems (2011). [Album] Germany: Ernst Karel
Tarzan and His Mate (1934). [Film] USA: Cedric Gibbons
Taste of Cherry (1997). [Film] Iran: Abbas Kiarostami
Ten (2002). [Film] Iran: Abbas Kiarostami
The Abyss (1989). [Film] USA: James Cameron
The Artist (2011). [Film] France: Michel Hazanavicius
The Beach (2000). [Film] USA and UK: Danny Boyle
The Bitter Tears of Petra von Kant (1972). [Film] Germany: Rainer Werner Fassbinder
The Blue Lagoon (1980). [Film] USA: Randal Kleiser
The Elephant God (1979). [Film] India: Satyajit Ray

The Great Dictator (1940). [Film] USA: Charlie Chaplin
The Jazz Singer (1927). [Film] USA: Alan Crosland
The Lover (1992). [Film] France, UK, Vietnam: Jean-Jacques Annaud
The Nomadic Listener (2020). [Album] Germany: Budhaditya Chattopadhyay
The River (1951). [Film] France, India, USA: Jean Renoir
The Terminal (2004). [Film] USA: Steven Spielberg
The Turin Horse (2011). [Film] Hungary: Béla Tarr
The Wayward Cloud (2005). [Film] Taiwan: Tsai Ming-liang
The Well-tempered City (2020) [Album] UK: Budhaditya Chattopadhyay
The Wind Will Carry Us (1999). [Film] Iran: Abbas Kiarostami
Times Square (1977). [Media Artwork] USA: Max Neuhaus
Titanic (1997). [Film] USA: James Cameron
Titas Ekti Nadir Naam (A River Called Titas, 1973). [Film] India: Ritwik Ghatak
TransMongolian (2012). [Album] Germany: Roland Etzin
Tropical Malady (2004). [Film] Thailand: Apichatpong Weerasethakul
Twentieth Century (1934). [Film] USA: Howard Hawks
20,000 Leagues Under the Sea (1954). [Film] USA: Richard Fleischer
Under the Roofs of Paris (Sous les toits de Paris) (1930). [Film] France: René Clair
Underwater (2020). [Film] USA: William Eubank
Vishwaroopam (2013). [Film] India: Kamal Hasan
Vive L'amour (1994). [Film] Taiwan: Tsai Ming-liang

INDEX

acoustic environment, 8, 30, 78–9, 114, 128, 141, 153, 157, 165
ADR (Automatic Dialogue Replacement), 55
aesthetics, 49, 53, 60, 62, 72, 152, 175
Against Ambience, 10
Althusser, L., 123
Altman, R.,15, 22
Alva Edison, T., 45
Alva Noto
  Cities and Memory, 181
ambience, 4–6, 8, 10–11, 17–19, 21, 30–1, 36, 40, 52, 60, 62, 67, 72–4, 77–8, 99–108, 110–111, 114–6, 122–4, 126, 129, 131, 143
ambient
  music, 10, 11
  sound, 4, 6–11, 14, 20, 27–8, 30, 32–3, 35–6, 40–1, 45, 47, 51, 53–6, 61, 63–5, 69, 132, 71–6, 78–9, 81–2, 94, 99, 118, 126–7, 136, 141, 148–52, 155–63, 171, 175, 178, 182
ambisonics, 98
Anand, C.
  Neecha Nagar (Lowly City), 50

Anand, V.
  Johny Mera Naam (Johny My Name), 59
Annaud, J. J.
  The Lover, 107, 173
Anthropocene, 6, 97, 169–70, 174
  anthropogenic, 7, 94, 117
Antonioni, M., 50
  L'Avventura (The Adventure), 116
Aravindan, G.
  Oridathu, 100
Arnheim, R., 49
Artemiev, E., 99
asynchronous, 91
audiographic realism, 53–4
audiovisual, 16–7, 19, 24, 32, 41, 89, 91, 125, 127–8, 143, 147, 152, 155, 163–4, 170, 175, 177, 179, 181
  culture, 16
auditory setting, 6–7, 20, 28, 31, 36–8, 40–1, 48, 51, 59–60, 67, 73, 76, 87, 90–1, 93–6, 100, 132–4, 137–8, 141, 148–51, 153, 156–8, 160, 162, 170, 173, 175, 179–80, 185

INDEX

Augoyard, J. F., 171
  Sonic Experience: A Guide to Everyday Sounds, 171

Balazs, B., 8, 15, 49, 79, 114, 157
Banerjee, D.
  Shanghai, 128
Barua, P. C., 47
  Devdas, 47–8
Beck, J., 18, 19, 22
Berliner, E., 46
Bertolucci, B.
  L'assedio (Besieged), 108
Bhutiani, S.
  Mukti Bhawan (Hotel Salvation), 114
Biancoroso, G., 17–18, 71, 158
binaural, 99, 110
Bioscience, 5
Bollywood, 61, 161
Borges, J. L., 56
Boyle, D.
  Slumdog Millionaire, 127
  The Beach, 117
Bresson, R., 50, 53–4
Bronowski, J., 169
  The Ascent of Man, 90
Browning, T.
  Dracula, 50
Burch, N., 27

Cage, J., 65
Cameron, J.
  The Abyss, 142
  Titanic, 117
Cascone, K., 176
Chakraborty Spivak, G., 123
Chandor, J. C.
  All is Lost, 117
Chaplin, C.
  Bali, 47
  Modern Times, 47
  The Great Dictator, 47
Chatterjee, S., 128
Chatterjee, J., 56
Chattopadhyay, B.
  Benaras, 113
  Decomposing Landscape, 40, 97

Elegy for Bangalore, 40, 120, 124–5, 156
Exile and Other Syndromes, 120
Eye Contact with the City, 40, 120, 124–5
Landscape in Metamorphoses, 39, 88–90
The Nomadic Listener, 138
The Well-tempered City, 122
Chaudhuri, A., 108
Chion, M., 8, 15, 17, 23–4, 152, 155, 176
  Audio-Vision, 17
Chopra, Y.
  Deewaar (The Wall), 59–60
cinema, 4, 8–9, 14–15, 17–18, 20, 22–4, 27–8, 38, 45–7, 49, 50–1, 55–6, 59, 61–3, 69–70, 73–4, 77, 79–80, 99, 115–16, 149, 151, 153, 155, 159–60, 165, 172, 174, 176–7, 182
Clair, R.
  Le Million, 50
  Sous les Toits du Paris (Under the Roofs of Paris), 48, 50
Cobussen, M., 167
colonialism, 47
Coppola, F. F.
  Apocalypse Now, 94, 173
Coppola, S.
  Lost in Translation, 128
Cooper, M.C.
  King Kong, 50, 93
Cousteau, J.
  Le Monde du Silence (The Silent World), 140
Cox, C., 65, 166
Cromwell, J.
  Of Human Bondage, 120
Crosland, A.
  Don Juan, 47
  The Jazz Singer, 46
Cuaron, A.
  Gravity, 76–7, 143
  Roma, 77, 129, 174

Dali, S.
  Self-portrait with Grilled Bacon, 110

203

INDEX

Das, J.
   'An Orange', 184
Dasmann, R., 89
Debord, G., 125
Demers, J., 11, 33, 37, 181–3
De Sica, V.
   Bicycle Thieves, 50
diegesis, 14, 24–8, 51, 55–7, 67, 71, 73–4, 76, 93, 134, 148, 155, 157–8
diegetic, 7, 100, 114, 116
digital, 8–10, 14–24, 27–31, 36, 38, 40–1, 56, 67–9, 71–7, 80–1, 88, 98, 127, 140, 148–52, 155–6, 160–5, 175–7
   surround sound, 16, 23–4, 69, 71, 74, 77
direct sound, 45, 47–51, 53, 70, 72, 90, 93, 98, 126, 132–3, 148, 151, 153
Doane, M. A., 20, 26, 29
documentary, 33, 48, 81, 106, 140, 161
Dolby Atmos, 23, 49, 76–7, 111, 117, 129, 142–3, 148–9, 163, 176
Dolby Stereo, 62, 69–70, 117
dubbing, 8–9, 21, 23–4, 36, 41, 52, 55–7, 59–61, 63, 69, 72, 74–6, 127, 148, 150–2, 158
Duras, M., 107
Dutt, G., 50
Dyson, F.
   Sounding New Media, 151

Ear | Wave | Event, 22
Eidnes Andersen, K., 95
Eisenstein, S.
   Bezhin Meadow, 90
Eno, B.
   Music for Airports, 10
environmental, 39–40, 77, 90, 97, 100, 107, 116
environmental sound, 3, 5, 53, 67, 73, 81, 91, 94–5, 98–9, 115
Etzin, R.
   TransMongolian, 132
Eubank, W.
   Underwater, 142

Fassbinder, R. W.
   The Bitter Tears of Petra Von Kant, 105
Fellini, F., 50
   La Strada, 126
   La Dolce Vita, 126
field recording, 32–3, 37, 39–40, 46, 81–2, 121, 140–1, 152, 155–6, 160, 165–6, 176
Fleischer, R., 142
   20,000 Leagues Under the Sea, 142
Flusser, V., 181–2
Foley, 55, 72

Gess, N., 164
Ghatak, R.
   Ajantrik, 173–4
   Jukti Takko Aar Gappo (Reason, Debate and a Story), 88
   Titas Ekti Nadir Naam (A River Called Titas), 116, 174
Ghaywan, N., 114
   Masaan (Fly Away Solo), 114
Ghosh, H., 128
Ghosh, R.
   Subho Muharat, 105
Gibbons, C.
   Tarzan and His Mate, 93
global cinema, 9
Godard, J. L., 50
   Breathless, 54
gramophone, 46
Gumbrecht, H. U., 164

Harari, Y. N., 184
Harman, G., 139
Hawks, H.
   Twentieth Century, 132
Henry, P., 52, 64
Hitchcock, A.
   Rear Window, 105
Holman, S., 30
Holman, T., 8, 15, 21, 67, 80
Hollywood, 8, 16, 49–50, 52–4, 60–2, 75–7, 79, 94, 132, 161
Hyatt, S., 140
hyper-real, 60, 75, 94, 172
   hyper-reality, 61, 63

Ihde, D., 22, 161
Ikeda, R., 181
Indian cinema, 8–10, 54, 56, 62, 64, 74–5, 77, 105, 114–15, 127–8, 159

Joon-ho, B.
  Parasite, 77, 110
Journal of Sonic Studies, 22, 165

Karel, E.
  Swiss Mountain Transport System, 132
Kerins, M.,15, 22–3, 27, 30, 61, 69, 71, 75, 77, 80
  Beyond Dolby (Stereo), 16, 61
Khan, F.
  Dharmatma, 59–60
Kiarostami, A.
  Taste of Cherry, 133
  Ten, 134
  The Wind Will Carry Us, 134
King, R., 180
Kleiser. R.
  The Blue Lagoon, 117
Kracauer, S., 20
Krause, B., 5

LaBelle, B., 32, 133, 160, 165–6
Lasse-Marc, R., 166
  Helgoland, 125, 156
  Sarajevo, 125, 156
Lastra, J., 36, 49, 60
Latour, B., 142
Lee, A.
  Life of Pi, 117
Levi-Strauss, C.
  The Savage Mind, 125
Linklater, R.
  Before Sunrise, 133
  Before Sunset, 133
location, 6, 9, 14–15, 18, 21, 23, 26–7, 29, 33, 37, 41, 46–9, 51–3, 55–7, 59–60, 63–4, 67, 69, 71–7, 79–81, 89–90, 93, 95–6, 98–9, 102, 104–7, 109, 113–114, 126–8, 136, 140–2, 147, 150, 152, 159, 169, 172, 174
Lopez, F., 166

Lorzig, H., 185
Lovatt, P., 95
Lucas, G., 62
  Star Wars, 62
Lucier, A.
  I Am Sitting in a Room, 64
Lumiere Brothers, 50

magnetic recording, 8, 21, 36, 41, 51–3, 55, 69–70, 75–6
Mamoulian, R.
  Applause, 47
  Love Me Tonight, 47
mediated ambience, 4
Melies, G., 50
Merleau Ponty, M., 22
mimesis, 14, 25, 28, 32, 134, 148, 165
Ming-liang, T.
  Vive L'amour, 107
  The Wayward Cloud, 107
mise-en-scene, 35, 48, 136
mise-en-sonore, 6, 36, 67, 69, 93, 106, 152, 163
monaural, 28, 36, 41, 47, 49, 51, 53–4, 62, 67, 70, 72, 75–6, 93–4, 100, 105, 113, 117, 126, 132, 136, 142, 148–50
Morton, T., 153, 157, 169
  Ecology without Nature, 30
Murch, W., 94, 171
Murray Schafer, R., 28, 65, 124

Namblard, M.
  F. Guyana, 95
natural ambience, 4
Neuhaus, M.
  Times Square, 64
neorealism, 50
Nollywood, 61, 161
Nouvelle Vague, 50, 54

performing arts, 46
phonautograph, 45
Polanski, R.
  Knife in Water, 116
Pookutty, R., 127
Prince, S., 165

INDEX

Rajadhyaksha, A., 74
Ray, S., 44, 50, 53–4, 56–7, 93, 99, 104–5, 108, 113, 120, 126, 174
   Agantuk (The Stranger), 104
   Aparajito (The Unvanquished), 113, 120
   Apu Trilogy, 113
   Apur Sansar (The World of Apu), 93, 113
   Aranyer Din Ratri (Days and Nights in the Forest), 57
   Ashani Sanket (Distant Thunder), 100
   Charulata (The Lonely Wife), 104–5, 173
   Kanchenjungha, 126
   Mahanagar, 126
   Nayak (The Hero), 57, 132
   Pather Panchali, 100, 173–4
   Pratidwandi, 108
   Seemabaddha, 104
   The Elephant God, 113
reality, 48–9, 53–4
rendering, 23, 31–2, 41, 51, 99, 128, 148, 152–5, 157, 180, 183
Renoir, J., 53
   La Chienne, 48
   The River, 108
Rosenbaum, J., 134
Rothenberg, D., 171
Roy, B.
   Do Bigha Zamin (Two Thirds of an Acre of Land), 50
Russolo, L., 65

Schaefer, P., 52, 64–5
Schoedsack, E. B.
   King Kong, 50, 93
Schryer, C., 170
Scott de Martinville, E., 45
Sen, R., 128
Sengupta, A. V.
   Asha Jaoar Majhe (Labour of Love), 106
Sergi, G., 63, 69–70
Sharun, V., 99
Shaviro, S.
   Post-Cinematic Affect, 177

Shinde, G.
   Dear Zindagi, 117
Sippy, R.
   Sholay, 63–4
site, 6–7, 15, 26, 32, 35, 37, 39, 41, 50–4, 56, 59, 63, 67, 71–2, 74, 79–80, 82, 112, 120, 128, 140, 142, 148–9, 156–8, 162, 165, 169, 178
site-specific, 4, 6, 8, 11, 14, 19–20, 22, 33–6, 39, 41, 45, 52–6, 61, 65, 71–3, 75–6, 79, 82, 90, 93, 95, 98–9, 107, 110, 113, 117, 126–7, 143, 147–8, 153, 156, 162, 184–5
Sobchack, V., 69, 80
Sokurov, A.
   Mother and Son, 90, 94, 173
Sonnenschein, D., 7, 15, 70
   Sound Design: The Expressive Power of Music, Voice and Sound Effects in Cinema, 70
sonic environment, 3–6, 11, 27, 30, 33, 35–6, 38–42, 48, 53–7, 69, 71, 73–4, 77–80, 91, 97–9, 109, 134–5, 137, 141–3, 148–9, 151, 156–7, 163, 165, 169–70, 172–3, 175, 182
sound art, 4, 7, 10, 17–19, 25, 28, 32–3, 37, 39, 42, 52, 64–6, 80, 95, 124, 132, 140, 152, 155, 160, 165–6, 176–7, 181, 183–4
sound effects, 20–1, 23, 46–7, 52, 55–6, 60–1, 63–4, 72, 76, 116, 127, 136, 157–8, 171–2
soundmark, 27, 30, 32, 77, 157, 162
soundscape, 4, 15, 25, 30, 32–4, 40, 65, 73, 77, 88, 98, 103, 124, 127–8, 142, 157, 162, 170
soundtrack, 17, 28, 44, 47–8, 50–3, 55, 61, 67, 70–1, 73, 76, 149, 151, 157–8, 162, 171–3, 176
Spielberg, S.
   Catch Me If You Can, 137
   Jaws, 117
   The Terminal, 137
stereo sound, 94, 127
stereophonic, 9, 16, 23–4, 28, 36, 41, 61–4, 67, 69–71, 74–5, 142, 148–52, 177

sound environment, 94
Sterne, J., 29, 109
  The Audible Past, 29
Subhash, B.
  Disco Dancer, 62
surround sound, 15–16, 18, 20, 23, 67, 69, 71–2, 74, 76–7, 98, 117, 128, 142, 163, 172
  design, 9, 22–4, 36, 41, 70, 72–3, 77, 80, 105, 127, 148–50, 162, 164
  environment, 23, 49, 95, 129, 151–2, 162
synchronisation, 46
synchronised (sync) sound, 36, 49–50, 54, 72, 74, 76, 105, 114, 127, 148, 150, 152, 159, 161–3, 182

Tarkovsky, A.
  Solaris, 142
  Stalker, 99
Tarr, B.
  Sátántangó, 100
  The Turin Horse, 100–1
Tati, J., 50
  Playtime, 136–7
The Journal of Sonic Studies, 22, 165
The Oxford Handbook of Sound Studies, 22
The Routledge Sound Studies Reader, 22
Thompson, E.
  The Soundscape of Modernity, 61
Truffaut, F., 50
  400 Blows, 54

Turgenev, I., 90
Tybjerg, C., 149

Universal Pictures, 50
urban, 5, 127
urban environment, 18, 120

Velez, D., 166
Vertov, D.
  Entuziazm, 50
Villeneuve, D.
  Blade Runner 2049, 76–7
Visconti, L., 50
Von Trier, L.
  Antichrist, 95, 173

Watson, C.
  Stepping into the Dark, 96
Weerasethakul, A.
  Tropical Malady, 95
Wenders, W.
  Alice in the Cities, 137
Westerkamp, H.
  Kits Beach Soundwalk, 64, 165
Whale, J.
  Frankenstein, 50
Winderen, J.
  Energy Field, 142
  Pasvikdalen, 142

Zemeckis, R.
  Castaway, 117